Dr. Johnson's Lichfield

Dr. Johnson's Lichfield

by

MARY ALDEN HOPKINS

HASTINGS HOUSE

PUBLISHERS   NEW YORK

Acknowledgments

GENEROUS ASSISTANCE has been given me by research workers, librarians and curators both in England and in the United States. In England, my special thanks are due Percy Laithwaite, Esq., Honorary Secretary of the Johnson Society, Lichfield, England, who placed at my disposal a collection of unpublished letters in the Johnson Birthplace as well as data which he himself has gathered from old deeds and documents. I am indebted to Dr. Ragnhild Hatton who searched for me London lists of Handelian singers and looked up other matters, and to Mr. C. E. B. Hubbard who found for me in the Birmingham court records the long-lost will of John Saville. A photograph of John Saville's miniature was sent me by Miss Mary W. Maguire and James R. Beard, Esq., along with family legends. Mr. and Mrs. Pennent of St. Asaph, Wales, most kindly had their portraits of Mrs. Johnson and Lucy Porter photographed for me. Professor Harold E. Butler and Miss Ruth Butler, grandnephew and grandniece of Maria Edgeworth, gave me copies of unpublished family letters about Lichfield affairs.

I appreciate the help afforded me by the late Dr. Henry Guppy, of the John Rylands Library, Manchester, England; Dr. C. K. Adams, Assistant Keeper of the National Portrait Gallery, London; Dr. C. H. Gibbs-Smith, Keeper of Museum Extension; by the Victoria and Albert Museum, London; and

v

the Maidstone Carriage Museum in Kent; Miss Sybil Rosenfeld; and Miss M. F. H. Ellis.

Permission to reproduce letters written by Anna and Sarah Seward and their father and by Joseph Greene has been given me by the Johnson Society of Lichfield, and George Birch, Esq., of that city allows me to quote the unpublished poem by Anna Seward. The John Rylands Library furnished me with photostats of letters written by Anna Seward and Mary Adey and gives me permission to quote from Pratt's letter to Dr. Johnson. The National Portrait Gallery, London, permits me to reproduce the picture of Mr. Day.

In the United States, my thanks are due to the University of Rochester for photostatic copies from the R. B. Adam Collection (now in private ownership), of letters written by William Hayley and Anna Seward. I have received assistance from Dr. Robert F. Metzdorf, of the Houghton Library, Harvard University; from Dr. E. Giles Dawson, of the Folger Shakespeare Library, Washington; Dr. James L. Clifford, Columbia University; Dr. Robert Manson Myers, Tulane University; Dr. George M. Kahrl, Elmira College; Mr. Arnold Mitchell, Stanford Research Institution; Mr. Robert C. Gooch, Library of Congress; Dr. Leslie W. Dunlap, University of British Columbia Library, Vancouver; Mr. Paul North Rice and Mr. Ralph H. Carruthers, New York Public Library; Mrs. Dorothy M. Peake; and Mr. Harry Gerstein. I thank Mr. Laurance Squire for constructing the charts of eighteenth-century Lichfield City and Close from various old maps and data. A detailed list of documents, manuscripts, books, etc., which I have consulted is given in the bibliography.

Chronology

1709   Samuel Johnson is born.

1712–16   "Sam" is taken to London to be "touched" by Queen Anne. He attends Dame Oliver's school and Browne's.

1717   David Garrick is born.

1717–25   Johnson attends Lichfield Grammar School.

1725–6   Johnson visits his cousin "Parson" Ford and overstays vacation. He is refused re-admittance to Lichfield Grammar School. He attends Stourbridge Grammar School for about half a year.

1726–8   Johnson is idle at Lichfield.

1728   Johnson enters Pembroke College, Oxford.

1729–31   After 13 months he returns to Lichfield where he stays two years. Fails to get ushership at Stourbridge Grammar School. His father dies.

1732–5   A period of depression and poverty. Is appointed usher at Market Bosworth Grammar School, but gives up the position after some months. Lives in Lichfield and Birmingham doing odd jobs of writing. Is briefly a tutor at Great Haywood.

1735   July 9—Is married.

1735–7   Fails to obtain headmastership at Solihull. Opens own school at Edial. Date of closing of school not known.

1737   Mar. 2—With Garrick to London. Brother Nathaniel dies. Garrick's father dies. Returns to Lichfield for wife before summer is over—exact date not known. Returns to London with wife toward end of year—date not known.

1739 A second period of depression and poverty—lacking definite dates. Applies for headmastership of Appleby Grammar School, Leicestershire. Fails. Spends some time in the Midlands (dates unknown). Visits Taylor in Ashbourne—meets Hill Boothby. Returns to his mother's house in Lichfield—meets Molly Aston. Receives some money as his share of mortgage on the Johnson house. Has a nibble at his play, *Irene,* from a London manager.

1740 Returns to London, month unknown.

1749 Seward family settles in Lichfield. Moves into Palace about 1751.

1752 Johnson's wife dies in London.

1756 Erasmus Darwin comes to Lichfield to live. Marries Mary Howard the following year. Honora Sneyd comes to live with the Sewards. Hill Boothby dies.

1759 Johnson's mother dies.

1760 Coronation of George III.

1761 Johnson visits Lichfield briefly.

1762 Anna Seward meets Col. Taylor.

1763 Lucy Porter inherits fortune from brother, Captain Jervis Porter.

1764 Sally Seward is betrothed to Joseph Porter. Sally dies. Anna Seward visits London; betroths self to Taylor; father breaks off engagement. First mention of John Saville in Anna's letters.

1765 Richard Lovell Edgeworth visits Lichfield. Anna Seward is wooed and jilted by Vyse.

1766 Lucy Porter moves into her new house, Redcourt.

1767 Johnson visits Lichfield.

1768 Taylor renews addresses; Anna not interested.

1769 John André comes to Lichfield from Buxton with the Sewards. Makes a second visit in October. Edgeworth visits Lichfield several times. Thomas Day adopts two orphans; takes them to France.

1770 André is dismissed by Honora's father. Honora goes to Bath for health. Mrs. Darwin dies. Day and Edgeworth take a house in Lichfield. Honora returns from Bath. Johnson visits Lichfield.

1771 Honora leaves Sewards to live with father and sisters now in Lichfield. Edgeworth brings his family to Lichfield. Day is refused by Honora. Day courts Elizabeth Sneyd. Day and Edgeworth go to France. André enters army. Johnson visits Lichfield.

1772   The Seward-Saville scandal explodes. Johnson visits Lichfield.

1773   Day returns from France; is refused by Elizabeth. Mrs. Edgeworth dies. Edgeworth returns from France and marries Honora. André visits Lichfield after Honora's departure. Saville separates from wife. Day leaves Lichfield.

1774   André goes to Canada. Dr. Johnson visits Lichfield.

1775   Dr. Johnson visits Lichfield.

1776   Edgeworth comes from Ireland to England. Johnson and Boswell visit Lichfield.

1777   Johnson visits Lichfield.

1778   Day marries Esther Milnes. Johnson visits Lichfield.

1779   David Garrick dies. Johnson visits Lichfield.

1780   Col. Pole dies. Mrs. Seward dies. Honora dies. André executed.

1781   Darwin marries Mrs. Pole. Johnson visits Lichfield.

1784   Johnson dies.

1786   Lucy Porter dies.

1787   Mrs. Piozzi visits Lichfield.

1790   Dr. Seward dies.

1803   John Saville dies.

1809   Anna Seward dies.

Contents

---

xi

CONTENTS

Illustrations

xiii

ILLUSTRATIONS

Dr. Johnson's Lichfield

CHAPTER I

Salve, Magna Parens!

THIS book is about the city of Lichfield, England, and the people who lived there during the lifetime of the great Dr. Johnson. The comrades with whom he associated while he was growing up and the friends with whom he fraternized later on when he came back for frequent, lengthy visits, belonged to professional and business families and also to the gentry. The lawyers and merchants resided chiefly in the city proper, while the clerical families dwelt in Lichfield Cathedral Close, and the gentry were scattered in family seats through the countryside of Staffordshire.

During his early years Samuel Johnson was not especially enthusiastic about his home town where he failed to find work for which he was adapted. After repeated disappointments and failures he went to London and there he won his fame. He lived in London, he loved London, he wrote about London. That is why we think, "Johnson—London," instead of "Johnson—Lichfield." Yet in his later years he returned nearly every other summer to spend weeks and even months renewing old acquaintanceships, visiting friends, walking the familiar streets, and reviving old memories.

Dr. Johnson was a man of many friends. In school he was

popular with his mates. As a young man he was taken up by the Staffordshire gentry. In the years of his fame he was in demand in London dinner clubs and at the conversation parties of the period. This difference is noticeable—in the "city" he associated with men and women equally, while in Lichfield most of his time was spent with gentlewomen. Dr. Johnson liked intelligent, well-bred women and they usually liked him, although he was ungainly in figure, uncouth in manner, awkward in gallantry, and often rude in conversation.

Best known in the honor roll of Johnson's favor is the name of Molly Aston—Molly, a beauty, a scholar and a Whig (Johnson was an embattled Tory). An evening spent in her company was rapture to Johnson. He said so. But one suspects that the feeling he recalled as ecstasy was really of an intellectual rather than of a deeply emotional character, and that this was a bantering flirtation pleasing to remember in later life. Very different was his passion for the middle-aged, faded Widow Porter, of Birmingham but with Lichfield family connections, whom he married in the face of universal disapproval. Hill Boothby, a later affinity, was still another type: very learned, very saintly, very holy. Her death interrupted a series of letters from Johnson breathing an admiration akin to adoration. Among his more tranquil Lichfield friendships, friendships as unexciting as satisfactory, were those with two sisters of well-remembered Molly Aston: Elizabeth Aston (by courtesy title Mrs. Aston) and Jane Gastrell whose deceased clerical husband had gained disrepute and fame by felling Shakespeare's mulberry tree which stood in the rectory garden at Stratford. And always there was Lucy Porter, his step-daughter, who cared for his widowed mother and remained his faithful though sometimes critical friend all her life through.

When Dr. Johnson came to Lichfield in his later years, a new group of young women were queening it, but, though they were beautiful, intellectual and amusing, Dr. Johnson

2

did not find their company particularly congenial. There was the lovely Honora Sneyd, who was later to marry Richard Lovell Edgeworth, and her lively sister Elizabeth; also Anna Seward, poetess of wide but fleeting renown, whose platonic love affair with John Saville was a Close scandal for thirty years. Among the men in this younger set were, beside John Saville, Robert Lovell Edgeworth, father of the noted Maria, who drove into Lichfield in a one-wheel traveling chaise of his own designing (Edgeworth was an intermittent resident of the town); John André who left his heart with Honora Sneyd when he went to die tragically in America; and Thomas Day who proposed to six women before he secured a Perfect Wife. There were other beautiful women and their attendant swains in this group, talented, educated, very much alive, some making music, some writing poetry or adventuring in science, and all with the habit of involving themselves in fantastic love affairs. In those days divorce could only be obtained by Special Act of Parliament. Whether this circumstance promoted marital complications or the contrary, is perhaps debatable. But complications were certainly not unknown. Edgeworth made love to Honora Sneyd although married and father of a family. John Saville separated from his wife on Anna Seward's account. Even the clergy were not immune. One reverend eloped with a married woman, another engaged himself to a young London female while his wife was still alive. Lichfield people were just as human as those of our own times.

Older than these young men and women of the intellectual clique, but sympathetic with them, was the amazing Dr. Erasmus Darwin, a remarkable man whose reputation has been overshadowed by his grandson, Charles Darwin. A cautious hostess was careful never to invite Darwin and Johnson to the same party because they were too much alike, and a meeting between them might lead to trouble.

In any case, Dr. Johnson had little in common with this lively, younger group. He met its members only occasionally, and when he did, his attitude was apt to be antagonistic. He preferred to spend his time with his old schoolmate and lifelong friend, Dr. John Taylor, in nearby Ashbourne, a clergyman who held five ecclesiastical appointments and raised blooded cattle. He also liked to take the friends he brought along with him from London to visit Mr. Greene, a surgeon-apothecary who had a locally renowned collection of oddities known as "Greene's Museum."

If it is true as we are sometimes told that each individual carries in his unconscious mind faint, compulsive memories of his racial history, the citizens of Lichfield were especially fortunate in their psychic inheritance, for Lichfield has a history of courage, independence, self-confidence and learning. These qualities were present in the Dr. Johnson group. He was not the only one who could cry, *Salve, magna parens!*

The very site of the city was determined, not by a navigable river, fertile fields, a harbor, or military advantage, but by the coming of a missionary bringing the word of God to the wild woodsmen of that locality. In those days priests were the scholars of a nation and monasteries were its universities. From the marriage of learning to religion were born music, architecture, sculpture, and writing. Law, politics, science, trading, and manufacturing came later and were for a long time vocations less honored than the ministry and literature. Had Dr. Johnson been born in Liverpool or Bristol the course of his life might have been very different.

Our knowledge of early centuries in Britain comes from myths and songs and legends transmitted from ear to mouth to ear until preserved by monastery scribes on sheets of vellum illumined in gold and red and blue. These early written chronicles are hardly more reliable than the minstrels' songs, for history was pure story-telling and the more inspired the narrator the greater his additions and deviations. We look back to that distant past through a golden haze of hero worship and no one knows how much fact lies hidden in the delicate mist. In those days England was sparsely settled. Northward from Lichfield lay Robin Hood's Sherwood Forest. To the south were the dells and glades of the Forest of Dean. To the southwest in Cornwall King Arthur's knights rode the greenwood trails. Close by in Warwickshire was the enchanted Forest of Arden. These forests included moorland as well as timberland.

The name Lichfield according to some scholars indicates that the section in which St. Chad settled was marshy, the word being originally *Licetfield* from the Saxon word *lece, lec, lich, lace,* from whence comes our *lake.* Others think that the word was first *Luitcoit,* which may be translated, "The Settlement by the Gray Woods."

A different derivation is given by Dr. Johnson in his Dictionary; "Lichfield, the field of the dead . . . so named from the martyred Christians." If he is correct in holding that the *lich* in Lichfield indicates death and not marsh, the word looks back to a persecution said to have occurred in the fourth century when Roman soldiers drove early Christian Britons in a great multitude into the forest waste where Lichfield now stands, to be murdered in a mass, their bodies being left to the beasts of the field and the fowls of the air. The corporate seal of Lichfield is blazoned as a representation of three slain martyrs, all proper. These figures are sometimes referred to as The Three Kings. The syllable *lich* with its meaning of death survives in *lichgate,* that roofed-over gateway to a church graveyard where a funeral procession, which came on foot chanting hymns along the roadway between the bared heads of passers-by, rested the coffin while waiting for the clergyman to come down the path from the church and turn

5

at the gate to precede the funeral train to the sanctuary, reciting a part of the service.

The tone of the somewhat unreliable history of early Lichfield is religious rather than romantic and the actors are not tilting knights and lovely ladies, but monks and saints and martyrs. Chief among them is St. Chad who was Bishop of Mercia about the middle of the seventh century. He was the youngest of four brothers with names like chiming bells—Cedd, Cynibill, Caelin, and Chad—all of whom were educated for the priesthood.

Seen through the half-light of mysticism which veils this early period, Bishop Chad appears more like a frescoed saint than a religious executive, but he was in truth a real political as well as apostolic force in the development of this section of England. The earlier part of his ministry was spent in Ireland, after which he spread the Gospel among the unconverted British and Anglo-Saxons in the Midlands. Thirty-one ancient dedications bearing his name indicate the extent of his accomplishments.

After he had been called by King Osway to become Bishop of Mercia, he fixed his See at Lichfield although this was an obscure, out-of-the-way locality. He chose this district not only because it was already hallowed by the blood of the martyred Christians, but because St. Augustine had visited the scene of the slaughter and pronounced it holy ground. Here Chad's predecessor had already built a church probably of wattles chinked with clay. Bishop Clad's great task was to reconcile the practices of the native British Christian groups with those of the invading Angles. So wisely and skilfully did he administer his See during the three remaining years of his life, that Lichfield was established as the ecclesiastical center of Middle England.[1]

Though we may not accept the authenticity of the legends which cluster about the memory of St. Chad, we could ill spare them, for they bear witness to the love and honor and reverence in which the saintly leader was held. Ancient chronicles relate how a flight of choral angels revealed to him his approaching death and how on the appointed death-day they winged and hymned their way to his bedside and bore him back with them to heaven. After his death many miracles were asserted to have happened. A lunatic, escaping from his keepers, spent the night on the saint's grave and in the morning was found restored to his senses. The very dust taken from his grave was a sure remedy for all disorders incident to man and beast.[2]

As years passed the hamlet of Lichfield became a village, a town, a city. Churches succeeded each other, each better built than the previous one, until finally, on higher ground, the cathedral of St. Mary and St. Chad rose to the glory of God. Century after century, buildings, additions, decorations, and restorations went on, until the Queen of English Cathedrals was completed.

Lichfield was a place to see visions in as late as the middle of the seventeenth century, as witness the experience of George Fox, the founder of the Society of Friends, in the market place of that city, in 1641. This is what he tells us in his journal:

"Thus being set at liberty again, [after a year's imprisonment in Derby for preaching] I went on, as before, in the work of the Lord; and as I was walking in a close with several friends, I lifted up my head and spied three steeple-house spires, and they struck at my life. I asked them what place it was, and they said, Lichfield."

He gave his friends the slip and went by his eye over hill and ditch till he came within a mile of Lichfield. In a great field there were shepherds keeping their sheep and he gave his shoes to the shepherds to keep, though it was winter. The shepherds trembled and were astonished. Reaching Lichfield he went into the market place, it being market day. He went to and fro in several parts of it, and made stands, crying,

"Woe to the bloody city of Lichfield!"

No one laid hands on him, but as he went thus crying through the streets, there seemed to him to be a channel of blood running down the streets, and the market place appeared like a pool of blood. Some friendly people came to him and asked,

"Alack, George, where are thy shoes?"

He told them it did not matter. When he had declared himself, he went out of the town in peace. He got his shoes from the shepherds but did not put them on until he came to a ditch and washed his feet.

George Fox began to wonder why he had been compelled to cry out thus. "For though Parliament," he says, "had had the Minister at one time, and the King another, and much blood had been shed in the town, during the wars between them, yet that could not be charged upon the town." He understood his compulsion when he learned that in Emperor Diocletian's time "a thousand Christians were martyred in Lichfield, and so," he understood, "I must go in my stockings through the channel of their blood, and into the pool of their blood in the market place . . . and so the sense of this blood was upon me."

Lichfield comes out of the era of song and saga into the period of dates and names and written records without losing preoccupation with religion. Weekdays as well as Sabbaths were filled with obligations to the stately Cathedral. Everyone was religious, although the passionate partisanship grew to seem more like politics than like piety.

When the Civil War, with God and King Charles on one side and on the other God and Parliament, swirled through

Staffordshire, the Royalists fortified the walled and moated Cathedral. Cannon mouths were thrust out through holes broken in the stone walls and soldiers manned the causeway across Minister Pool. The Earl of Chesterfield took command.

The opposing forces of Parliament under Robert, Lord Brooke, set their barricadoes and gun mounts facing the southeast gate of the Close. Lord Brooke, wearing a purple plush cassock, prayed God for a sign of approval and ordered the fire to open. When in the excitement of directing the assault, he pushed up the visor of his steel-barred helmet, Dumb Dyott, a mute, perched on the Cathedral battlements, put a bullet into Lord Brooke's eye. The Royalists wrote it down in history that Lord Brooke had asked for a sign from God and God had signed him in the forehead because he was desecrating the holy Church. This happened on St. Chad's Day, March 2nd, 1643. Nevertheless the Parliamentarians took the fortified church in three days. They took it, lost it, regained it. The Cathedral endured three sieges.

The destruction went on for a month. The invaders plundered and both sides destroyed. The Royalists asserted that the impious Puritan Parliamentarians, when in possession of the Cathedral, hunted a cat with hounds through the sacred chapels and that the soldiers, standing in the nave, shouted to hear the echo from the vaulted roof. By the time the war was over, one spire was down, images of the holy saints were mutilated, windows smashed, carved stalls broken and bells stolen. What was valuable was carried away and what was left was ruined.[3]

After the mad excitement of destruction came the slow atonement of rebuilding. John Hacket, the first Bishop after the Restoration of the Monarchy, was a practical man willing to work with his own hands. The morning after his arrival in Lichfield he mustered his carts and his coach horses, hired others, gathered his servants and the farmers from round

9

about, and set to work removing the rubbish. He solicited subscriptions from every village in the Diocese of Lichfield and Coventry, from the nobility of the entire kingdom, and from the Ministers of State. The canons gave half their salaries. Bishop Hacket not only gave large sums from his own fortune, but, standing at the door of the inn, begged twenty-three thousand pounds from travelers in eight years. His Gracious Majesty, King Charles the Second, gave one hundred fair trees out of Needwood Forest, a lord gave candlesticks, a lady provided the communion utensils, and someone saw to the south steps.

When the repairs to the edifice were completed, there were still bells to be cast. The bishop put his hand in his pocket and invited the nobles and commoners to do likewise. Some gave coin; others trees—the best tree on the land, or as good a tree as one had, or a very good tree, or simply a tree. From these timbers were hung ten sweet bells where only six had hung before and a society of bell ringers was formed, called The Loyal Youths.

The Cathedral was reconsecrated with impressive services: processions, music, prayers, and anthems, concluding with the collection of another contribution. Bishop Hacket gave three noble entertainments in the new prebendary house with its great gallery. One gathering was for the members of the church, another for the nobles and gentry, and a third for the bailiffs and magistrates of the city.

By the time Samuel Johnson was born this noble religious enthusiasm was a thing of the past. The Church of England had settled into a coma of respectability, the routine of religious observation taking the place of spiritual awareness. The awakening of the church through the rude impact of Methodism had not yet occurred. Conscientious clergy preached erudite sermons, melodious organ music billowed through the arches, and the choir was the equal of any in England. The people were proud of their building, their clergy, and their music, but they had lost the active spiritual faith of their fathers. Nevertheless this hallowed edifice, built by unquestioning faith, wrecked by rival zeal, rebuilt with sacrifice, consecrated by devotion, was a spiritual shrine to those rare souls who struggled toward God without much human assistance.

CHAPTER II

The Johnson Family

BY THE time of Johnson, Lichfield had emerged from a tangle of woods, wars, saints, and plagues, although the crude discipline of stocks, ducking stools, and bridles for scolds persisted. The population was over a thousand, the city was surrounded by large estates belonging to old families some of whom had also town houses, coach roads ran to other cities, streets had been laid out, a good water system safeguarded health, and a famous grammar school was graduating boys who attained prominence in the church, the law, parliament, and as writers. Lichfield had become a cultural center.

Daniel Defoe wrote a guide-book four volumes long entitled *A Tour Thro' the Whole Island of Great Britain*. Although he gathered his material before his death in 1731 and the work was completed by Samuel Richardson soon after, the city altered so slowly that the portrait was a likeness for many decades. He found Lichfield a fine, neat, well-built, and pretty large city. He wrote: "There is a kind of a flow, sluggish, Lough or Water, which runs or rather glides heavily through it. . . . This water parts the city in two; one part is called the

Town, and the other the Close; in the first is the Market-place, a fine School and a very handsome hospital dedicated to St. John, well endowed. This Part is much the larger, and the most populous: but the other is the fairest, and has the best buildings in it, and, among the rest, the Cathedral Church, one of the finest and most beautiful in England. . . . There are in the Close, besides the Houses of the Clergy Residentiaries, a great number of well-built and well-inhabited Houses; which made Lichfield a Place of good Company, above all the Towns in this or the neighboring Counties of Warwickshire or Derbyshire." [1]

Lichfield was in advance of most other English towns in the conveniences it afforded its inhabitants. Clear, cold water was piped from outlying springs to reservoirs, called conduits, placed at points convenient for housewives. Public wells in addition to private ones supplemented the supply, and cisterns for rainwater helped out. As the open reservoirs were an irresistible temptation to housewives to do their washing right there in the pools, the city fathers built public roofed wash-houses at brookside stations.

This fine supply of water was a safeguard against the fires which were so common when chimneys, built of stone and clay or wattles and clay, pierced roofs thatched with straw, and wood fires leaped on hearthstones. Each house had its own leather buckets and, dotted about the town, were stores of additional buckets, ladders, and long poles with hooks on the ends for pulling burning thatch into the street. Watchmen patroled the streets all night. These watchmen in early days actually woke each householder once a night to sniff for smoke.

Only one writer of the period speaks slightingly of the city. Carl Philip Moritz, a German touring England on foot, asserted that the town had narrow, dirty streets and the people were unfriendly, but he was prejudiced in advance because the daughter of a Sutton landlord had warned him that the Lichfield folks thought too well of themselves. Moritz paused only to buy bread at the bakeshop and walked on, noting that for the first time he saw round window panes.[2]

The Johnsons were not an old Lichfield family. As time of residence was reckoned they were new-comers, having dwelt there only two generations. William, Samuel's grandfather, had brought his family from Cubley, a village some twenty miles away. When he died, leaving a widow and three boys, the town came to the assistance of the bereaved family, as it came to the aid of all needy, industrious, respectable families, especially those with promising sons. The Johnsons received help first from a church charity and later from the Lichfield Conduit Lands Trust. This trust was a unique institution created originally to safeguard the city water supply and carried on by a succession of officials so capable and trustworthy that its income from land rentals increased until it was able to devote large sums to civic betterment. By the time the Johnson family came to Lichfield to live the Trust was contributing not only to the care of streets, sewage, fire prevention, but also to the relief of poverty, to medical care for the poor, and to education. The Trust became a sort of a fairy godfather to the city and no shame was attached to accepting its assistance.[3]

Among the Trust benefactions, education was considered important. The agency built or helped build schoolhouses, paid or helped pay teachers' salaries, provided textbooks for needy pupils, paid some tuitions, and for the promising sons of worthy but impoverished citizens paid the indenture fees for apprenticeships to master craftsmen. The three Johnson half-orphans, Samuel's father, Michael, and his uncles, Andrew and Benjamin, were among the lads in whom the city invested money. Michael was apprenticed for eight years to

Richard Simpson of St. Paul's Churchyard, London, a master bookbinder and bookseller. Benjamin was later sent to the same man for seven years. When Benjamin was on his own, Andrew, after a preliminary apprenticeship to a baker, was bound to Benjamin to learn book selling. So Samuel's father and two uncles were all booksellers, furnishing a literary atmosphere in which the little boy grew up.[4]

When Michael, Samuel's father, was twenty-four he opened his own business in Lichfield, expanding it rapidly until he was bookseller, bookbinder, and in a small way a publisher. He grew to be a man of great stature, good intelligence, and recurrent depressions, all three of which characteristics Samuel inherited. He also possessed what his son did not inherit, namely, good health. Not till he was forty-nine did he marry and his bride, Sarah Ford, was thirty-seven. The marriage settlement indicates a degree of prosperity. The following year he built himself a noble edifice which was both shop and home at the corner of Market Street and Breadmarket Street in the busy market place where marts had been held Tuesdays and Fridays from the twelfth century on. We have many prints of English markets of that period, all similar, all featuring stone buildings with windows and doors from which burst fat laughing women and thin viragoes with brooms, squalling babies falling down steps, brats in the gutters, loitering shopboys wearing aprons, impudent postboys in smart red jackets and polished boots, dogs fighting, peddlers brawling, and perhaps a dandy in satin picking his disdainful way. Along the cobbled market streets rumbled heavy traveling coaches with postillion and outriders, market carts with smocked carriers snapping long whips, two-wheeled light gigs, and sometimes the chaise of a traveler-in-a-hurry drawn by six galloping horses. Even though the Lichfield market was quieter than those Hogarth drew, it had resemblance, with the addition of a scattering of black-clad

15

clerics in flat hats stalking through the riot of noise and color and motion.

In the midst of such a hurley-burley, in the spot where trade was best, Michael Johnson bought a dilapidated building for the sake of the lot on which it stood. He tore it down, leased additional street footage from the Lichfield Corporation, and put up a four-story edifice which contained a large shop, two parlors, two kitchens, and eleven bedrooms. That building today is a museum and is known as The Birthplace in honor of Michael's son Samuel.

The city was divided into three Parishes: St. Mary's—where Michael built—Stowe, and St. Michael's. St. Mary's, conterminous with the ancient city, held the most important buildings and shops, the Three Crowns Inn, the Guildhall where Mrs. Siddons acted for the first time after her marriage, the Corn Market, Dame Oliver's School, the excellent Grammar School where Dr. Hunter flogged and taught, dwellings, and after 1766 Lucy Porter's fine new house.

To the northeast lay the Parish of Stowe, or St. Chad's or Chad-Stowe, which took its name from the Saint, his cell, and his well. Michael Johnson built here the parchment works which contributed to his financial undoing, and here beside Stowe Pool was the famous tree, probably not planted by Michael but called the Johnson Willow.

In St. Michael's Parish was situated, just outside the South gate of the City, St. John's Hospital, an old building with its row of ancient chimneys outside the walls like the shell of a crustacean, an almshouse for poor old men who could qualify as God-fearing, non-drinking paupers, neither leprous nor mad, but of earnest and chaste conversation.

The Johnsons had been three years married when Samuel, their first child, was born, Wednesday, September 7, old style (or September 18, new style), 1709. This year was a momen-

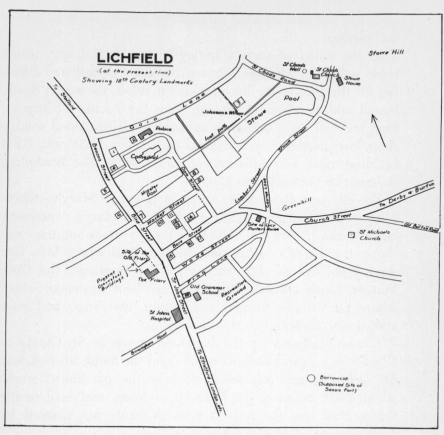

LICHFIELD

(at the present time)

Showing 18th Century Landmarks

Stowe Hill

St Chad's Well
St Chad's Church
Stowe House
St Chad's Road

To Stafford

Gaia Lane

Johnson's Willow

Lost path

Stowe

Pool

Beacon Street

Palace

Cathedral

Stowe Street

Minster Pool

Dam Street

Market Street

Lombard Street

Greenhill

To Derby & Burton

Church Street

Old Burton Road

Old Street

Bore Street

Wade Street

Site of Lucy Porter's House

St Michaels Church

Site of the Old Friary

Present Conventual Buildings

The Friary

St John Street

Frog Lane

Old Grammar School

Recreation Ground

St Johns Hospital

Birmingham Road

To Stratford London etc.

Borrowcop
(Supposed Site of Saxon Fort)

KEY

1 Vicars' Close
2 Deanery
3 The Parchments
4 Erasmus Darwin's House
5 Site of David Garrick's House
6 The Swan
7 The George
8 Brooke House
9 Site of Dame Oliver's School
10 Greene's Museum
11 Dr. Johnson's Birthplace
12 Three Crowns Inn
13 Site of Elias Ashmole's House
14 St. Mary's Church
15 Minors House
16 Tudor House
17 Guildhall
18 John Hunter's House

PLATE I

Plan of Lichfield in Johnson's Time

Drawn by Lawrence Squire from eighteenth century data

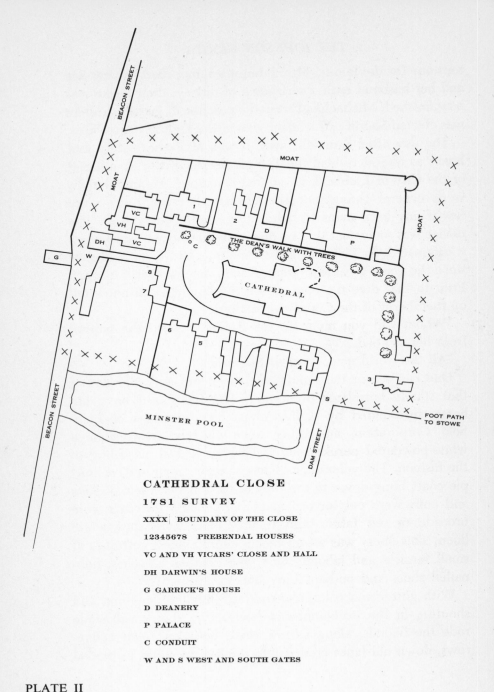

CATHEDRAL CLOSE

1781 SURVEY

XXXX   BOUNDARY OF THE CLOSE

12345678   PREBENDAL HOUSES

VC AND VH VICARS' CLOSE AND HALL

DH DARWIN'S HOUSE

G GARRICK'S HOUSE

D DEANERY

P PALACE

C CONDUIT

W AND S WEST AND SOUTH GATES

PLATE II

Plan of Lichfield Close

Drawn by Lawrence Squire from an eighteenth century chart

tous one for the family. Mrs. Johnson's father died leaving her and her husband each a small sum of money; their house was now finished; Michael had started a parchment factory; and he was elected Sheriff of Lichfield, one of the highest civic offices.

The day after Samuel's birth, it was his father's duty and honor as Sheriff to lead the Perambulation of the Boundaries of the City of Lichfield, an annual ceremony. Perambulations were general throughout the country because there were few if any local maps to delineate accurate boundaries. The device was so ancient that no one knew how or where or when it originated. In Lichfield Perambulations had been held ever since the place became a "county" with its own sheriff in 1547. Prior to that date the onus of settling boundary disputes fell on the Sheriff of the County of Stafford.

"Whom will you invite to the Riding?" asked the mother from her sickbed.

"All the world now," replied the father.

One can see in the mind's eye the pomp and splendor of that stately horseback procession. The big sheriff on a big horse, surrounded by bailiffs, constables, members of Lichfield Corporation, and other town officials, wearing huge white-powdered perukes and large hats cocked according to the fashion. The voluminous skirts of their green, red, or purple coats hung down to the tops of their boots, their pockets and cuffs were cut for ornamentation, their waistcoats were brocade or red fabric, and their cravats were snow-white linen. This finery was set off by the more modest costumes of small farmers and laborers who wore leather breeches, hobnailed shoes and perhaps blue smocks.

With glitter and color, clanking and jingling, laughing and shouting in the exuberance of health, the showy calvacade rode the bounds, along narrow roads between green hedgerows, down old lanes eroded into ditches, by villas in tended

17

grounds, as well as windowless hovels, by gravel pits, black peat meadows, stretches of clay soil, rich marle, and fruit orchards, through all the lovely countryside.

The circuit began at a place called the Cross and Hand. The course was laid down from the Cross and Hand to "a street called Bacon Street and from thence goeth northward along the lane leading to Longdon Church unto a little lane at the further side of Oakenfields and so along that little cross-lands unto another lane . . . and then into another little lane between Stitchbrooke Ground and Gifford's Crofts; and so along that little lane at the further side of the Lady Lea-sowe, being the land of Zachary Babington, Esq., and down that lane to a brook called Pone's Brook, and so on over that Brook into another lane called Steppingstones Lane . . . turn into a field of Lichfield, called Whisich, at a stile going into the fields called Browne's Fields; and so taking in the field, called Whisich, then go by the closes, called Browne's Field Hedge, unto the grounds called God's Croft Hedge; and so along that hedge. . . ."

Other landmarks were Gosling's Lane; Matthew Coal Lane; the nearer end of Gorsty bank; Burton-turnings; lanes here and lanes there, some to enter, some to pass; and when nearly home, along the brook in Pipe Green, into "a little lane that buteth upon the lane that leadeth from Lichfield to Pipe" and so on back to the Cross and Hand.[5]

A great feast was held after the Perambulation, perhaps in the Sheriff's proud new house where the day-old baby lay in his mother's arms; perhaps in an Inn; perhaps in the Guildhall where there was more room. The feasts in those days were gargantuan. Beef and lamb and pork and venison and game and fish were put on the table along with puddings and tarts and jellies and sweets and breads of every sort. Food was washed down with draughts of famous Lichfield ale.

This day was the high point of Michael Johnson's life. His

son Samuel when himself an old man liked to tell how all the town was feasted with uncommon magnificence and how Michael Johnson was the last but one to maintain the splendor of the Riding.

It was not a happy household into which the boy was born. The parents had sterling virtues but not the graces of life. Mrs. Johnson was a worrying woman and she had plenty to fret about. The husband who had been so prosperous at the time of his marriage, over-expanded his business and never caught up with his debts. But however unwisely he managed his financial affairs, he never lost the esteem of his fellow citizens. He was elected to positions of trust, serving a term as Warden of the Conduit Trust; he was Warden of St. Mary's Church; and until his death he held the office of Magistrate.[6]

The strain was increased by Mrs. Johnson's conviction that she had married beneath her station. When rich, dominating, conservative Mrs. Robert Harriott of Trysull, cousin to Mrs. Johnson on her mother's side, came to visit, the atmosphere was thick with disapproval. Mrs. Harriott seems to have given financial assistance at times, but Mr. Johnson was so exasperated with her that he asserted his independence by working his horses on the Sabbath, although he was usually a strict Sabbath observer. He escaped from the critical women by getting on his horse and riding away to canvass for book orders.

Little Samuel's wretched health increased the family gloom. His Aunt Ford, a good-hearted but tactless woman, commented that he was such a sickly baby that she wouldn't herself have picked him up in the street. Mrs. Johnson so cherished this ailing child of her middle age, borne with difficulty, that it was hard for her to put him out to nurse, according to the accepted custom. She visited him every day and because other mothers laughed at her anxiety, she went furtively, by different routes. The pitiful, near-sighted, scrofulous child was taken to doctors without avail. When he was two and a half his mother traveled to London with him to have him touched by Queen Anne, the Royal Touch being reputed a cure for scrofula. The Touch worked no miracle but Samuel came home richer by a speckled linen frock which he called his London Frock, a silver cup, and a silver spoon, marked "Sam," to distinguish them from the rest of the family silver which consisted of two spoons. Poverty had not yet taken a permanent seat at the Johnson hearthstone. One other child, Nathaniel, was born to the parents.

Samuel learned his letters from a hornbook at an infant school in Dam Street nearby, kept by Dame Anne Oliver, widow of Peter Oliver who had been a shoemaker. Samuel was so near-sighted that one day when he was making his difficult way home alone, his teacher came upon him actually crawling along the gutter on hands and knees. When she went to his assistance he fell into a rage at the idea of being helped. He was no more docile as a child than later as a man. At the age of six he was advanced to a school kept by a man, Thomas Browne, an ex-shoemaker. The master had a desk and a chair, but the pupils sat on the floor when they were not standing for recitation. We need not assume that because Browne had been a shoemaker he was an illiterate man, for workmen in those days were craftsmen and frequently had excellent brains as well as skilful fingers. Indeed, Browne had written a spelling book which he dedicated To The Universe. When Samuel was seven and ready to study Latin he went on to Lichfield Grammar School, headed at this time by the famous Dr. John Hunter.

Young Samuel was under the assistant master as long as he was in the lower forms. When he advanced to the classes taught by Dr. Hunter personally, he got on very badly indeed with that harsh disciplinarian. Dr. Hunter was perhaps tyrannical even according to the pedagogical customs of the time. A cane was as much a part of a teacher's equipment as a book, and to Hunter it was even more important. With it he flogged Latin with unusual success into a number of boys who grew up to be distinguished men, including seven who later sat contemporaneously as judges in the superior courts at Westminster. Johnson looked back on him as a brutal, unjust bully. Since other men who were students at the same time spoke highly of him as a teacher, it seems possible that personal antagonism existed between the two, although one was a dignified, elderly schoolmaster of distinction and the other an obstreperous cub of a schoolboy.

Samuel was more popular with his schoolmates than with the master. Handicapped by poor eyesight and the inertia which beset him all his life, he could not join in school games, although he developed great muscular strength. His Uncle Andrew Johnson, a champion in these arts of whom a boy could boast, gave him instructions in boxing and wrestling and his father taught him to swim, a somewhat uncommon accomplishment in those days. To offset failure in sports, Samuel made good in class work. Only one pupil in the school rivaled him—the son of a local plumber. Stories have come down to us of the boys carrying Samuel on their shoulders in honor of his classroom feats and of giving him slides on the ice, pulled by a rope around his middle. Three boys were closer to him than the others. John Taylor of Ashbourne was his lifelong friend. Next in his regard stood Edmund Hector, a Lichfield boy who later moved to Birmingham. A less intimate companion was Robert James, belonging to a Lichfield family given to the medical profession; later on he became known as the inventor of James Powders which some people recommended as a cure-all, while others denounced them as poison.

Outside the school young Johnson, a city boy, was to a limited extent received by the clerical families in the Cathedral

Close who formed a clique separate from City social life. The city of Lichfield was at first only an adjunct to the Cathedral Close, all government being vested in the ecclesiastical body. The manorial rights of the Manor of Lichfield were a valuable perquisite of the Bishops of the diocese until 1547 when these rights were transferred to the bailiffs and citizens in return for certain reserved rights and privileges and an annual rental of fifty pounds which is still paid to the Bishop.

The Close was smaller than the city, having in 1781 only forty-three houses in contrast to the City's seven hundred and twenty-two. Its population was two hundred and sixteen inhabitants while in the city dwelt three thousand five hundred and fifty-five persons.[7] The Close was entirely exempt from civic jurisdiction. It had its own magistrates and constables, its own local by-laws, water supply and so on. It was the more learned section, with its prebendaries, canons, deacons, archdeacons, chancellors, precentors and other cathedral officers. There was the smell of Latin, Hebrew and Greek in the Close. Many of the clergy had traveled and some spoke French, Italian and even German, in addition to keeping Latin a live language on their tongues. The Close tended to look down on the City because the ecclesiastical families were in general of a higher social rank than the City folk, but there was more wealth and a sprinkling of titles among the latter. Although this cleavage existed, the relationship was friendly and some families were at home in both sets.

We know much more about the people who lived in the Close than about those in the City, because the Close wrote more letters, histories, and biographies. The City built schools, churches, and almshouses, constructed water works, drained marshes, surveyed land, built causeways, recruited troops—in short built a city. Although the Close did some repairing and a little building within its narrow bounds, it interested itself chiefly in music, writing, and theorizing. The Townsmen pretty well restricted their writing to official reports, while the Gownsmen wrote poetry and prose in several languages, on many subjects. The religion of the Cathedral Close was so undeviating as to be stolid. The mysticism of the Quakers and the rising vigor of the Methodists were repulsed by a wall of religious conservatism. If any of the clergy had spiritual natures it was not they who held the highest preferments.

The atmosphere of the Close contrasted sharply with that of the City. The hubbub of trade was replaced by the rhythm of chimes floating away over the countryside, the chant of ritual and the music of men's singing voices. Against the dignity of the red sandstone Cathedral, among Tudor houses and Georgian mansions with flower gardens, strode somber clergy in black kneebreeches, black wool stockings, voluminous robes, full-bottomed, powdered wigs, and round, low-crowned, broad-brimmed felt hats. Hoop-skirted ladies in bright silks strolled along the shaded Dean's Walk. Children dressed like little men and women played in the gardens and dashed along the precincts.

Young Samuel while still a lad gained entrance to this fastidious coterie through the patronage of Gilbert Walmesley, Registrar of the Ecclesiastical Court of Lichfield Cathedral. Mr. Walmesley was a bachelor, living in the Bishop's Palace and making his home a center of social life. He possessed that form of social talent which makes a party both a social treat and a mild festival, and his hospitality was extended to those who needed recognition as well as to his friends and equals. He liked to help the more promising youngsters of the town. The group which he gathered about him was a fore-runner of present-day extra-curricular activities and character-forming organizations. Prominent among the youngsters were Samuel Johnson and David Garrick. It was not hard to foresee a pleasing future for a clever, friendly boy like David, but it took perspicuity to detect behind the screen of awkwardness and arrogance the quality of Samuel's mind. Both boys were much in Mr. Walmesley's home.

Their patron was able to live in the Bishop's Palace because the Bishops of Coventry and Lichfield, up to 1868, rented out the building; they themselves lived in Eccleshall Castle near Stafford. The Palace was one of a group of beautiful ecclesiastical buildings, a spacious stone edifice north of the Cathedral and next to the Deanery. It had been built under odd circumstances, by the Right Reverend Thomas Wood, bishop nearly a hundred years previous, a peculiar man, who lived away off in Middlesex and neglected his cathedral duties to a degree even beyond what was allowed to the clergy in those easy-going times. When he refused to make necessary repairs on what was after all his official residence, the Archbishop of Canterbury suspended him and imposed as a punishment the building of the Palace. The handsome stone house, because of its central position, wide outlook, and large rooms, was well adapted to be a gathering place.[7]

Mr. Walmesley paid especial attention to Samuel Johnson and to David Garrick. When Johnson turned the Palace dinner table into a debating society, Walmesley, a Whig, argued courteously with Sam the young Tory. Why was Sam a Tory when Lichfield Close breathed the favor of the Whig ministry? Perhaps for that very reason. Or because Sam young and Sam old hated change too deeply to accept the House of Hanover. When Garrick needed a theatre, the Palace drawing room was his. Here he staged his first play, Farquhar's *The Recruiting Agent*. Samuel was to have written a prologue, but procrastinated too long. The two boys were both talented, but the contrast between them was spectacular; Samuel was large, clumsy, and myopic, while David was small, agile, and notably graceful. In temperament they were equally dissimilar; Samuel being slow, philosophical, and melancholy; while David was quick, shrewd, and merry.

There was French blood in the Garrick family, David's grandfather having been a Huguenot who fled to England with his family. His oldest child, Captain Peter Garrick, became a recruiting agent in the English navy, met and married Arabella Clough, daughter of one of the Lichfield Cathedral Vicars Choral, and our David was one of their seven children. The Garricks had as much sickness and poverty as the Johnsons. Mrs. Garrick became an invalid suffering acute pain which could be quieted only by opium. She had what David called Ugly Little Fainting Fits and Fever on her Spirits. David's sister Jenny had long illnesses and, according to a letter the boy David wrote his absent father, the housekeeper-help was given to rolling on the floor with the cholic and tying up her head with a napkin. The grandmother was ill but hoped, wrote David, to live until the Captain's return. The father was "a jolly man." Things went wrong when he was away recruiting.

So much money went for sickness that the family was always in straitened circumstances. When the landlord had been paid and the baker, there was not enough for the butcher. In spite of patching, planning and contriving, the young Garrick ladies were in great want of lace for their heads and suffered from wearing plain headcloths. When David had a present of buckles, his breeches were ragged.

Mrs. Garrick was a gentle, loving, dependent woman, deeply in love with her husband after many years of marriage. He was fond of her and of his children, who in turn adored him. There may have been no more affection in the Garrick than in the Johnson family, but the Garrick love was articulate. Moreover, seven brothers and sisters are less susceptible to their parents' difficulties than two, having more activities of their own to take up their attention. There was laughter and wit and merriment in the Garrick home.

Both David and Samuel benefited from Walmesley's recognition of their exceptional talents. It afforded Johnson contact with culture and gayety which supplemented the treasures of his father's bookshelves. Association with people of birth, riches and breeding helped him develop self-confidence that stood him in good stead in his later life. While less important to Garrick, Walmesley's encouragement must have increased his faith in himself and helped him to withstand his family's disapproval when, after his mother's death, he dared choose the stage for his career. Walmesley's active friendship for both boys ceased only with his death.

Johnson, at Dr. Hunter's dictum, left the grammar school earlier than he intended. During a vacation the boy visited his cousin Cornelius Ford, later Rector of South Luffenham. "Parson" Ford was a university man, dissolute, extravagant and sophisticated, but brilliant. Sam had such a good time with this blithe and clever relative that he stayed on after the school term opened. When he finally appeared at school Dr. Hunter refused to take him back. Samuel hung round his father's bookshelves for a time, attended the Stourbridge Grammar School for a time, and returned to Lichfield to brood and read and work on a blank verse tragedy. From a morass of despondency he was rescued by the death of purse-proud Mrs. Harriott. This cousin who loved Sarah as much as she hated Michael, left Sarah one pair of her best flaxen sheets and pillow coates, a large pewter dish and a dozen pewter plates. Also forty pounds for her own separate use. Since Samuel entered Oxford eight months later, it seems probable that his mother decided to invest her inheritance in her son's education, the sum being about enough to support a university student for a year. The winter of 1728-9 Samuel spent at Pembroke College. When he returned to Lichfield at the end of thirteen months at Oxford it was evidently with the expectation of going back later on, for he left his books behind. This was not to be. Either money could not be raised or his health, bad at this time, would not permit it.[8]

. Now began a period of very great unhappiness. He was seriously handicapped by his appearance and manner. He was tall, emaciated, and big-boned. His face was marked with scrofula. He was untidy in his dress. His uneasy pride made him truculent. Although Gilbert Walmesley never ceased his efforts to advance Samuel's interests, the young man was difficult to place.

For two years he stayed at home with his nose in a book, adding to his massive store of learning. He tried for the position of usher at Stourbridge Grammar School and failed. He succeeded in obtaining an ushership at Market Bosworth Grammar School, but unable to endure the subservience required of him, gave up the job. After another stay in Lichfield, he went to Birmingham where he lived for a time with his schoolfellow, Edmund Hector, and here he began his writing life by working on the *Birmingham Journal*, but without marked success. This was a dark period of uncertainty, depression and poverty, interrupted by his marriage in 1735 to a Birmingham widow who had some money, but not sufficient to put an end to his financial difficulties. He failed to obtain the headmastership of a school at Solihull, near Birmingham. He opened a school of his own at Edial, near Lichfield, with funds his wife brought him, but despite Walmesley's exertions, failed to get enough pupils to support the venture.

All Johnson had to rest his hopes upon was a half-written tragedy, *Irene*. Walmesley, who never lost faith in Johnson's capacities, advised him to take *Irene* to London and try for theatrical production. Leaving his wife in Lichfield, Samuel set out early in March 1737 for the great city with David Garrick who had been one of the pupils at Edial and who was now going to study at Rochester.

In later years the two liked to recall their youthful poverty, especially how they traveled on one horse by the ride-and-tie method. They somewhat exaggerated their hardships as self-made men are wont to do, looking back from comfortable achievement. Johnson would say:

"That was the year I came to London with two-pence half-penny in my pocket."

Garrick would hand him his cue,

"Eh? What you say? With two-pence half-penny in your pocket?"

Johnson would repeat:

"Why, yes; when I came with two-pence half-penny in *my* pocket, and thou, Davy, with three half-pence in thine."

As a matter of fact their circumstances were not then so desperate. Enough money was left from Mrs. "Tetty" Johnson's dower to support her and her daughter, Lucy, in Lichfield; one may assume that some small portion was allotted to the London adventure, as had been the case in setting up the school. As for Garrick, his father was expecting to pay his son's expenses while studying for the bar. Dire need came soon enough. Samuel's brother, Nathaniel, who was to help in the bookstore, died a few days after Samuel's departure. He seems to have been a problem son and there is a suspicion that he died by his own hand. David's father died within a week.

The two young men worked at whatever odd jobs they could get in London and Johnson drudged on *Irene*. Before the end of the summer Johnson went back to his mother's house in Lichfield where he remained for three months. When he returned to the assault on London again he took his wife with him. This time he secured work from Edward Cave, founder, publisher and editor of *The Gentleman's Magazine*. Johnson helped edit, translated articles from foreign languages, and wrote pieces on various subjects. His earnings were so small that he applied for the headmastership of a school at Appleby in Leicestershire, and went there for personal interviews. Again he failed. After this he spent several months wandering in the Midlands, visiting his friend, John Taylor, in Ashbourne, and later his mother in Lichfield, in the winter of 1739-40. We know little about this period of his life. It was a time of discouragement and slackened effort. Mrs. Johnson to whom he had been married now for some years remained in London. There is indication of a temporary lack of sympathy between them, and little if any correspondence.

CHAPTER III

Three Ladies
Tetty, Hill, and Molly

JOHNSON'S marriage to the Widow Porter was fantastic. Elizabeth Jervis Porter (Mrs. Harry Porter) was twenty years his senior and the mother of three children. Johnson met the Porter family during Harry's lifetime, while he was staying in Birmingham with Edmund Hector in 1734. He had become acquainted with Lucy, the daughter, when she visited her aunt, Mrs. John Hunter, the schoolmaster's wife, in Lichfield. Lucy introduced Samuel to her mother, and the mother was favorably impressed with him. She told Lucy, "This is the most sensible man I have ever met." Evidently Johnson was equally pleased, for when Harry Porter died that same year, Johnson married the widow only ten months later. He was then twenty-six and his bride forty-six. Johnson asserted that it was a love match on both sides, and we have no reason to doubt his statement in spite of the fact that Mrs. Porter's possession of a small fortune made the marriage possible.

The bride came of a good line of Leicestershire squires on

her father's side and on her mother's from landed stock of equal respectability. From her maternal grandmother she inherited money, household chattels, and jewelry to the value of about eight hundred pounds.[1]

Much of the information about her is unreliable because it is colored by prejudices which existed against both her and Johnson. Their marriage united and increased these antagonisms. The feeling against Johnson sprang chiefly from the old hostility between him and his former schoolmaster, Dr. Hunter. The Hunters and the Porters were related and shared each others' dislikes. Practically everyone in Lichfield belonging to the middle class and minor gentry was related by blood or marriage or both, to everyone else, and family ties were strong. The complaint against Mrs. Porter was that she was the cause of her husband's bankruptcy. Her in-laws accused her of extravagance. We do not know whether this was a reasonable charge or whether it rose from the natural desire to excuse a relative's failure by blaming an outsider. In any case Mrs. Porter did not improve her standing with her deceased husband's family when she so hastily married young Johnson who had never been able to earn his own keep, let alone support a wife. Her in-laws were confirmed in their belief that she was a trifling, irresponsible creature.

There is some confirmation of the charge that Mrs. Johnson was extravagant, from Mrs. Desmoulins, penniless widow of a writing master and daughter of Johnson's godfather, Dr. Swinfin. Mrs. Desmoulin spent some time with Mrs. Johnson when the latter was living in lodgings in Hampstead for the sake of fresh air, while Johnson remained in London. Mrs. Desmoulin said later that Mrs. Johnson indulged herself in nice living at unsuitable expense while her husband was drudging in London smoke, and that she by no means treated him with that complacency which is the most engaging quality in a wife. However, one remembers that, when destitute Mrs. Desmoulin and her daughter were supported in Johnson's own home, she kept the household by the ears with her bad temper. The pot was calling the kettle black.

Plenty of people spoke ill of Tetty—to give her the name by which her husband always designated her. David Garrick was one of the pupils in the school which Johnson set up at Edial, near Lichfield, immediately after his marriage, financing it with Mrs. Johnson's dowry which had not been swallowed up in her first husband's bankruptcy. Garrick held that she was a silly, affected woman; fat, over-painted, full of girlish airs and graces and over fond of cordials; but schoolboy Garrick naturally found a middle-aged bride in love with a young husband an absurd object. His mimicry of her later on in select companies was doubtless very funny, but not convincing evidence.

That as a younger woman she was lovely to look at is proved by a little-known portrait which depicts her in her early thirties.[2] Even allowing for the usual portrait-painter's flattery, the woman comes near being a beauty. Soft fair hair is parted and puffed to reveal an unusually high forehead; her face is a long, narrow oval, and the eyebrows are arched above well-formed eyes. The expression is gentle and a trifle whimsical. Her shoulders slope and her very low-cut dress is charmingly simple. She looks like a gentle, loving woman. If one wishes to pick flaws and deduce how the face might alter in later years, one can suggest that the forehead is too high, the chin softly weak and the nose over-long. It is not a strong face nor one that would weather well.

Tetty had taste for good reading and a pretty wit. She read comedy aloud to Johnson's liking, but he criticized her in tragedy. Certain stories which have come down to us from different sources indicate that she was intelligent and quick-witted. When Johnson with a lover's humbleness said he was not worthy of marriage with her for several reasons, including having had an uncle who was hanged, she replied that though she had not had a relative hanged she had fifty that deserved hanging. (She may have been thinking of the Hunters who scorned her.) When Johnson one day began to say grace she interrupted him with, "Nay, hold, Mr. Johnson, and do not make a farce of thanking God for a dinner which in a few minutes you will protest is not eatable."

One of Mrs. Johnson's friends was Anna Williams, the poetess. We know her best as a member of that ill-assorted family which Dr. Johnson gathered under his benevolent roof after his wife's death. She is less famous as a verse-maker than as a tea-maker who when she was old and blind gauged the fullness of teacups by keeping her finger inside as she poured. She said that Mrs. Johnson had a good understanding and great sensibility but was inclined to be satirical. Johnson, on the other hand, said she was so sympathetic that she encouraged people to feel sorry for themselves when they had never before thought themselves ill-used. He said, also, that she was patient in illness. She seems to have been an easy-going, self-indulgent woman, with a kindly disposition, who was as lenient to her husband's failings as to her own.

She had a good deal to put up with. Johnson was more successful as a friend than as a family man. He was kind, loving, and steadfast, but he was not domestic-minded. He was easily vexed and snappish, but had not that insistent continuity of obstinacy, called firmness, which is necessary to govern a household. As with many argumentative natures, his first impulse was to take the opposite side, a trait that makes for lively conversation but not for harmonious living.

This lack of adaptability came out even on their way to the altar, a trip which they took on horseback from Birmingham to Derby. The bride was in a capricious mood, perhaps a bit on the hysterical side as even a second-time bride may be, and complained that the groom rode too fast and she couldn't keep up, and when he slackened pace, that he was a laggard and she could not go so slow. Johnson resolved not to be the slave of caprice but to begin as he meant to end. He pushed on briskly till he was out of her sight, knowing that she could not miss the road which ran between two hedgerows. When she had had her lesson he slackened speed and she came up in tears. Boswell admires this as "manly firmness," but it was more like calling out the fire engine to extinguish a candle.

A certain independence of spirit she must have possessed, and a warm-hearted nature, or she would not have defied her friends and relatives by marrying Johnson. Her tenderness was sufficient for her to overlook his appalling aspect and bad manners. Other women in later years endured these traits, but that was after he was famous and it gave a woman prestige to be seen with him. His wife was able to love him for his good qualities in spite of his peculiarities. He, on his side, never faltered in his devotion to her, and after her death he kept the anniversary of his loss with tears and prayers.

It is odd that a man unprepossessing in appearance, slovenly in dress, rough to the point of rudeness, and gluttonous, should have won the esteem of gentlewomen. Certainly not all of them cultivated his friendship only because of his literary renown. Peter Garrick, David's older brother, told James Boswell that a lady had confided in him that Dr. Johnson was "a very seducing man." The secret lay in the deep tenderness which he felt for women and his protecting attitude toward them. His letters to female correspondents are charming.

A few years after his marriage, Johnson met a woman whom he much admired although his close association with her did not come until after his wife's death. This was Hill Boothby, a well-born, high-bred gentlewoman. He made her acquaintance in the winter of 1739-40, when he was visiting John Taylor in Ashbourne toward the end of his second period of poverty and severe depression. This sojourn with his old friend was a welcome break in what was an otherwise dismal winter.

During this visit he associated with a group of county families living around Ashbourne, related by blood or marriage or interests or by all three ties. These families included the Taylors of Ashbourne; the Boothbys of Ashbourne Hall; the Meynells at Bradley, a mile and a half northeast of Ashbourne; the Fitzherberts at Tissington Hall, four miles to the northeast of Ashbourne; and probably the Ports, at beautiful Ilam in the foothills of the Peak mountains. Each family lived on its own estate. Staffordshire, Derbyshire and the adjacent counties held to old-fashioned methods of farming. The land was divided into large and small estates and the lords of the manor rented their acres to tenant farmers who lived for generations in the same houses and ploughed the same fields. Even when through some unusual circumstances an hereditary estate came into strange hands, the tenants usually stayed on undisturbed in their possession. The method was inefficient and wasteful compared with the great agricultural projects being developed in Norfolk, where tenants were ousted, their farms thrown together, and common land enclosed, for intensive cultivation. Under that new system crops were great, cattle heavier, and expense of production reduced, but tenant farmers were depressed to the status of day laborers. The change was beneficial to the nation as a whole, but it wiped out the yeoman class.

Staffordshire and Derbyshire and other counties with swift-running streams and unexploited coal mines were fated for an industrial rather than an agricultural re-fashioning, equally beneficial to the country at large and equally disastrous to many individuals, and ruinous to the sweetly smiling landscape. This change was in the future; the railroad had not yet come, and slow-moving canals winding from lock to lock were the apex of engineering skill.

The leisurely, placid social life of the inter-related county families fitted into this lovely setting. The position of John Taylor's house in Ashbourne village made it a natural social center and the standing of the Taylor family was good enough to admit its members and guests into aristocratic circles. John Taylor had been carrying on his father's law practice since the death of the latter, but this year he gave it up and entered the church, becoming rector of Market Bosworth. Although he had not yet acquired his later wealth and numerous ecclesiastical preferments, he was already a person of importance.

It was Johnson's first experience of associating with the gentry on equal terms, for in Lichfield he had been a protegé of Walmesley and his friends, rather than a comrade, and appreciation by these people who were his social superiors was good medicine for a discouraged heart. He found the Meynell family especially congenial. Mr. Littleton Poyntz Meynell, the father, has survived as the man who made a memorable remark which Johnson used to quote with a chuckle, namely, "For anything I see, foreigners are fools." His wife and his daughter Mary were of a higher intellectual capacity. They were bound in closest friendship with Hill Boothby, all three being very religious. Johnson greatly admired these ladies and his feeling was returned.

Hill Boothby belonged to an ancient family that could trace its lineage back some three hundred years. The family seat was Ashbourne Hall, on the outskirts of the village of that name. Most of the family fortune, the girl's odd name of "Hill" and her father's baptismal name "Brooke," came from Hill's grandmother, the Hon. Hill Brooke, second wife of Sir William Boothby.

Correspondence concerning the connection between Hill's grandfather and Samuel's father has come to light.[3] The letters deal with delays in the arrival of books from the Johnson shop, criticism of the bindings, and more personal matters.

Sir William asks Michael to investigate the character and attainments of a Frenchman teaching school in Lichfield and report as to his suitability as a tutor for Brooke, then fourteen, later Hill's father. Another time Michael is requested to look up a Mr. Pike in Uttoxeter, to discover if he knows Latin, writes a good hand, understands business, is honest, and comes of a respectable family, as Sir William is considering engaging him as a private secretary.[4]

Though Sir William died two years before Samuel's birth, it seems quite possible that the name of so good a customer was sometimes mentioned in the Johnson family. Hill Boothby was less likely to know of the Johnsons, unless the Boothby family continued to patronize the Johnson bookshop. She must have been deeply influenced in her own scholarly trend by her grandfather's library which was so noted that it was mentioned on his tombstone; the inscription records that he "... was a man of learning, evident by his collection of nearly six thousand books, now regularly placed in a convenient and graceful library in Ashbourne Hall, to remain to his posterity there." Sir Brooke, the fifth baronet, Hill's brother, is said to have ordered sent to him a copy of every book that was printed.

Hill Boothby was the first learned lady with whom Johnson was well acquainted. She was a student of ancient and modern languages, mathematics and natural philosophy. This last term was somewhat loosely used to indicate such matters as astronomy, chemistry, botany, and other sciences. Her handwriting was especially admired and a Hebrew grammar which she compiled for her own use was as beautiful as the parchment manuscripts of the middle ages.

Her nephew Sir Brooke, the sixth baronet, who was ten or eleven when she died, remembered her beauty, grace, and elegance. He described her as having "much feminine softness" and excelling at active exercises. The active exercises in

which elegant females indulged were chiefly walking and battledore. Sir Brooke, years later, when turning over to Mrs.
Piozzi Johnson's correspondence with Hill, wrote, "She had
the appearance of that extreme cleanliness which one cannot
help supposing to be connected with purity of mind." Anna
Seward, who as a little girl doubtless knew Miss Boothby in
her last years, expressed a similar feeling, though in deroga-
tory terms, speaking of Miss Boothby as Johnson's "spiritua-
lized mistress." [5] Johnson himself emphasized "the purity of
her mind" and "the graces of her manner" when describing
her to Mrs. Thrale.

Johnson's other women friends were likewise all good
women but they were not so heavenly-minded. Hill Boothby
lived with God to a degree which embarrassed some of her
friends. Her nephew apologized for her spiritual ardor on the
ground that she was perhaps a little misguided by the enthusiasm or hypocrisy of the men she chose for the directors of
her faith. Anna Seward dubbed her puritanic, and even Dr.
Johnson admitted to Mrs. Piozzi that Hill Boothby had
"pushed her piety to bigotry, her devotion to enthusiasm." She
was doubtless influenced, probably indirectly, by the religious
awakening brought about by the open-air preaching of Whitefield and the Wesleys which finally resulted in the formation
of the Methodist Church. This new zeal in religious matters
was at the time shocking to most members of the conservative
Established Church. To call a person "enthusiastic" was an
insult which could not be smiled away. Hill Boothby was
perhaps admired not for her piety, but in spite of it.

We do not know with what relatives or friends Hill
Boothby made her home at the time Johnson first met her.
Later on, when Mary Meynell, after her mother's death,
married William Fitzherbert of Tissington Hall, Hill Boothby
went to live with her. Another member of the household was
the Rev. Richard Graves, a domestic chaplain. Mr. Graves

THREE LADIES, TETTY, HILL, AND MOLLY

wrote a book, and in that book he gives us a respectful but lively picture of Miss Boothby. Mr. Graves admired the lady, but he did not take her as seriously as did some of her friends.

The book was entitled *The Spiritual Quixote: or, the Summer Ramble of Mr. Geoffrey Wildgoose. A Comic Romance,* the narrative of an ambulative summer in the life of one Wildgoose, an itinerant preacher. The slight thread of his wandering binds together essays, short fiction, descriptions of life on the road, and meetings with members of all social classes. Its theme is satire on Whitefield, whom Graves, a scholar and a man of taste, found offensive.

One of the episodes is a picture of life at Tissington Hall. Mr. Fitzherbert is called Sir William Forrester; Mrs. Fitzherbert, Lady Forrester; Hill Boothby, Miss Sainthill. Several other members of the family are introduced and guests, including Col. Rappee, whose actual name was Col. Deane.

Wildgoose, traveling afoot with a companion of lower social standing and education than himself, in a lovely part of the Dove Valley, came upon a genteel party of well-dressed people, picnicking in a cave halfway up a mountainside, amusing themselves with German flutes, singing, reading, and Rhenish wine, while servants stationed at proper distances among the trees, enlivened the scene with strains of music from French horns. The well-dressed revelers, discovering that the shabby wayfarer was a man of parts, shared with him the cold collation of ham, fowl, tongue, oranges, cheesecake and other portable provisions and invited him and his companion home with them for a visit of several days. Mr. Fitzherbert loved unusual personalities and was entirely without snobbishness.

Upon their arrival at the venerable pile of Gothic building, fitted up in modern taste, Mrs. Forrester (Fitzherbert) went immediately to the nursery, accompanied by Wildgoose, to hear her children's prayers. Mrs. Molly, the nurse, met them

39

at the nursery door with the youngest who "being the most helpless, possessed of course the largest share" of his mother's affection. This was little Alleyne Fitzherbert, later Lord St. Helens, Ambassador to Russia, who when he was an old man indicated the real persons behind the aliases of the story. The children said their prayers and were blessed, after which the adults met for their own evening prayers in the hall. Sir William Forrester (Fitzherbert) before marriage "had led a remarkably gay life, and had even been tainted with many of the fashionable opinions of the age." Regard for Lady Forrester (Fitzherbert) and a sense of the importance of religious principles made him so domestic a man that he read prayers every evening "even when in town."

Dr. Johnson describing Mrs. Fitzherbert to Mrs. Thrale said that she was handsome enough for a queen; her beauty had more in it of majesty than of attraction; more of the dignity of virtue than the vivacity of wit. Her first care was to preserve her husband's soul from corruption and her second to keep their estate entire for their children. When asked if the husband returned the regard, Dr. Johnson said, "He felt her influence too powerfully; no man will be fond of what forces him daily to feel himself inferior. She stood at the door of her Paradise in Derbyshire, like the angel with the flaming sword, to keep the devil at a distance. . . . She died, and her husband felt at once afflicted and released."

After Prayers came an interlude of "Repartees," during which Miss Sainthill (Boothby) a very sensible maiden lady, a friend and companion of Lady Forrester (Fitzherbert) rallied Col. Rappee (Deane) on absenting himself from Prayers. Col. Rappee (Deane), for whom everyone felt dislike and contempt, but who for some reason had to be endured as a guest, had a distasteful trick of ridiculing religion (in that house!), matrimony (before Mrs. Fitzherbert!), parsons (before Mr. Graves!) and old maids (before Miss Boothby!), in a way that shocked the delicacy of his hearers. Sir William (Mr. Fitzherbert) egged Miss Sainthill (Boothby) on to snub the upstart and applauded her Repartees.

Attacked on his absence from Prayers, the Colonel replied without much originality that one could pray in private as well as in public. Miss Sainthill (Boothby) went farther, and agreed that one could pray even in a warm bed, but was in danger of dropping off to sleep.

The Colonel gathered his wits for defense. He stated that he never forgot to thank God for three things.

"I suppose the first is, that you are not an old maid," said Miss Sainthill, probably with an arch look.

"No, that I was not born in Russia."

Airy persiflage followed, revealing at length that it was not the Russian cold the Colonel disliked, but the arbitrary government.

The Colonel's second cause of thanksgiving was that he had not been born a cheesemonger, as he disliked the smell of cheese. Miss Sainthill (Boothby) warming to the fray suggested smartly that he should not have been bred a soldier as he did not love the smell of gunpowder. The Colonel bowed and smiled and dealt the final blow. "I am glad that I have not a very long nose," he cried. Miss Sainthill (although Miss Boothby was an acknowledged beauty) courtesied and took a long pinch of snuff, "being conscious how liberal nature had been to her in that respect." She congratulated him because a long nose would expose him in battle to greater danger.

"Well fought, Miss Sainthill," said Sir William. "Colonel, leave off whilst you are well."

Supper was now laid on the side-board; anchovies, olives, and some other trifles. And so to bed.

If this pleasantry is faded and stale, consider how stupid our own jocoseness will seem two hundred years from now. Humorous writing is the least enduring of all literary forms. We have however established the fact that Miss Boothby had a reputation among her friends for wit as well as for learning and goodness.

Mrs. Johnson's death in 1752 threw her husband back into the loneliness from which his marriage had at least partially freed him. His need of loving was great and his affections turned toward Hill Boothby whom he had probably then known for some thirteen years. He had not been in Lichfield since the winter when he must have first made her acquaintance, but it is likely that she spent time in London with the Fitzherbert family, although Mr. Fitzherbert was not returned to Parliament from Derby until a few years later. This is conjecture, but plausible. The letters which survive were all written soon after Mrs. Johnson's death and near the end of Miss Boothby's life. They have a warm tone of tender intimacy which indicates an attachment of long standing. Perhaps it was uneasiness at the familiarity of Johnson's expressions that caused early commentators to emphasize that the relationship was wholly platonic. Perhaps the circumstance that Miss Boothby was so very religious made incongruous such expressions as "my dearest dear" and "my sweet angel." One letter closed, "Dear angel, do not forget me."

One does not know how this passionate friendship would have developed had Hill Boothby lived. She must have been fond of him; certainly she was not holding him at arm's length. It is hardly probable that a lady so splendidly regular, so dutiful, so pious, allowed many men to address her as "Dearest dear." Both were a few years under fifty when the attachment flared into increased warmth, on Johnson's side at least. At that age emotion has not atrophied nor hope been wholly lost. She died at the age of forty-eight, but of what illness, in what circumstances or where, we do not know. Nor do we have any record of the grief that her death must have caused Johnson.

A likeness exists between the personality of Hill Boothby

and that of Aspasia, a character in Johnson's play *Irene*. The role of Aspasia was not suggested by Miss Boothby, as the play was written some years before the playwright could have met her, although the drama was not produced on the stage till later. Aspasia is portrayed as beautiful, learned, poised, courageous and filled with religious fervor; all qualities in which Hill Boothby excelled. In Aspasia, Johnson drew his ideal woman. In Hill Boothby he may have recognized his Aspasia.

Mary Aston, the third woman who captivated Johnson, was the sister of Magdalen Walmesley, wife of Johnson's friend and patron. Molly had auburn hair, fine complexion, graceful figure and quick wit. It has been incorrectly assumed that Johnson's adoration was an affair of calf-love. Doubtless it was a daydream which no one took seriously, but it was the daydream of a married man in his late twenties. Anna Seward, who saw life romantically and sometimes spitefully, is responsible for the error. She says that the noble-minded Walmesley endured at his table the low-born squalid youth. "It was here that Molly Aston was frequently a visitor in the family of her brother-in-law, and probably amused herself with the uncouth adoration of the learned, though dirty stripling, etc." In another letter she sets down the series of the women he admired as: ". . . first the rustic Lucy Porter, before he married her nauseous mother;—next, the handsome but haughty Molly Aston;—next the sublimated, methodistic Hill Boothby. . . ." [6]

The difficulty in accepting these statements lies in the improbability of Samuel's having met Molly at Walmesley's home when he was a stripling, for her sister Magdalen did not marry Gilbert Walmesley until 1736, when Johnson was twenty-seven and was himself married. Anna was always hazy about dates and as all this took place before her birth, it is probable that she was painting a picture rather than recording a fact.

The youthful Samuel Johnson must have enjoyed Mary

Aston's company at her brother-in-law's after his visit to Taylor in Ashbourne when he went to stay with his mother in Lichfield. This was toward the end of 1739. Molly might easily have been then visiting the Walmesleys. This explains Mrs. Johnson's discomposure when a fortune-telling gypsy, whom the Johnsons once met on the road while walking out with two or three friends, announced after reading Johnson's palm at his wife's insistence, "Your heart is divided, Sir, between a Betty and a Molly: Betty loves you best, but you take most delight in Molly's company." Mrs. Johnson would hardly have wept about a woman whom her husband had adored as a schoolboy, but a young woman whom he admired rather frantically after his marriage was a different matter.

Molly was the lightest of Johnson's loves, although the adjective "light" is incongruous in connection with any of Johnson's emotions. He remembered her with delight rather than affection, and since it was during a particularly unhappy period that she brightened his days, he could well be grateful. He told Mr. Thrale that the happiest time of his life was that year in which he spent one whole evening with Molly Aston. "That indeed was not happiness, it was rapture; but the thought of it sweetened the whole year." If Johnson spoke thus to Mrs. Johnson of the siren—and he was not a secretive man—no wonder the poor lady wept at the gypsy's confirmation. It was a happy, open admiration which young Mr. Johnson felt for the charmer, but a letter which he wrote to Tetty this same winter bears witness to his loyal passion for his wife.

The Astons were an interesting family. The father, Sir Thomas, had one son and eight daughters. Catherine, the eldest, married Hon. Henry Hervey, fourth son of the Earl of Bristol, which brought the dissolute Hon. Henry and his equally genteel and dissolute brother, Thomas, into the circle of Dr. Johnson's acquaintanceship. Molly, the second daughter, was nearest Johnson's age, being only a year older. She married David Brodie, but not until she was forty-seven years old. (Late marriage ran in the family; sister Sophia was a bride at forty-two and Margaret, at thirty-nine.) Elizabeth, the third sister, with the courtesy title "Mrs.", was the only one who died a spinster. Magdalen who married Walmesley came next. Jane married the Rev. Francis Gastrell, the Vicar of Frodsham, in Cheshire, with interests in Stratford, where he gained immortality by cutting down Shakespeare's mulberry tree to disoblige the pilgrims to that shrine. When Johnson visited Lichfield in later years, Elizabeth and Jane, who had settled there, were his particular friends.

Johnson had a tenacious affection for members of this family. It was Catherine's high-born, disreputable husband of whom he said, "Harry Hervey: he was a vicious man, but very kind to me. If you call a dog Hervey, I shall love him." It was to Thomas Hervey who was "vicious and genteel" that Johnson wrote, begging him not to separate from his wife. Johnson's London friend, Topham Beauclerk, was related to the Astons on his mother's side.

This desultory winter, brightened in his memory by the beginning of acquaintanceship with Hill Boothby and a sprightly flirtation with Molly Aston, was brought to an end while he was staying with his mother and Lucy in the big house his father had built in the marketplace. The family financial strain was eased by a loan of eighty pounds, secured by a mortgage on the property, from Theophilus Levett, a prosperous man and an old family friend. Twenty pounds of this was Samuel's share and this twenty pounds he immediately sent to his wife in London with an affectionate letter. A second cheering event was a communication from Garrick telling him that his blank-verse tragedy *Irene* had been accepted for production at Drury Lane Theatre either in the current season or the following one, and there was an offer for publication after the production. This was heartening news at the time.

Johnson returned to London in high hopes, sometime in the spring of 1740. The *Irene* project, however, fell through and the play was not then put on the stage. Nevertheless he stayed on and established his permanent residence in the metropolis. He did not return to Lichfield till 1761.

CHAPTER IV

Lichfield Social Life

RESIDENTS in Lichfield Cathedral Close and gentry living in the city proper occupied themselves with a wide range of employments. Lichfieldians wrote poetry, studied botany, cultivated gardens, discussed philosophy, experimented, invented, and delighted in walking, dancing, visiting, and making music. Traveling theatrical troups put on Shakespeare and modern plays at the Guildhouse. Music lovers went to Birmingham, Manchester, and Sheffield for concerts and oratorios; to London for drama and musical festivals; and to various health resorts to make new acquaintances.

Lichfield was at this time engaged in a local renaissance which, although it showed itself in literary, musical and scientific activities, nevertheless was instigated by the political and religious restlessness which agitated all England. The country was shaken from without by the direful restlessness of the French and stirred within by the preaching of Whitefield and the Wesleys. The names applied to this period are significant of changes going on: the Age of Revolution, the Age of Reason, the Romantic Revival, and the Evangelical Movement. These phases were different aspects of one great wave. England was rousing herself from the long spiritual lethargy following on the Restoration. Great projects were afoot in industry, agriculture, and engineering. Political reforms were germinating. The study of sciences was accelerated. Education was seeping downward into the masses. Living conditions were becoming more comfortable. In this vast reorganization, Lichfield folk played their inconspicuous part.

The continuous influx of new families coming to live in Lichfield a longer or shorter period was especially favorable to a healthy social life. It kept the community from ossification and incidentally, by affording a supply of out-land husbands, to some degree lessened the consanguinity of the inhabitants. An eighteenth century cathedral town contained ecclesiastical families who formed a permanent colony and also what might be called an itinerant ecclesiastical population. Families like the Smallbrookes, the Woodhouses, the Whites and the Vyses had so much influence in church circles that their members were appointed to office generation after generation and they were able to place their sons and nephews and daughters' husbands as curates and rectors and vicars in neighboring parishes. The members of such families often stayed on in Lichfield after their actual connection with the Cathedral was broken; as in the case of Gilbert Walmesley's sisters-in-law, Mrs. Aston and Mrs. Gastrell.

An influx of young clergymen fresh from the university arrived to fill minor positions. Non-resident prebendaries who came annually to keep their two-month terms were accustomed to rent their houses in the Close to elderly members of the country gentry, dowagers and their daughters and relatives or friends. Such a tenant either moved out for a prebendary's two months of residence each year or received him as

PLATE III
Stowe Pool and St. Chad's Church
Minster Pool and the Cathedral

E. Stringer del 1763.

View near Lichfield, including a most remarkably large Willow Tree.

T. Cook f.

PLATE IV

Drawing which shows the Johnson Willow, the houses of Mrs. Aston and Mrs. Gastrell, and St. Chad's Church

From Rev. Stebbing Shaw's *History of Staffordshire (1798)*

a guest. Lichfield was a military center as well as a Cathedral town and officers brought their families to stay while their regiments were quartered in the town. Additional flexibility was given to the social life by smart wealthy visitors attracted by military maneuvers, concerts, balls, hunts, races, and other gaieties. Lichfield was almost as popular as the health resorts.

The serious activities which engrossed the largest number of devotees—apart from professional duties connected with the Cathedral—were writing and music. The most popular recreations were dancing and horse-racing.

Conditions in Lichfield were favorable to authorship. Gentry and clergymen were not obliged to scramble for a living, as the former inherited wealth and the latter were secure in lifetime appointments. Thanks to estate stewards working for one class and curates for the other, there was leisure for cultivating talents, although many of these softly-bedded gentlemen, balancing effort against inertia, chose elegant laziness.

Impromptu verse bubbled up freely; some of it so melodious that one suspects secret preparation of lines apparently composed on the spur of inspiration. In the older generation, William Vyse, Canon-residentiary of Lichfield Cathedral and Archdeacon of Salop, father of the general and of the rector of Lambeth, was especially gifted at improvisations. One specimen from his ready pen especially acclaimed was a eulogy on Charlotte Lynes, a very beautiful woman who was visiting his wife. The verses were written at "a convivial meeting of Lichfield gentlemen" when the drinkers were required to praise their toasts in epigram or ballad. The first verse ran:

> Shall Pope sing his flames
> With quality dames,
> And duchesses toast when he dines;
> Shall Swift verses compose
> On the Girl at the Rose
> While unsung is my fair Charlotte Lynes!

The hymn of praise oft repeated set Miss Lynes to preening herself and this annoyed the author. When complimented on the verses in a large company, he said:

> Charlotte the power of song can tell,
> For 'twas the ballade made the belle.

The clergy seldom published their verse, feeling that it would detract from their dignity. Dr. Seward was an exception. He allowed his verse to appear anonymously in Dodsley's collections.[1] His longest poem is *The Female Right to Literature*, a letter addressed to a young lady from Florence. The burden is that in Asia the female sex must bow their fair necks to slavery's galling yoke, but in happy Britain conditions are better, though many a man still fears a learned wife. Dr. Seward is for female learning but nervous about female vanity.

Sermons were a staple commodity. Many clergymen published a few for prestige, somewhat as present-day college professors put out erudite papers to prove scholarship. In The Birthplace at Lichfield is a copy of "A Sermon preached at Lichfield, on Sunday, Dec. 7, 1755, by T. Seward, Canon of Lichfield. The late dreadful Earthquakes no Proof of God's particular Wrath against the Portuguese."

Sermon writing had certain peculiarities. A discourse was not always the work of the man who delivered it from the pulpit. When Johnson was desperately poor during his early years in London he ghosted forty sermons for cash, conscientiously destroying the original manuscripts. Burning the first draft was his method of transferring ownership. As an act of friendship he wrote for Dr. Taylor sermons which after Taylor's death were published by his executor as Taylor's own. Dr. Johnson's style was recognized by his admirers and there was a mild literary scandal.

We can postulate a minor school of writers to be called The Lichfield Group, made up of Lichfieldians who achieved publication and others who frequently visited the town and were influenced in their development although they did not live there. Johnson and Garrick would be honorary members only, for they headed schools in their own right with their own standards and followers. They were, one might say, alumni of Lichfield. Active members would be Sir Brooke Boothby (verse and political pamphlets), Erasmus Darwin (verse and scientific works), Anna Seward (verse, biography, and correspondence), and Dr. Thomas Seward (verse and sermons). Qualifying as members-at-large—temporary Lichfield residents—would be Richard Lovell Edgeworth (didactic and educational prose), Thomas Day (verse, didactic prose, and juveniles), Thomas Sedgewick Whalley (drama, verse, and novels), and William Hayley (poetic plays and verse).[2]

The Cathedral with its excellent organ and talented choristers naturally inclined Lichfield taste toward serious music. Lichfieldians were passionate Handelarians. Performers and listeners never tired of his oratorios. *The Messiah* held first place in all hearts. Haydn's *Creation* was approved but not so loved.

As St. Cecelia is the tutelary saint of music, festivals were held in her honor on her feast-day, November 22. This day was observed in Lichfield from 1742 until the beginning of the next century. The thirty-second annual concert at the Vicar's Hall at eleven o'clock in the morning "was performed to the politest and most crowded audience ever remembered on the like occasion." An announcement of 1777 gives an idea of the musical standard: "The Band will be very full, the stewards having engaged some principal performers on the trumpets, kettle-drums, clarinets. First violin by Mr. Clark."

The following program for another year shows what were favorite selections:

DR. JOHNSON'S LICHFIELD

CONCERT

AT THE

VICARS HALL in LICHFIELD;

MONDAY, January 4, 1779.

ACT I.		ACT II.	
Overture.	Ditters.	Overture.	Vanhall.
Song.	Dr. Arne.	Song.	Arnold.
Quartetto.	Lidel.	Solo Bariton.	Lidel.
Song.	Handel.	Song.	Sacchini.
Harpsichord Con:	Bach.	Overture.	Ditters.

SONG, In Judith. Dr. ARNE.

Not unto us, but to his name
   The praise, the thanks bestow,
Who form'd above the starry frame,
   And sunk the deeps below.

Who gave the seasons, day and night,
   By turns to rise and fall;
Who out of shade created light,
   And out of nothing all.

             Da Capo.

SONG, HANDEL.

  In Alexander's Feast.

Softly sweet in Lydian measures
Soon he sooth'd his soul to pleasures.

SONG, Dr. ARNOLD.

Come Hope, thou Queen of endless smiles,
Whose aid the woes of life beguiles,
With thee I'll rove, with thee I'll rest
Amidst thy sweet enchantments blest.

I feel, I feel thy gladsome ray
Dawn on my soul like rising day;
My heart no more shall feel its care,
For joyful Hope inhabits there.

SONG, In Cresco,
       Sig. SACCHINI.

Tergo il pianto,
Idolo mio,
Soffri in pace,
Il mio morir.

Se tu nutri
Amor in seno
Calma il duolo,
E serba almeno
Al mio cenere i sospir.

Sergi il pianto,
Idolo mio,
Soffri in pace,
Il mio morir.

Ah mi scoppia
Il cor d'affano
E'un addio
Troppo tirano
Troppo atroce
E' il mio languir.

Sergi il pianto,
       etc.

           Da Capo.

Another concert included overtures by Abel, Vanhall, Toeschi and Haydn, songs by Handel, a harpsichord concerto, and a concerto by Handel.

Concerts given during Race Week were of a lighter character. *Aris's Birmingham Gazette,* in September 1769, reports under Lichfield News: "The Company was entertained at the Public Breakfasts by a fine Band of Music from London, by Order of the Stewards. . . . The Concerts under the direction of Mr. Saville gave general Satisfaction as the several Catches, Glees, Roundelays, etc. which were performed at the Jubilee at Stratford were very properly introduced."

The Catches, Glees, and Roundelays to which reference is made were a part of the Shakespeare Jubilee which Garrick had put on at Stratford earlier in the month. This early, crude form of what developed later into our impressive historical pageants was an unhappy fiasco. The Stratford villagers, not experienced in making a good thing out of a merry-making crowd, as did the Lichfield people accustomed to Race Week, musical festivals, and like celebrations, resented the influx of London nobility and neighboring gentry as a personal affront, and their churlishness was exceeded only by their cupidity. Rain ruined the costumes, dampness choked the elaborate fireworks, and the Avon innundated the grounds so that the coaches rolled hub deep to the theatre and ladies walked gangplanks to enter. Nevertheless Garrick salvaged and improved the entertainment for the London stage the following winter and got back the large amount of money he had put into the project.

All of Lichfield folk who could get to Stratford must have attended the watery festival. Afterward, in Lichfield, Peter Garrick, according to *Aris's Birmingham Gazette* of November 6, 1769, gave "a Genteel Entertainment to a select Number of his Lichfield Neighbors, who attended the late Jubilee at Stratford-upon-Avon. Among other Pieces of Music, the Songs in the Dedication Ode, and in Shakespeare's Garland were introduced by the Gentlemen of the Choir, Choristers, etc. who assisted Mr. Garrick's Band at Stratford; the whole was conducted with the greatest Regularity, and afforded the highest Satisfaction to everyone present."

The solos had been sung at the Jubilee by actors from Garrick's Drury Lane Company. The choir and choristers who assisted must have been from Lichfield Cathedral. Two of the songs which were among those sung at Peter Garrick's party, were Garrick's "For the lad of all lads was a Warickshire lad," and "The pride of all nature was sweet Willy O." The unfortunate episode of the slaughtered mulberry tree was featured in a song, sung by a soloist who held in his hand a goblet carved from wood of the sacred tree, with a refrain:

> Bend to thee,
> Blest Mulberry,
> Matchless was he
> Who planted thee,
> And thou like him immortal shall be.

The ladies of Lichfield were taught dancing as a branch of Deportment. The cotillion, the ecossaises, and the minuet were popular. The cotillion was a French folk dance (cotte was the short petticoat worn by peasants) and won immediate favor when brought to England in 1770. The ecossaises was similar to the English country dance but more energetic and faster in tempo and was often danced to Scottish tunes. A ball usually opened with a promenade march around the room in couples. Minuets were first danced, followed by country dances. Among the most popular country dances were three more slow and dignified than the others: *Green sleeves, Christchurch Bells* and *Joan's Placket,* the word placket designating either a pocket or a petticoat.

A brilliant series of subscription balls was held each winter in Lichfield under the direction of some high-born lady or gentleman. Of all the dances, the annual Hunt Ball was the most splendid affair, the gentlemen wearing their orange-pink hunting coats, although die-hard Jacobins danced in the Stuart plaid long after the failure of Charles Edward's cause. (Some gentlemen, for years after the Jacobean uprising of 1745, went so far as to hunt with hounds dressed in the Stuart tartan foxes which had been put into replicas of the red coats of British government soldiers.) At Hunt Balls, the ladies, full blown in hoopskirts, were splendid in every color. This rainbow was set off by the black of the clergy and ladies in mourning. Black ribbons were worn for friends, kinfolk of the farthest degree, and members of the royal family, but even sable garments did not interfere with social gaiety. On one long-talked-of occasion, ladies came in white frocks decked with ribbons and scarves to match the gentlemen's hunting coats.

All the dances which had ever been held were surpassed by a masque-ball given by Sir Nigel Gresley after he became the seventh baronet, living in the turreted villa on the banks of the River Trent, within driving distance of Lichfield. One of the large rooms in his villa was decorated with murals representing trees which arched over the ceiling, while between the trunks one saw flowered banks and winding paths. An actual paling fence with an unlatched gate shut off the pictured scene from the room. The opposite wall depicted a mountain scene and another showed fields. The fourth side was a wall of windows. The chimney was a rock grotto ornamented with mineral specimens and sea shells.

Sir Nigel could dominate this extravagant background. He was a fine figure of a man, over six feet tall, and this night he was dressed as a Grand Seignior. As he was at this time a widower, his sister Louisa, elegant and witty, acted as hostess. Sir Nigel had boasted that he would assemble forty beauties from Staffordshire and Derbyshire and he kept his word. The men of those two shires were proud of the beauty of their women.

Private balls were supplemented, equalled, and sometimes surpassed, by the subscription Balls of Race Week—tickets not transferable. Young ladies from all over Staffordshire made their debut on this occasion and men came in coaches, chaises, and on horseback to dance with the belles and toast them by name at the Race Dinner. At one such dinner, in the middle of the century, the guests included one Duke, three Earls, four Lords, sixteen Baronets, besides Honorables and Esquires; two hundred and thirty-three gentlemen in all. To be toasted at a dinner like this was something to boast about to one's grandchildren.

Race Week held annually in September was the gala event of the year. The races themselves were the most important feature, but they were accompanied by public and private entertainments of all kinds including cockfights and bull-baiting. For some time after the 1745 flare-up of Jacobin rebellion, political feeling ran so high that the Whigs held their races for three days, while the Tory races came off for two days a week later. The 1769 races were especially successful. The famous racer Eclipse, winner that year at Epsom, won the King's Place at Lichfield on Tuesday, September 19th, one of the nine races won the first year of Eclipse's career. The notable horse won eighteen consecutive races during the following years. This successful Race Week closed with a great Dinner for Gentlemen at The Kings Head, a Concert at which the Jubilee music was repeated and a Grand Ball.

A picturesque feature of all social gatherings was the age-scale of the participants, who ranged from girls in their earliest teens to dodderers with canes. Difference in years was less of a barrier between generations than it is nowadays. It was not necessary for character-forming organizations to stage Mother-and-Daughter parties or Father-and-Son dinners, for mothers, daughters, fathers, and sons were accustomed to attend social events as family groups rather than as individuals. At subscription balls the young people danced while their parents played whist in the card room. In Jane Austen's *Pride and Prejudice,* written toward the end of the century, Sir William and Lady Lucas went with their daughters to Bingley's ball and only eccentricity prevented Mr. Bennet from accompanying Mrs. Bennet and their five daughters.

When the Lunar Society, a group of savants, inventors, manufacturers, and scientists, some of whom were Lichfield men, sat down to dinner at Five Ways, the home of Samuel Galton, a wealthy Birmingham man of letters and science, the children of the family were present. At one such dinner a small black and yellow snake was discovered slithering round the room. "Mary Ann, go catch that snake," said Mrs. Galton to the child who was later Mrs. Schimnelpennick. Mary Ann caught it and one of the guests claimed it. He had found it frozen by the roadside and slipped it into his pocket to take home to dissect, but the warmth of the room had brought it back to life.[3]

It would have been difficult to split families along age groups because of the custom of elderly men marrying girls in their teens. The great mortality among wives (from tuberculosis and childbirth) combined with the longevity of leisure-class husbands, frequently enabled a man to beget broods by successive mothers, so that in exceptional cases the first-born children were older than the newest mother. Maria Edgeworth called each of her father's four wives "my mother," although the last one was much her junior.

During the period when Lichfield social life was forming the pattern we have been describing, Dr. Johnson was absent from his home town. After he once tasted London life that city became his chosen home. He returned to Lichfield to conduct his wife to London; came back in 1739 when he formed

his friendships with Hill Boothby, the Fitzherberts in Ashbourne, and later that same winter with Molly Aston in Lichfield; but was not again in Lichfield until the winter of 1760-1,
the year after his mother's death. In 1767, he received a pension from the King, which enabled him to move about more.
That same year he made a long stay in his home town and
from then on he returned often and stayed as long as six
months at a time.

During the period of Johnson's absence he lost touch with
the social and intellectual life of the city. When he was again
associated with Lichfieldians, he was indifferent, almost antagonistic to the young people. Why this should have been,
one does not know. In London six of his most intimate friends
were separated from him by chasms of thirty years and more.
He could enjoy a frisk with Bennet Langton and Topham Beauclerk, find companionship in the company of Fanny Burney,
converse for hours for the edification of James Boswell, ex-
pand in Hannah More's adulation, and lean on Mrs. Thrale's
daughter-like affection, but the truly delightful young ladies of
Lichfield did not attract him nor did he find fellowship among
the talented young men. A possible exception was Henry
White, who besides holding ecclesiastical offices was an anti-
quarian and a brilliant talker when his interest was aroused.

However, in a small town like Lichfield, it was inevitable
that there should be encounters, if only occasional and accidental, between the Doctor and members of the Cathedral set.
Mary Martha Sherwood, author of *The Fairchild Family* and
other books from which we learn a good deal about Lichfield,
tells about such a meeting between Johnson and her mother.
Martha, senior, was an unattractive intellectual little orphan,
living with three unusually beautiful women—the Woodhouse
sisters. She had, however, a fortune of ten thousand pounds.
As her daughter tells the story, Dr. Johnson met her mother

in the Dean's Walk, beside the Cathedral, a favorite strolling place for gentle exercise. The vigorous lime trees planted by Dr. Binckes long before, made a roof overhead.

It was—and is—a lovely spot. Lichfield Cathedral is the smallest of the English cathedrals, but in the opinion of some of its admirers, one of the loveliest. The building has charm rather than grandeur, a cathedral to take to one's heart. It stands a little removed from the center of the city, on a rise of land, and is set off by Minster Pool in which its three graceful spires are reflected on a bright summer's day. Around it cluster Tudor dwellings and Georgian residences set in green turf and flowering gardens.

In these idyllic surroundings Martha met the great man.

Martha was of dwarfish stature with a long, pock-marked face and large features. Dr. Johnson wasn't handsome either. As he came rolling heavily toward her under the leafy roof of lime-trees, his near-sighted gaze was attracted by something that pleased him, namely, a book in her hand. Seeing a book, he instinctively reached for it. It was a volume of *The Rambler*, or it may have been *Rasselas;* Martha could not remember which. It would seem a happy circumstance to be caught with one of the great man's books; but not so. Dr. Johnson opened it, looked into it, and without a word—flung it away among the graves, from whence Martha later retrieved it. Dr. Johnson's moods were often unpredictable.

The ugly little Martha deserves, perhaps, a short postscript. Mary, the loveliest of the Woodhouse girls, had become engaged to George Butt, the Prince Charming of the Cathedral Close. Mary died. After an interval, George Butt's father and Martha Sherwood's father arranged a marriage between the handsome young man and the ugly duckling. George, whose true love was dead, took Martha and her uncomely face and figure, her brilliant mind and her ten thousand pounds. It was not a happy marriage, but the children inherited the mother's brains and the father's looks. Mary Martha, who wrote books, was the oldest of the brood; following the Lichfield endogamous custom, she married her cousin, Sherwood, and is known to fame and posterity as Mary Martha Butt Sherwood.

CHAPTER V

Joseph Porter Comes to Lichfield

SAMUEL JOHNSON acquired three stepchildren by his marriage to Mrs. Porter in 1735: Jervis Henry, named after his two grandfathers, Henry Porter and William Jervis; Lucy, named for her paternal grandmother, Lucy Porter; and Joseph, called after his father's rich merchant brother in Ironmonger Lane, London. Jervis, already in training for the Navy, repudiated his mother and so far as one knows never saw her after her marriage. He once called at her house in London when she was ill, but before she could dress to receive him, his filial impulse had vanished and he had left the house. He rose to be a captain in the Navy and inherited from Uncle Joseph (for whom his brother was named) a fortune which he in turn left to his sister, Lucy, in 1763.

Lucy, aged twenty, accepted her mother's marriage and adapted herself to the situation with the philosophy and commonsense which she showed under all circumstances, pleasant or unpleasant. When her mother and stepfather moved to London she remained with Johnson's mother in the big house in the market place. With the two of them lived Catherine Chambers, a devoted servant, perhaps a poor relative. This odd family group carried on the bookshop. They were desperately poor, and Johnson, struggling in London, could send them no money. Lucy carried her share of the burden with the courage and blunt honesty which marked her entire life.

The third child, Joseph, was only ten when his mother remarried. He did not live with his mother in London, nor in Lichfield under Lucy's wing (she was nine years his senior) but was cared for by his father's family. Eventually he lived on good terms with his stepfather, as in later years he is mentioned in Dr. Johnson's letters to Lucy. Joseph became a merchant in Leghorn, Italy. He returned to Lichfield in 1764, after long years of absence, to marry Sarah Seward. This alliance was arranged by his sister, Lucy, and Sarah's father, Dr. Seward.

That Reverend Thomas Seward, Prebendary of Salisbury and Canon-residentiary of Lichfield Cathedral, should affiance his young daughter to a man whom he had never met, but knew only at second-hand as respectable and prosperous, does not indicate that Dr. Seward did not tenderly love his child, nor that he was especially mercenary. A parent in those days was nervous when a daughter was still a spinster at the ripe age of twenty. Dr. Seward could not dower his daughter, which narrowed the choice of a husband. He thought well of the Porter family with whom he had connected himself by marriage. Of course this general approval did not extend to "Tetty" who married Johnson in such unseemly haste after her first husband, Harry Porter's death, but did seem to include Joseph. Lichfieldians preferred endogamous marriages, and Joseph was, no doubt, considered one of the Seward clan, although only a step-cousin-once-removed. The difference in age between Joseph and Sarah did not seem a detriment to her parents, for, though the marriage of middle-aged "Tetty" Porter to young Samuel Johnson had shocked her family, yet the converse, Sarah's marrying a man her senior by the same number of years, was considered an admirable arrangement.

Parents made engagements and daughters acquiesced. On the Porter side there must have been complacency because a member of a City family which had been for years under a financial cloud, was now rich enough and socially important enough to marry into one of the most prominent Close families.

Prebendary Seward had brought his family to Lichfield in 1749 to live in Market Street until a few years later they moved into the Palace and carried on the tradition Walmesley had established, keeping the house the center of social, literary, and musical life. The family consisted of Dr. Seward, who held ecclesiastical offices beside his prebend; his handsome wife, Elizabeth; Anna, called Nancy, auburn-haired and amber-eyed, passionate in love and in hatred; the tender and exquisite Sarah, called Sally; and a young half-orphaned relative, Honora Sneyd. The Canon had marked social talent, his wife was hospitable and efficient; all three girls were exceptionally beautiful and talented.

Dr. Seward, though not of illustrious birth, being the son of a steward to a noble lord, had traveled abroad as tutor to the lord's heir, associated on friendly terms with other members of the nobility and was entertained at their houses. The Duke of Grafton, his patron, had obtained for him the livings of Eyam in the Peak District and Lingsley in Staffordshire. These livings he retained in plurality after his appointment as prebendary to Lichfield Cathedral. He wrote pleasant verse and brought out an edition of Beaumont and Fletcher.

One cannot tell very much about his personality from his portrait, for his great white wig and the yardage of his ample canonicals conceals his individuality. He was corpulent, with large features and bags under his eyes. He was a kindly man, prudent in his finances, optimistic, civil to everyone, but petulant when crossed, over-talkative, fond of social life, a minor writer. He was generally esteemed, but in two men he roused hearty dislike. Dr. Johnson said he was gross in his habits and dominating in conversation—the very criticisms often aimed at himself. Horace Walpole, whose double distinction comes from being the son of Robert Walpole, the great statesman, and from being himself an author of note and the builder of Strawberry Hill, met Seward first in Italy and was later annoyed at finding him a fellow guest at Rangely Hall, the Earl of Hertford's seat in Warwickshire. Walpole looked down his aristocratic nose at the doctor, considering him a social climber who needed snubbing. Boswell, on the other hand, found him genteel, well-bred, and dignified, and Richard Lovell Edgeworth, who was much at the Palace, considered him a man of learning and taste, good-natured and indulgent to others' foibles, and fond of conversation.

Mrs. Seward was a handsome woman. Her portrait, painted when she was forty-two, shows a lady with a very straight back, charmingly dressed in a satin gown made with a stiff bodice, full sleeves, and broad embroidered collar. Dark hair is drawn back from a high forehead. Her eyes are dark, her features regular, her expression slightly supercilious. She looks like a witty woman with a sharp tongue, but of this there is no record. We do know that she was generous, sensible, and devoted to her daughters; that she was quick-tempered, had periods of depression, and was at times emotional to the point of hysteria.

It is possible that the occasional peevishness of the canon, the excitable disposition of his wife, and the vehement, undisciplined nature of Anna, produced a somewhat discordant home life which was painful to gentle Sarah and young Honora, but it is obvious that the family was bound together by devotion and admiration. All domestic strain was swept away when company came. Dinner parties, tea parties, supper parties, card parties, and musical evenings followed each other in swift succession. The young people were early accustomed to visiting and receiving guests and to holidays at watering places. When Dr. Seward made his annual trip to Eyam where he was still rector, the family stopped for a visit at Buxton, which had a hot bath, saline springs, and genteel society from all over England. Dr. Johnson said that Canon Seward went to Buxton because he loved to lord it in a limited group, the intimation being that London was too much for the canon to take on.

On a Wednesday afternoon in April, 1764, Mrs. Seward was giving a card party to twenty ladies. Joseph Porter, Sally's unknown fiancé, was reported to be lingering in London on his way home from Italy and therefore should not have been due in Lichfield for a week or so. The Seward family evidently planned to get this party out of the way before his arrival. Mrs. Seward, Anna, Sally, and Honora were all busy supervising servants in the kitchen, arranging tables and chairs in the drawingroom, getting out cards and bustling about as hostesses do just before a party, whichever the century. They were disconcerted to receive at one o'clock a note from Lucy Porter saying that her brother had arrived from Italy and she would bring him to tea. She knew that there was a party on, for she had been invited, and she knew that the Sewards would much prefer to meet Joseph privately first, but she could not resist the triumph of flaunting her rich brother in the faces of ecclesiastical ladies, some of whom perhaps somewhat looked down on the Johnsons and Porters who had been in trade, although there was not at this time in Lichfield the snobbish attitude toward retail trade which later developed all over the country. It was hard on Sally to inspect her betrothed for the first time before the eyes of twenty interested neighbors.

One must not assume that this engagement was in opposition to Sally's wishes. She was docile, fragile and reticent. Like all the Sewards she had strong emotions, but unlike the others she hid her disappointments under quiet acquiescence. A mild desperation inclined her to accept this elderly lover whom she had never seen, for she had been twice in love and each time the affair had come to nothing. John Sneyd, young Honora's first cousin, had loved her, but his family objected because Dr. Seward could not dower his daughter. Dr. Seward had a fair income from church livings held in plurality, but there was a large house to keep up, a staff of servants to maintain, wife and daughters to dress, and continuous social entertaining to pay for. It is true, the Sneyd family was a large and wealthy clan. But at the time he was wooing Sally several lives interposed between John and inheritance of the family fortune.

The freedom of younger sons was sadly curtailed by their economic dependence. Commissions in the army and navy could be bought and the church was open to them, but advancement depended chiefly on the influence their families or patrons could bring to bear. Law and medicine were less popular with easy-going young men because they demanded not only preliminary university education, but ability, courage, and perseverance.

John's love for Sally must have been in his early youth, perhaps in the nature of "calf love," for by the time he was twenty-three he could have married as he chose, having inherited the property of his branch of the family after the death of his father and elder brother. So John Sneyd married a proud beauty with a fortune and the proud beauty very naturally alienated him from the Seward family. After her death his second wife healed the breach and the Sneyd and Seward families were again on visiting terms.

Sally's other love affair was not a matter of general knowledge. We have an account in a letter written by her sister Anna to an unknown correspondent. Anna Seward's published letters are written in a stilted style fashionable in the period. During the later part of her life, when her friends had persuaded her of what she was not loathe to believe, namely, that her poetry was deathless and all that pertained to her important, she rewrote many letters for posthumous publication in a fashion which made her ridiculous.

Nevertheless, much of our information concerning Lichfield people, their personalities, and the events of their lives, comes to us from the six volumes of Anna Seward's correspondence, published by Constable in 1811, two years after her death and twenty-one years after Dr. Johnson died. These letters were not actually edited by Sir Walter Scott, although Anna appointed him as her literary executor to his surprise and discomfort. He did, however, go over them and cut certain passages. Sir Walter had entered into correspondence with her when he first began writing and in those early years had valued her praise and encouragement. When he called on her in 1807, he found her so attractive and entertaining, in spite of her absurdities, that what was to have been a passing call lengthened into a two-day visit at the Palace. Nevertheless he was dismayed when her will was read two years later and he learned that she had unloaded on him a vast bulk of writing for a Collected Edition of her works. The mass included not only the books and poems already published, but corrected, rewritten correspondence sufficient for twelve volumes, six years output of Juvenile Letters, four sermons and other prose, and some of her father's work. Eventually Constable, after conferring with Sir Walter who did some pretty violent pruning, brought out six volumes of letters. Although one appreciates Sir Walter's dilemma, one regrets not having all the letters, for in spite of her inaccuracy and prejudices, Anna Seward fills in many gaps in our information.

The pseudo-gothic manner in writing as well as architecture was considered uncommonly tasty by some people. Regina Maria Roche's *Children of the Abbey*, published in 1796, is a fine example of the style. If one is going to like Anna Seward at all (and those who scorn her miss a delightful acquaintance) one must accept at the outset the fact that she pushes her affectations to absurdity. Her sentimental, declamatory style must be forgiven her. When deeply and recently moved by love or sorrow, Anna wrote simple touching English and the conventions of certain types of poetry forced her into simple language. She wrote a few excellent sonnets, constrained by the unyielding rules. Her ballads are not bad and some of her descriptive verse deserves to live. Too often she adorned her sorrow and hung it on the wall for passers-by to weep at. In verse the monody was her favorite form, lending itself to apostrophe, hyperbole and exclamation.

Anna at her desk chose a feathered pen from a sheaf of neatly cut quills and wrote in a clear fine hand on enduring rag paper, in ink which faded with the years, the following epistle, to an unidentified friend called Emma:

(undated)

Suns beheld the expanding sweetness of another tender partiality self-repressed in the heart of my Sarah. A gay agreeable young officer, of Noblesse extraction, danced with her at our Assemblies, and was always by her side in the public walk.

His attentions to her were perfectly respectful, but it became known that he indulged the excesses of a Libertine Disposition. After this discovery she had resolution to shun him invariably, danced with him no more, avoided him in our walks, nor was he any longer admitted to our little conversation parties.

The gentle spirit made not such spirited exertions without pain—but I think the repeated disappointment influenc'd her in Mr. Porter's favour; for when (on the proposal being made) I said to her:

"Ah, my sister, reflect that if marriage is not preceded by enamoured tenderness, it must forever exclude that charming sentiment, or admit its approaches at the price of peace, if not of innocence, of censure, if not of absolute dishonor."

She replied—"My heart has been so luckless in its

68

choice, I am resolved not to trust it any more. Shou'd I be enabled to esteem this Gentleman, without feeling personal disgust, I believe I can perform my duty. Thou knowest I am not avaricious, but a noble fortune will put it in my power to do generous things, and to have about me a pleasing Society, formed by the Friends I love. If I possess the means of doing good, and of making happy, I trust I shall not want the inclination to employ them worthily."

"Thou art an angelic Creature," exclaimed her Anna, "and I hope thou wilt be able to love thy prim Batchelor into the bargain. It will, as I conclude, inevitably be his misfortune not to inspire thee with passion, but it will be his fault (the irrevocable ceremony pass'd) if he does not gain thy affection."

. . . They are to live every alternate year in Italy, since Mr. Porter does not chuse to resign his Business. That is well, his mild Help-mate will have the less trouble in amusing him. . . . I am to be permitted to accompany them to Italy. If your Anna shou'd find a Friend in a Brother, she will enjoy many pleasures from a sister's affluence, and journies to the Continent, wtihout paying for them that high price—her liberty.

It is time to bid you adieu.—My sister has brought my workbag with her own, down for the evening. The Curtains are dropt—the Candles shine cheerily, and the fire burns bright in the hearth. Little Honora draws her chair to the table—Hawkesworth's *Almoran and Hamet* in her hand. What a beautiful story, how sublime its moral! Honora looks upon me with eyes full of intellectual avidity. Her young mind must not want its evening's repast.[1]

The oriental tale which was to be Honora's evening repast is a two-volume novel by John Hawkesworth, of the Arabian Nights variety, in which chaste constancy and constant chastity is in continual danger of rape. The plot is sensual and the sentiments moral.

That Sally made a satisfactory pretence of accepting willingly her unknown fiancé seems evident from a letter written her by her father when she was absent from home about three months before Joseph came to claim his bride. The date is January 14, no year. The phraseology of the letter is as artificial as that of his daughter Anna, although this letter was not rewritten for publication as were her stilted ones. He says that his darling is appointed to Disappointment, but that it is an excellent thing to exercise female Patience—a Virtue of no strong Constitution in her Sex, subject to Rickets unless necessity sometimes puts it upon its legs. Hers must stand a tip-toe till the following Wednesday at least, when perhaps he might let it sit down on an Elbow Chair. He treats her to an account of a Mr. Rawlins who was coming to have a curious Peep at her sister, reconnoitering before he laid close siege; he tells her about his cough and philosophizes on Distempers increasing in the Down-Hill of Life, but assures her that parents have a Renewal of Youth and many internal Joys while their Darlings enjoy a full share of Health and Youthful Happiness; in a postscript he gives her leave to apply to her sister Nancy [Anna] for the Solution of her Suspense and gives Nancy permission to tell what she knows of the matter. It is not a comfortable letter.[2]

When gentle Sally learned that her unknown fiancé had arrived in Lichfield before he was expected, she cried a little and retreated with her sister to the suite which they shared.—This consisted of three rooms, one of which, called the dressing room, was an upstairs sitting room where they entertained their friends. The room was hung in blue and the fire-place was framed in Dutch tiles depicting Bible scenes, showing Moses, Aaron, and Balaam's Ass and other worthies. The windows looked westward toward the Cathedral and the outlook was delightful.

To this lovely room came the two beautiful women; one pensive and resigned, the other angry and jealous. Sally wiped her eyes and prepared to meet her fate. Little comfort she received from her sister. Anna was in a nasty mood. She had a stronger personality than her sister, inheriting her father's brains and her mother's emotionalism, to which was added an imperious nature. She possessed a vibrant beauty and a wild exuberance of spirit. When she entered a room it was as if life itself had come in at the door. She was generous, affectionate and considerate as long as she was allowed to dominate a situation; when thwarted by circumstances, she was a treacherous shrew. This day, far from sympathizing with her despondent sister, she punished her for accepting the proposed marriage.

"Look, love," she says she said,—though she probably said nothing of the kind, for her tongue was not so high-falutin as her re-write pen—"that calm and gilded rain promises flowers and fruit in abundance; may those kindred tears prepare thy mind as that shower prepares the earth, for the flowers and fruits of wedded happiness."

Sally was a long time dressing, not from special care, but to put off the decisive meeting. She no longer wept, but shook her head at her reflection in the mirror, sighed, and breathed, "Ah, Heaven!"

"Bless me!" exclaimed the pitiless sister, "one would think thou wert adorning a victim, and not a mistress. If that idea has passed across thy mind, prithee, put a stop to this business at once! Study a pretty harangue of dismissal, full of esteem, wayward heart, and so forth."

Sally tied on her ribbons and fastened a gypsy hat on her coiffure and was ready to meet the eyes of the twenty inquisitive ladies. "Oh, Heavens!" sighed Sally and accompanied her jealous sister to the drawing room.

The Palace drawing room where the ladies assembled was a charming apartment, looking eastward over still leafless shrubbery, across the valley to Stowe Pool, on the border of which rose the Church of St. Chad. Through the bare, graceful

71

tree limbs, one saw Mrs. Elizabeth Aston's house and that of Rev. Mr. Hinton which Mrs. Gastrell later occupied. In the middle of the vale the giant Johnson willow reared its bulk, near the old parchment works once run by Michael Johnson, Samuel's father. On either side of the great willow was visible the gleaming water of Stowe Pool, beautifully clear in spring. Very little of the City could be seen from the windows; the view was chiefly of villas and gardens.

One can make a pretty good guess as to who attended the party. Someone must have come from Dean Addenbrooke's family living next door in the Deanery; while from the row of prebendary houses to the west and south of the Cathedral, bordering on what was once a moat, doubtless came representatives of the Smallbrookes and the Woodhouses and the Vyses—families toward whom ecclesiastical preferment rushed like tacks to a magnet. From families moving in the Cathedral set though not holding office, would be ladies from the Garrick family living in the old Clough house on Beacon Street, which had been David's grandfather's home. Also from Beacon Street would come frail, charming Mrs. Erasmus Darwin. Mrs. "Moll" Cobb of the Friary was probably present and Mrs. Elizabeth Aston. Since the Cathedral Close housed mercantile and professional households as well as clerical, the Seward party may have included someone from the medical-apothecary family of the Salts, the popular Butts, the rich Newton family, and the Bailye clan. All the ladies knew of the proposed Seward-Porter alliance, the progress of negotiations, and the arrival of the candidate, thanks to Canon Seward's habit of telling all to everyone.

The older ladies sat down to cards and the younger ones got out their needlework. In this heyday of needlework ladies busied themselves knotting fringes, netting purses, tatting lace edging, knitting stockings, garters, gloves, ropes for skipping, play reins, balls for babies. They embroidered ruffles, neckcloths, caps, undersleeves, aprons, and entire dresses that took a year or more to finish. There was gros and petit point for chair backs and seats; bugle work with shiny black beads; tent stitch for larger pieces.

We know how the ladies were dressed. Hoops were in the half-way stage. They had formerly been so wide that the wearers had a problem in passing through doorways, a problem similar to moving a dining table from one room to another. When the Vicars' Hall had been opened with a ball a few years before, the announcement read: "As there is reason to expect a good deal of company the ladies are desired to appear without hoops." (This was the ball in which John Sneyd danced in the same set with three ladies who afterward became his successive wives.) Even with moderated hoops, the dresses were cumbersome with draperies and puffs and ruffles and streamers. Empire styles did not come in until later, after the French revolution. That mode, in startling contrast, lured ladies into drying their muslin dresses on their bodies in order that the close-clinging folds might reveal curves so long and so discreetly hidden. Some of the ladies powdered their hair, but the extremes of London coiffures were not in favor in country districts.

The last guests to arrive were Lucy and Joseph Porter. The presentation of her rich brother was a triumph for Lucy. She had shown so much fortitude during a hard, poverty-stricken life that people in general respected her and overlooked her odd ways and sharp tongue. After her mother had married Dr. Johnson and gone to London, Lucy lived with Johnson's mother, helping her behind the bookshop counter. Conditions became easier after Lucy inherited ten thousand pounds from her brother, Captain Jervis Porter, who had himself inherited from Uncle Joseph, the rich London merchant, but she had

held over from the hard days the terrible directness and tact-
lessness which sometimes develops in those who see their
duty plain and pursue it vigorously.

Lucy and Joseph made an odd-looking pair. She was a
woman of fifty, with a round face, faded flaxen hair and eyebrows, and a worn complexion. Now that she had money she
dressed elaborately but without taste. Today she wore a blue
and white tissue with Brussels lace.

Brother Joseph was below middle height, thin, stooped, and
sun-dried. He was garbed in a fashion strange to English
eyes: a black velvet coat, a gold tissue waistcoat embroidered
with colored flowers, a bag wig, curled and powdered white
as snow. His teeth were good but he was not in a smiling
mood. He was ill at ease as his sister presented him to twenty
strange curtseying ladies. He had, however, enough self-
possession to assert that in all the cities through which he had
passed he had never seen such beautiful women as England
produced. In this he was speaking truth, not flattery, for this
group was made up of unusually lovely young ladies.

We have a list of girls who "bridled" to Joseph; that is, drew
in their chins before they sank to the floor in deep curtsies,
their hoop-skirts making cheeses around them. Nannette
Sneyd, with large, languishing hazel eyes, warm cheeks, and
a tender fascinating smile, was doomed to an early death from
tuberculosis. Helen White, a cousin of the Sewards, celebrated for her resemblance to Raphael's Madonna, was a gad-
about and gossip. Eliza Woodhouse, scarce sixteen, with dark
hair, acquiline beauty and an air of grandeur, and her lovely
sister Mary, were doomed like Nannette to early death. Very
likely present although not mentioned among the beauties
was the Woodhouse girls' little foster-sister, Martha Sherwood,
who had a fortune to compensate for her pock-marked, horse-
like face. Among the popular girls was Mrs. "Moll" Cobb's
niece Polly Adey, whose figure was fine and whose air was

74

spritely. Anna herself was beautiful, although she did not think so, being very conscious of her over-plumpness. Every description of her records her brilliant eyes, her vivid personality, her quick tongue, and her dominating personality. Honora Sneyd, still a child, was there. She was eight years younger than Sally and resembled her in pensiveness and loving devotion, but had greater intellectual power.

Sally's young elegance held its own among all these nymphs, these houris. Yet the man who had traveled from Leghorn to Lichfield to make her his bride paid her slight attention. He was fascinated by her vibrant, aggressive sister. To Sally's embarrassment at meeting an unknown fiancé in front of sharp-eyed neighbors was added the humiliation of not pleasing him. He ignored Sally and gave his attention to Anna. The ladies must have exchanged glances and lifted eyebrows at Joseph's conduct. The child Honora, staying close to Sally's side, looked up into her face with a tender understanding.

Anna, humiliated at being unbetrothed though the elder, stole the attention of her sister's suitor, thus proving to herself and to twenty ladies that she was not unattractive to men even though her younger sister was to be married first and leave her to coif St. Agnes' tresses. She had an angry conviction that she had been personally betrayed and she soothed her pride by taking Sally's suitor away from her right under the eyes of twenty neighbors. Anna could take second place to none and as Sally's bethrothal made Sally important, Anna took a vicious revenge. Where Anna loved she idolized, but she could be cruel in proportion to her love. She tried to quiet her own pain by hurting the beloved.

When the two Porters had gone to supper with the Whites who were relatives also, the guests hurried off to spread the news of Joseph Porter's extraordinary conduct. Sally turned to the sister who had diverted her lover's interest and begged

75

ironically that Anna would kindly invite her to go to Italy as
her guest after she had married Joseph. It was the only reproach the gentle creature made her unfeeling sister. Anna
tried to smooth things over by explaining that Joseph had devoted himself to her in order to spare her fiancée the embarrassment of being publicly wooed.

The following morning, Helen White, a cousin, beautiful
as a goddess, thoughtless as a child, came rushing in agog
with a packet of gossip. Helen probably felt her intrusion at
this critical moment could be justified under the pretext of her
being related to both parties. (No matter how she was related!
The intricacies of Lichfield family relationships could only be
clarified by a series of genealogical charts.) She was naturally bubbling over with excitement. One may take one's
choice in considering Helen as spiteful or insensitive. She
spoke romantically, at least so Anna reported in a letter to a
confidant:

"It is verily and even so! this irresistible Madame Anne!
Sarah must wear the willow, but I think it will not be with a
very aching heart."

Sally was annoyed but she was able to smile as if it were a
joke.

Without any apparent sense of guilt, Anna asked, "Who
told you this?"

"My Uncle White," Helen informed them, "told me he had
asked Mr. Porter how he liked Mr. and Mrs. Seward.

" 'Extremely!'

" 'And Miss Seward?'

" 'I think her charming,' and expatiated on Anna's charm.

" 'The youngest?'

" 'She seems a modest, pleasing young woman.' "

Young Honora stood up for Sally, as Anna should have
done and did not. She cried out,

"I don't believe he likes Nancy best!'

Dear, sensitive young Honora must have been often buffeted in that turbulent household. Anna proceeded to provoke more trouble. Mrs. Seward was so exasperated with her eldest daughter that she took snuff with unwonted energy and her eyes darkened and flashed. Anna had that same peculiarity of eyes darkening when angry. The beauteous Helen scampered off to tell the neighbors.

The day was not a pleasant one in the Palace. The Sewards and Porters exchanged polite notes about health but did not meet. Before night the rumor was widespread that Mr. Porter had jilted Sally and made proposals for Anna's hand. Anna preened herself and Sally did not reproach her.

Mr. and Mrs. Seward, jolted by Joseph's unexpected behaviour, assured Sally that no pressure would be brought to bear on her to fulfill the engagement of marriage. When she replied that she wished to go on with the affair, they begged her to reject Joseph if he was not "perfectly agreeable to her."

At eleven by the clock on the following morning, the situation changed completely. A different Joseph appeared at the Palace with Lucy. The mountebank had vanished and a proper Englishman in a sober brown coat invited the young ladies to walk with him and his sister to Lucy's new house. That April Friday was a day made for walking, with the trees in pale green leaf and scores of chaffinches singing on the orchard boughs. Joseph's mood had changed. After long absence he was in England in April. Besides, he was probably subdued by a trouncing from his blunt-tongued sister who did not hesitate to lay down the law even to the fearsome Dr. Johnson. Sally, Anna, young Honora, and the ubiquitous Helen White accompanied the Porters.

We can see the group of five ladies and one man as they left the Close and crossed the causeway to the city. The younger ladies were all beauties: handsome, chattering Helen White; Anna of the radiant hair and brilliant eyes; serene and lovely Sally; quiet young Honora; and happy, faded Lucy, complacent in her rich brother and her new house. Full, bright-colored skirts swung on hoops; gypsy hats perched sidewise on elaborate hair-dos; scarves fluttered, ribbons waved, and gewgaws glistened.

The charming group went down Dam Street and Conduit Street. They passed the house where Lucy's famous stepfather had learned his letters in Dame Oliver's school; crossed the Market Place where still stands the Johnson house and went round the corner to Tamworth Street where Lucy's new house, Redcourt, was abuilding. Her stepfather disapproved of this project, advising her to lease a suitable residence and put her money out at interest.

The chastened Joseph devoted himself to Sally exclusively. Somewhere between the Palace and unfinished Redcourt he found a chance formally to offer his hand and heart to the lady he had come to woo. He was formally accepted. Joseph and Lucy returned to the Palace and spent the day with the Sewards.

As the Sewards became better acquainted with Joseph, the parents who had been keen on the marriage grew doubtful. Anna found in him an impolite impatience of contradiction, a jealousy without the excuse of love, and considerable pee- vishness. It may be that Joseph punished Anna for beguiling him; and it may be that Anna disliked him the more because she had a guilty conscience over having flirted with him. Meantime Sally was showing signs of illness, with feverish at- tacks. The parents grew more and more worried and from assuring Sally that she need not marry against her wish, they came to begging her to break the engagement. The daughter who had always been so docile, definitely refused their advice. She persisted in going on with the match.

A letter to her dear friend, Mary Adey, asserting that she

loved Joseph Porter does not ring true. It sounds like the pious fraud of an unhappy girl:

Lichd May the 29 1764

Thank you my dear Polly Adey for your kind Letter, impute not to neglect my not answering it sooner, nor think it proceeded from an insensibility of the favor, believe me I am incapable of either, my Love and Esteem for You makes me infinitely delighted with every testimony of Your affection, You who have a Heart capable of rejoicing with transport at the Felicity of your Friends, will I am sure feel a most lively pleasure in the completion of an Event which promises so much happiness to all our Family: for my own part I am almost asham'd to own even to Polly Adey, how entirely Mr. Porter has possession of my Heart, I blush to think how quick a progress he has made in so short a period, yet the tenderness and affection he has expressed for me, His desire of doing everything that can be conducive to mine and my Relations happiness, and the fair Character He bears will surely justify the soft confession. . . . Tis impossible to tell you with what joy I behold the delight that sparkles in Miss Porters Face on the near completion of Her kind wishes, or with what gratitude I hear her repeat the many affectionate things She said upon this occasion. I know you are glad I do not quit Lichfield. I hope we shall spend many happy days together. . . . Be sure you keep your resolution of coming down the beginning of next Week, for I would fain have you present when the indissoluble knot is tied, You know You are to be my Bride Maid, We shall only stay in London to equip ourselves with Cloaths and that cannot be very long. I have been much indisposed for some days past with a feverish complaint, which prevented me from writing sooner to you, but I am now with the help of the Bark got tolerably well. All this Family join with me in love to Yourself, Your Aunt, and Uncle Cobb, our compts. attend Mr. and Mrs. Ryson and their sweet girls. Adieu my Dearest Polly Adey. S. Seward.[3]

Joseph had arrived in April. Early in June was the date decided upon for the wedding. Anna was to accompany the bridal couple to Leghorn to stay two years. But when the appointed day arrived, the bride was dying of either typhoid or typhus fever. Dr. Erasmus Darwin attended her. There was almost no hope for Sally from the onset of the violent fever. Her distracted family haunted the sickroom and Mr. Porter sat by the window, head on hand, but Anna thought he was more vexed than grieved. Sally was so patient and resigned that one feels she was not unwilling to leave a world that did not give her the love she needed. She had no will to live.

When it was clear that Dr. Darwin could not save the patient, Mrs. Seward sent a chaise and four at full speed to bring from Worcester a clergyman by the name of Bayley who had acquired some fame for administering James's Powders, then considered miraculous, later held a poison. Dr. James, having been a student at the Lichfield Grammar School under Dr. Hunter and a protegé of Gilbert Walmesley, inclined Mrs. Steward to favor his cure-all.

When Mr. Bayley arrived, handsome, distracted Mrs. Seward fell on her knees and clasped her arms around him crying, "Dear angel-man, save my child!" The clergyman burst into sympathetic tears, but he did not save the patient. Dr. Darwin persuaded him that James's Powder was not suitable to the case and Sally died without the assistance of the poison.

The violence of the family grief was in accordance with its members' usual vehemence of feeling. The father who up to the very end optimistically expected recovery dropped into despair, but recovered cheerfulness after a few weeks of unhappiness. The mother after keeping up as long as funeral duties required her effort, sank into an apathy akin to melancholia. Honora, so like Sally in selfless personality, lost herself in sympathy for the others. Anna, poor Anna, was as un-

Published by Dawson & Hobson, Ashbourn.

ASHBOURN HALL,
The Seat of Sir William Boothby, Bart.

Printed by T.W.& C. Fairland, London.   Published by Dawson & Hobson, Ashbourn.

TISSINGTON HALL.
The Seat of Sir Henry Fitzherbert Bar.t

PLATE V

Ashbourne Hall

Tissington Hall

From *Ashbourne and the Valley of the Dove (1839)*

PLATE VI
Dr. Johnson in his Travelling Dress

able to control her grief as she had been to control her jealousy. She was noisy in her anguish and by that same token the sooner threw it off.

Sarah Seward's funeral was simple and touching. The coffin was covered with a white pall and borne by six girls dressed in white. It was customary for a bereaved family to wear black hoods and each member of the funeral party black scarf, gloves and hatband. It was also customary to feed the mourners after the funeral as many of them had long drives before they could reach home again. A funeral was both a religious rite and a social occasion. The mortality among young women was appalling; five sisters in one family, three in another, and so on. Sally's burial service must have awakened tragic echoes in the hearts of many of the guests, because in so many families girls and young mothers had died of tuberculosis, fever or childbirth.

CHAPTER VI

Mr. Taylor Comes to Lichfield

THE hero of a book about Lichfield is perforce Samuel Johnson. The heroine is Anna Seward although some people would cast her as the villain. She was handsome, talented, passionate in hate and in love, and oh, so very sure of herself. Friends and enemies alike admitted she was beautiful. Friends considered her a genius and she agreed with them. Her poetry won her the title, "The Swan of Lichfield." The phrase when bestowed was honest encomium; today it is spoken with a smile.

Anna was vain, jealous, prejudiced, dogmatic. Yet to those she loved, she was kind, generous, and self-sacrificing. All she asked of her loved ones was complete possession of their hearts and their attentions. She would not, could not, share. If she saw no good in those she hated, she saw no flaws in those she loved. Such she was as a girl; such she was as a woman.

Seventeen hundred and sixty-four was a full year for Anna Seward. In the spring she was upset by Joseph Porter's arrival and Sally's determination to fulfill her matrimonial engagement; in the early summer she was devastated by Sally's death;

in the fall her family packed her off to London for her first visit to that exciting metropolis. To complete the year she proceeded to fall tempestuously in love.

Her suitor was a young military man to whom she referred in her letters as "Mr. T—"; later as "Col. T—". She met him in Lichfield before Sally's death and had at first been sentimental over him rather than deeply concerned.

Lichfield was a center for military recruitment and maneuvers were often held there because the city was adjacent to Cannock Chase where there was amply room for extensive operations.

Young Taylor, for Taylor seems to have been his name, was a good-looking youth with a pensive air and a dignified seriousness most attractive in contrast to his gaudy military uniform. He wore a red coat, a long waistcoat embroidered in gold, white breeches, white stockings, and black shoes adorned with huge buckles. White frills at the neck and wrists were of spotless linen or of thread lace. His large broad-brimmed hat, cocked into a tricorn, sat on a wig white with powder, the queue tied with a black ribbon. His chin was held up by a stiff leather collar and he may have been adorned with cockades, a watch fob heavy with seals, with gold coat buttons, gold lace, and a gold-plated sword hilt. Such a costume stood out brilliantly among the ecclesiastical black robes and black pancake hats of the Lichfield clergy, like a parrot among rooks.

This serious young man had the distinction of being hopelessly in love. His brother officers gravely named Georgiana, daughter of Evelyn Chadwick of West Lake, Nottinghamshire, as the object. While Taylor's regiment was stationed in Lichfield, Anna, with her usual desire to have a finger in every pie, told him she heard the lady was to be married. His jealously and suffering were so intense that she immediately confessed that it was a false rumor and Mr. Taylor poured out to her the story of his hopeless love. From that time he sought her for sympathy and confidences. Before his regiment left Lichfield he hinted that his heart was no longer Georgiana's but Anna's, but he only hinted. Juliet had succeeded Rosaline. Anna did not take the affair seriously; still it served to give her position among the other young ladies of the Close and provided a subject for gentle sighs.

When she met him later in London his heart had grown fonder and his tongue bolder. He declared his passion and sought her hand. Anna plunged into her first love affair impetuously. She engaged herself to marry him, but cautiously stipulated that her father should not know. They corresponded after her return to Lichfield until the matter was brought to her father's attention by zealous friends. Canon Seward was very angry and wrote an irate letter to Taylor. Taylor's income was not sufficient to allow of his marrying. His guardians stated that the expense of his education, the purchase of his commission, and his living expenses since he had gone into the Army had reduced his fortune one-half. He was now twenty-four and had been four years in the Army. Anna was infuriated with her father and wrote her friend Mrs. Sykes, "My mother has behaved with extreme kindness in this business." [1]

Mr. Seward wished his daughters to marry, but he realized more clearly than did his love-sick daughter that while a broken heart was painful, marriage without an income was disastrous. There was no way a wife could earn money unless both woman and circumstances were unusual, as in the cases of Mrs. Barbauld who helped run her husband's school, and Mrs. Trimmer who wrote primers. Anna's talent for verse was not a financial asset. A parent's choice for a daughter's husband was one with an estate sufficient to provide adequately for offspring, sisters, younger brothers, aunts, cousins, superannuated servants, and all other family dependents, or else a young man with prospects: that is, coming inheritance or patronage. A youth in the church, if only a curate, was sometimes a fair financial risk. In Jane Austen's *Pride and Prejudice* there was no financial objection to that preposterous cleric, Mr. Collins. By the time Anthony Trollope was solving this problem for his lads and lasses he had the help of political secretaryships, but even those salaries were insufficient for romance, as witness the fate of Lily Dale, and remember that Johnny Eames rose to position only after he became an earl's protegé. Patronage was more effective than native ability.

Anna's restless heart, driven by great need of loving, soon detached itself from Mr. Taylor, and bestowed itself upon Cornet Richard Vyse, back home after six years' military education. He was tall, dignified and handsome, his uniform was elaborate, and most becoming.

The British Army afforded promising careers to young men of energy. Despite the conclusion of the Peace of Paris with France in 1763, Pitt was busy preparing for all eventualities. It was necessary to keep considerable military forces in America, recently wrested from the French, and also an army in Ireland, area of continuous trouble. Militia was augmented for home defense, and regular troops enlisted for service abroad. The army was undergoing thorough reorganization, with great attention to training of officers, recruited largely from the nobility and gentry. Those who survived the rigorous schooling, were rapidly promoted.

Cornet Richard Vyse belonged to a Lichfield church family. His father was a Canon-residentiary of the Cathedral and Archdeacon of Salop. His mother was the daughter of the Right Reverend Richard Smallbrooke, Lord Bishop of Lichfield. His older brother William, who in the fulness of years became Chancellor of the Diocese, Canon-residentiary of the Cathedral, Archdeacon of Coventry, and Rector of Lambeth, had been an infant sweetheart of Anna, but in later years they sniped continuously at each other. Connections like these would help a young man in any line where advancement depended chiefly on patronage, and young Richard had as sure a future in the Army as his brother had in the Church. Canon Seward would not have refused his daughter's hand to an applicant with such family connections and Anna would not have repulsed the tall young man who with the charm of youth had poise beyond his years, when he came home from Ireland, lonely for English ladies.

The courtship proceeded happily for three months under the eyes of an interested Close. Vyse's father and sisters approved. Suddenly the Cornet's behavior altered from enamored fervor to cool civility, bordering on neglect. Anna believed that a friend of his who was no friend to her had remonstrated with him on marrying a dowerless maid. Quite likely, for the Close was like one great family, its members meddling in each other's affairs. Cornet Vyse rejoined his regiment in Ireland without bespeaking Anna's hand and on his next visit to England married one of Anna's friends, Anne Susanne Spearman of Bishop-Middleham, Durham, a pleasing but not beautiful young woman with a fortune in her own possession. She was Honora's first cousin. Anna had known her well and was now rueful at the memory of heart-broken confidences to her about Vyse's dereliction. However Anna attended the wedding and when the young wife died in childbed a year later Anna wrote a monody on her death and put it away to be published years later in her collected works. Along with it she saved an elegy addressed to young Vyse, and a couple of ballads about sailor lovers on the billows. An odd circumstance in relation to the publication of the elegy is mentioned in a letter written years later (June 14, 1802) by Anna to her publisher, R. A. Davenport, Esq. in London.

> I very much approve of your plan, if it can be done, of having the five omitted stanzas printed immediately and

86

sent to the booksellers to be pasted into the volumes wh. are not already sold. I own I shou'd be infinitely mortified that this Elegy shou'd meet General V—'s eye shorn of those benedictions for his welfare, wh. it possessed, when I gave it to him in our mutual youth. This elegy is likely to excite more public curiosity than any other of *my* little poems in your vol., at least amongst the large circle of fashionable People in wh. *he* is known.[2]

This early elegy was a fore-runner of the monodies on which Anna's later fame partially rested. The sea ballads have the self-conscious sadness to which that form of verse is susceptible. The first verse of one is:

> The stormy ocean roving,
> My William seeks the foe;
> Ah me! The pain of loving,
> To war when lovers go!

"William" being a generic name for swains in ballads.

Anna had several proposals of marriage from men whom her father considered eligible, but she refused to bestow her hand without her heart. Moreover the fact that her father approved a suitor may have had the tendency to set Anna against him. Canon Seward had a difficult daughter.

Let us now return to Mr. Taylor and his fantastic love. Dates will help. He first met Anna in Lichfield in 1762. They betrothed themselves in London in 1764 and the engagement was broken early the following year. Then came the Vyse interlude. When Anna was again in London in 1768, Taylor revealed to her that he had inherited a fortune which would satisfy her father. Anna confessed to him that his constancy surpassed her own and that she did not now wish to marry him. Mr. Taylor appeared to take her refusal philosophically although it was seven years before he married. He brought his wife to Lichfield on their honeymoon while Anna was absent in Nottinghamshire. Mrs. Seward reported that the wife was young, beautiful and pleasing. Anna was sorry to have missed the call, but dismissed the matter from her mind, having no inkling of Mr. Taylor's tendency to prefer a charmer who was absent to one within his grasp.

Twenty-eight years after the last time Anna had met Taylor she received from his wife a most astonishing letter. Anna was at this time terrifying herself with the ungrounded fear that she had cancer of the breast and she talked a great deal about it as she did about everything which concerned her. Mrs. Taylor wrote that she had heard of Anna's trouble and could not resist writing to say that she was suffering from the same pain and apprehensions. (In her case also the symptoms were from some other cause.) She was starving herself as a cure; she wished it were possible for her to take upon herself all Anna's pain and pay the death penalty in her stead; she felt intimately acquainted with Anna because her husband, now a colonel, had talked so much about her; she had obtained Anna's poems as they appeared; she had sought information about her from every source. Would Anna please send her picture, for she united with her husband in his unswerving devotion to the woman he could not forget. She enclosed verses she had written in praise of Anna Seward.

Anna, distressed and astonished, replied kindly and sensibly, but this did not close the correspondence. Mrs. Taylor was persistent. Came other letters telling of Col. Taylor's sorrow over losing—some thirty years previous—a ring given him by Anna; his belief that she had given away a locket which he had presented to her—she had not—; and his brooding resentment that she had been socially gay the year he married. Anna especially resented this last allegation as that particular year had been an especially unfortunate and unhappy one, although Mr. Taylor's marriage had had nothing to do with her sadness.

The Taylors were known to Mrs. Sykes, née Miss Rogers

of Dronfield, Derbyshire, a friend of the Seward family since the days when they had lived in Eyam. Mrs. Sykes had written verse and a novel and had a vast flow of language. She was able to inform Anna that Mrs. Taylor had not exaggerated her husband's dejection of spirits. His melancholia was attributed to his unrequited love for Anna. Anna had a grounding of commonsense under her romanticism and she refused to accept this theory of Taylor's blighted life. Moreover this did not explain Mrs. Taylor's odd behavior. When that lady had realized that her married life was to be lived in the shadow of her husband's consuming passion for Anna, she had taught herself to love her rival as much or more than he did. She had outdistanced him in frantic admiration. Mrs. Taylor's worshipful letters made Anna uncomfortable, but worse was to come.

Col. Taylor journeyed to Lichfield and called at the Palace.

He sent up his card by the manservant. The housekeeper passing through the hall was startled to find a strange man standing at the foot of the stairs, gazing upward with earnest, melancholy eyes. He retreated to the parlor under the housekeeper's scrutiny, but when the manservant returned to tell him that Anna would be down directly, Col. Taylor had vanished.

The explanation came later in a letter from his wife to whom he had related the circumstances upon his return home. He told her and she told Anna: "The momentary gratification must have been followed by regret and pain that would sufficiently have punished the temerity of attempting to see her at all. I had no sooner entered the house than I became sensible of my perilous state of feeling, and fled with precipitation."

The curtain now falls to indicate the lapse of seven months. Anna was entertaining friends in the book-room above stairs when the manservant told her that a stranger-lady was waiting to see her alone. On her way to meet the caller Anna passed John Saville in the gallery and he whispered as he passed her, "Mrs. Taylor, or I'm mistaken!" If one enjoys guessing at details one can imagine Anna's start of consternation; her, "Impossible! What makes you think so? Oh, you are only teasing!" Nevertheless when an elegant, faded beauty with an animated, pleasing countenance, rose with the greeting, "At this instant the vision of my life is realized!" Anna replied, "Mrs. Taylor, I am sure."

Mrs. Taylor had come to Lichfield to live near Anna! She had brought one of her daughters with her. One assumes the husband dead, for he is not again mentioned. His widow had taken from his dying hand the torch of love for Anna! Anna was constrained to accept responsibility for the Taylor family's social life in Lichfield. Mrs. Taylor was a pleasant lady. The daughter who accompanied her played the harpsichord and the pianoforte brilliantly. A younger daughter still at school was said to have an exquisite voice.

Mrs. Taylor had been educated and had lived until her marriage in France. Some relatives and many friends perished on the guillotine, her husband was cold to her, her darling, gallant son ran the family into debt, and her health was impaired. She related these depressing circumstances without dejection of voice or countenance. The gaiety of French manners, Anna noted, prevailed over the infelicities of fortune.

Anna rather liked Mrs. Taylor, but found her excessive admiration an inconvenience. Perhaps she suspected that the lady was shrewdly utilizing her defunct husband's infatuation to insinuate herself into a desirable coterie. Under Anna's reluctant wing she cuddled down in the midst of a cultured, pleasant, Cathedral group.

CHAPTER VII

Richard Lovell Edgeworth Comes to Lichfield

RICHARD LOVELL EDGEWORTH, heir to an estate in Ireland, was twenty-one years old when he came to Lichfield in 1765 for the first time. That was the year after Dr. Seward had broken off the secret engagement of his daughter, Anna, to Colonel Taylor, and the same year that Cornet Vyse failed to cap his courtship of Anna with a marriage proposal. It is to be assumed that the wounds inflicted by these disappointments were superficial and healed rapidly, since she was ready for a flirtation with the attractive Irishman when they were introduced at the Darwins.

Edgeworth later became an important member of Lichfield's group of intellectuals; but the purpose of this early visit was scientific rather than social. He had come to discuss the art of carriage-building with Dr. Erasmus Darwin. Today we identify Edgeworth chiefly as the father of Maria Edgeworth, the Irish novelist and writer of tales for children, but he was himself a man of parts. He was a pioneer along several lines; in the education of children, in scientific theories of various purposes, and in the invention of agricultural and transportation devices. In the course of his life he worked on the perfecting of the "Tellograph"; he designed a horizontal mill for grinding flints which was used by his friend Josiah Wedgewood; an improved lamp; an improved candlestick; a manifold writer; a knitting loom for stockings; a weighing machine; a surveying machine; a canal lock; a pump; and "a flying bird."

Young Edgeworth drove into Lichfield in an extraordinary rig which he had designed. Men were especially interested in carriage construction because the roads were so bad that the vehicles had to be very good. In Edgeworth's Ireland the roads were hardly more than trails through bogs and tracks over hills. The English highways had been improved during the century but backroads and byways were narrow, rutted, pitted with bogholes, and dangerous with stumps. All roads were dusty in dry weather and muddy in wet. Many were so narrow and rough that they could be traversed only on horseback. The problem on which both Edgeworth and Darwin were working was to make a vehicle lighter than the clumsy, lurching coaches which were always overturning, and stronger than the usual chaise used for local travel. None of the conveyances were comfortable. Dr. Darwin was concerned because he had a widespread medical practice that necessitated long hours on the road, and Edgeworth was moved by youthful restlessness increased by the desire to get away from his wife who was of a despondent nature most depressing to his own buoyancy.

He traveled into Lichfield in a one-wheeled, one-horse, one-seated vehicle built according to his own original design. The large wheel was set in the center of an axle with shafts extending from either end of the axle. A seat was slung from the shafts, between the horse and the wheel. The seat was not over thirty inches above the ground, to bring the center of gravity low. One may understand better if one visualizes a wheelbarrow, drawn instead of pushed, with the wheel much enlarged, the body shrunken, and the handles elongated into shafts to accommodate a horse between them. There was some arrangement to raise the swinging seat to avoid stumps and rocks in the roadway and a leather apron protected the driver's legs from mud. The vehicle attracted a good deal of attention.

When Edgeworth heard of an unusual turn-out designed by Darwin, he came to Lichfield to inspect it and to enjoy with the inventor an exchange of vehicular theory which they had begun by letter.

Edgeworth proceeded to Dr. Darwin's home on Beacon Street. Dr. Darwin was out making his medical rounds when Edgeworth arrived, but Mrs. Darwin welcomed the guest cordially. Mr. Edgeworth was slender and graceful. His high forehead sloped backward in a line with his elegant nose, his chin was firm, his lips full and his expression eager. His approach was friendly, his manner confident, his mind inventive, and his heart affectionate. He wore a long-skirted coat of bottle green or purple or some other gay color and knee breeches. One feels sure that he had the watch, the cane, the snuff box, and the rings necessary to a young man of fashion. Edgeworth was a ladies' man, marrying four wives in the course of his lifetime, beside having annulled a marriage he had never made. The story of Edgeworth's marriages comes later.

Mrs. Darwin had been Mary Howard, a member of one of the Cathedral Close families. She had married at eighteen and was now about twenty-eight, witty, poised, delicate in health, and in love with her husband.

The guest commented favorably on the prints and books in the room where he was received and he and his hostess were soon absorbed in a discussion of literature. Mr. Darwin was delayed. Edgeworth suggested leaving and returning when the Doctor had arrived. Mrs. Darwin said this was unnesessary as they had expected him for several days and a bed had been prepared. They went on talking about literature.

When they had almost finished supper, a terrific rat-tap-tapping resounded at the door. A maid answered. When a bustle ensued, Mrs. Darwin went to see what had occurred. Edgeworth, hearing her exclamations, joined her. A very large man was directing and aiding in bringing into the hall a man apparently dead.

"No, he is not dead. Only dead drunk," explained the large man who was obviously Dr. Darwin. "I found him nearly suffocated in a ditch; I had him lifted into my carriage and brought him home to take care of him."

When candles were brought, Mrs. Darwin recognized the unconscious man as her brother. He was drunk. Every one exclaimed that he had never been like this before.

After the brother had been put to bed to sleep it off, Darwin and Edgeworth had leisure to get acquainted. Dr. Darwin was at first puzzled when he learned that his wife had been entertaining the guest all the afternoon and evening. After some conversation the doctor explained with a great deal of amusement that from Edgeworth's letters about carriage building, he had assumed that Edgeworth was a coachmaker.

"Ah, Doctor," replied Edgeworth, "you see how superior in discernment the ladies are to the most learned gentlemen; I assure you I had not been in the room five minutes before Mrs. Darwin asked me to tea."

Mrs. Darwin admitted that she had immediately seen that Mr. Edgeworth was a gentleman and had instructed the maid to prepare a chamber more sumptuous than the one which had been assigned to the supposed coachmaker, and Edgeworth then understood a slight confusion which had ensued when Mrs. Darwin had given the maid some low-voiced instructions.

Dr. Darwin was above middle height, with stooped shoulders, overweight and clumsy in movement. He had heavy features, a pock-marked face, a saturnine expression, wore a full-bottomed wig. He had an impediment in his speech. Beneath his unattractive appearance, surface irritability, and a tendency to sarcasm, he was generous, sympathetic and amiable. When he entered a room his heavy face lit up and his slow, stammering speech was worth listening to if one appreciated wit, irony, imagination, and lively information. Everybody respected him and many loved him. He was the son of a private gentleman near Newark, Nottingham, and had come to Lichfield in 1756 soon after he finished his academic and professional training at Cambridge and Edinburgh. He was not only a skillful physician, but also stood high as a botanist, zoologist, geologist, and writer. The learned doctor and the young sprig from Ireland had in common a passionate interest in mechanics. They were both inventors and each had invented fantastic machines.

The morning after Edgeworth arrived, the two men inspected each other's carriages. Dr. Darwin's was constructed on a different plan from Edgeworth's but was equally strange. The best description of it is given in a hitherto unpublished manuscript written by Rev. Richard George Robinson, Chancellor's Vicar of the Cathedral from 1770 until his death fifty-five years later, in his eighty-ninth year.

This eight-page document, dated Ashbourne, 27th October, 1812, without salutation other than "Errata and Observations," is a critical review of Anna Seward's *Life of Erasmus Darwin.* Rev. Mr. Robinson had been on friendly terms with Anna in the early years and she wrote an epitaph for his first wife, Hannah Wild of St. Mary's Parish, Lichfield, beginning:

> "Ere ten short months have run their swift career
> Three lovely sisters press the untimely bier!"

95

Mr. Robinson writes:

> She [Anna Seward] gives a strange and very inaccurate
> description of a carriage which the doctor constructed.
> It was in the form of a garden chair, fix'd upon the axle-
> tree; the foot-board terminated in an elastic pole, which,
> as she describes, went through a ring fix'd on the saddle,
> and which she very improperly calls a kind of Proboscis,
> through which various insects take their food, and by
> which the elephant conveys it to its mouth. The fact is
> the Doctor had told me some gentlemen at Mr. Mundy's
> [the poet, F. N. C. Mundy, living in Needwood Forest]
> had made themselves very merry with his carriage, and
> one of them had said it was like the proboscis of an ele-
> phant. I had told her this.
>
> The wheels were of the ordinary size; it would other-
> wise have been impossible to have got into it, but from
> behind. The Doctor had a coal-cart with exceedingly
> high wheels, the body of which was fix'd under the axle-
> tree, and this probably ran in her head, when she men-
> tioned his one-horse carriage having very high wheels.
>
> She mentions his breaking the patella of his right knee
> by a fall from it, in the year 1768, and that this uncom-
> mon accident happened also to herself, and Mr. Levitt
> in the course of one year. All this is very erroneous; and
> also that he had been thrown from it several times. It
> was the first time. Two days before, I went from Burton
> on Trent, where I was on a visit to my relations, to dine
> with Sir John Every[1] at Egginton, which is four miles
> from thence; and staid all night. The next day the Doctor
> call'd there to see Lady Every, who was under his care
> in the inoculated smallpox. He took me with him to Bur-
> ton in this carriage, and the horse took fright on the road
> at a barrow of gravel, thrown down by a labourer, em-
> ployed in making the canal, called the grand trunk; and
> ran one of the wheels on the top of a hedge, a yard or
> two. The carriage received a violent shock, which I really
> believe injured the axle-tree; for it broke the next day
> in one of the streets of Rugeley when the knee pan of the

doctor was broken. He never used the carriage after-
wards.[2]

Edgeworth could describe to Darwin experimental vehicles
which he had designed other than the one in which he was
traveling. He had built a phaeton of uncommon lightness,
constructed so that each wheel could rise separately over ob-
stacles in the road. He had experimented with a sail-carriage
propelled by breezes but this frightened horses on the road
and once when it got away from him and sailed off with no
one at the helm, he managed to climb on board at the risk of
his life and steer it into a field in time to avert its smashing
into a stage coach. His most spectacular vehicle was a huge
broad wheel inside of which was another wheel six feet in
diameter. The driver walked within the inner wheel somewhat
as a horse works a treadmill (but inside instead of outside),
the effect of the walker's stride being increased by the size of
the outer wheel. Before the inventor had added machinery for
control, some yokels borrowed the invention to try it out sur-
reptitiously. One got in and started the wheel down hill. The
momentum increased until the velocity was terrific. The rider
was barely able to throw himself out, when the machine
crashed into a quarry and was smashed to smithereens.

Edgeworth's imagination was not limited by carriages; he
constructed a huge umbrella for covering haystacks, a machine for cutting turnips, a machine which would lay down
its own road (fore-runner of the caterpillar tractor), and a
wagon in two parts (precursor of the trailer). Many of these
inventions were brought out later when he had settled down
in Ireland to farm his estate. His mother was concerned at
the hop-skip-and-jump nature of Richard's employments. On
her deathbed she warned him that his inventive faculty
would lead him into new plans, and dazzle him by new
schemes before he had fairly tried what he had begun. She

97

begged him to resolve to finish and never to procrastinate.

The second night after Edgeworth arrived Mrs. Darwin gave an impromptu supper party at which the guest met some of the Cathedral families. Though a supper was more informal than a dinner, it was no simple meal. The English gentry at this period did themselves well in the way of food. Breakfast was usually at nine o'clock and as a family had been up and active for several hours, it was a hearty though informal meal. Dinner was in most country homes at two in the afternoon, and was a tremendous repast.

Mutton was the standing dish. An informal invitation was often worded, "Will you eat your mutton with us?" but the guest was not restricted to that one meat. To Rev. James Woodeforde, rector of Weston Longville, Norfolk, at this time, we are indebted for much ecclesiastical culinary information. When, dressed in his gown, cassock, and scarf, he dined with his bishop at Norwich, in a party of twenty, they sat down at table somewhat after three and rose at six-thirty to adjourn to the drawing room for coffee and tea. They had been served two courses of twenty dishes each followed by a dessert of twenty dishes, accompanied by red wine and white wine and Madeira.

This was a bishop's dinner, but Mr. Woodeforde, though only a parson, set a good table himself. A dinner which he served to four brother clergymen to meet Mr. Mellish, a new young clergyman at Tuddenham, was by no means niggardly. It was nearly four o'clock before they sat down to the table, one guest being late, perhaps the one who brought a "brace of cucumbers" as a gift. The first course was a fine cod's head and shoulders boiled with oyster sauce, pea soup, roast saddle of mutton, potatoes, "colli-flower-brocoli," and the cucumbers. The table was cleared and there followed: roast duck, macaroni, a sweet batter pudding with currant jelly, blancmange, and raspberry puffs. Then came a desert of oranges, almonds, and raisins, nuts and dried fruits. The drinks were port and sherry, porter, strong beer and small beer. Small beer contained less alcohol and was usually provided for servants. After tea and coffee the company played Limited Loo and "spent on the whole a very agreeable day."

At Mr. Mellish's return dinner, ten guests sat down to the table, each with his own servant standing behind his chair. As this was "a time of scarcity," no wheat flour was used in preparation of dishes, which eliminated pastry and tarts and white bread. A combination of brown meal (perhaps whole wheat) and barley flour was used. The first course consisted of salmon with shrimp sauce, white soup, roast mutton and cucumber, lamb fries, tongue, ragout of veal, rice pudding and stewed beef. The table was then cleared and the second course served, consisting of: roasted sweetbreads, jellies, macaroni, frilled oysters, and small crabs. We should serve these foods in separate courses, but at that time meats and sweets were included in each course. Tea and coffee were served in the drawing room, followed by cards. Those who wished played and the others were "setters by."

The list of foods in Parson Woodeforde's diary includes over eighty items running from almonds to woodcock and including such oddities as swan, fawn, and udder. His beverage bills were for ale, beer, brandy, claret, cocoa, coffee, cyder, Geneva gin, Madeira, mead, port, rum, sherry and tent wine. He bought brandy and rum by the tub and bottled it himself.[3]

Everyone who could afford it ate meat at every meal. In *Pride and Prejudice,* when Darcy's sister entertained Elizabeth Bennet and her aunt and uncle who were making a morning call in "the sacred shades of Pemberly," Darcy's country seat, cold meats were served as a light repast as well as fruit. Glassed hot houses were coming into use and gentlemen who possessed them shared fruit and vegetables with their friends and, though there was no ice, salmon and oysters were evidently somehow transported, for the letters of the time often mention sending them as presents.

Every well-kept house had a closet, filled in summer and emptied in winter, where were stored jams and jellies of strawberry, raspberry, gooseberry, apricot, plum, currant, and peach; also candied orange peel, currants and raisins; along with pickles of gherkins, beetroot, onions, and the like.

Hours up to dinnertime were designated as morning and were sacred to work: domestic tasks for the ladies and for the landed gentlemen riding over their estates. After the two or three o'clock dinner was evening and given over to social relaxation. This was an especially happy arrangement in winter when the day closed in so early, and if it seems that this gave an unduly short work day, one should remember that the day began early—long before the nine o'clock breakfast. Moreover these are the hours of the gentry and not of the farmers.

At Mrs. Darwin's supper party given in honor of Richard Edgeworth, Anna Seward was seated next to the guest. When Anna was present a party was always a success. The ladies of the Close must have been often exasperated with her, if not actually jealous and resentful, for when Anna entered a room she dominated it by right of her full-blown auburn beauty, her talents, and most of all by her exuberant joy in living. She had superb health and a voracious appetite for whatever was going on at the moment. If nothing was going on, she started something. She was a marvellous woman. She was vain, dominating, sentimental and self-centered; she was also beautiful, impulsive, affectionate, honest and courageous.

We have a description of her from Mary Martha Sherwood: "Miss Seward," Mary Martha tells us, "had that peculiar sort of beauty which consists in the most brilliant eyes, glowing complexion, and rich dark hair. She was tall and majestic, and was unrivalled in the power of expressing herself." She was "extremely greedy of the admiration of the other sex. . . .

She was, in a word, such a woman as we read of in romances; and had she lived in some dark age of the past, might have been charged with sorcery, for even in advanced life, she often bore away the palm of admiration from the young and beautiful, and many even were fascinated who wholly condemned her conduct." [4]

Edgeworth and Anna led the table talk, the gayety and the laughter. They competed in repartee, quotations and literary allusions. Most of the company had memories well stocked with verse. A number of them could, and did, break into impromptu rhyming on frequent occasions.

When Anna quoted lines from Matthew Prior's *Henry and Emma,* pausing at the couplet,

> To bind his wounds my finest lawns I'd tear,
> Wash them with tears and wipe them with my hair,

Edgeworth commented that tearing finest lawns showed tenderness and washing wounds with salt water was beneficial, but protested vigorously against using tresses as a towel, an action neither sanitary nor elegant. From this he went on to compliment Anna on her own magnificent auburn hair, which was the more striking because it was almost the exact color of her extraordinary eyes.

Mrs. Darwin and the other ladies grew restive under this duet which was more pleasurable to Richard and Anna than to the others. Ladies found Anna's exuberance annoying at times. Mrs. Darwin may have felt that Edgeworth had appeared as a single gentleman long enough, for she suggested that the company drink Mrs. Edgeworth's health. Anna was caught off guard. Her face showed surprise, even consternation. The others burst into laughter in which there may have been a little malice.

Edgeworth was not only married, but he had been divorced before he was ever married at all. The unusual circumstance occurred this way: When he was about sixteen he was one of a group of young people who were having "a raking of tea." That is, they were drinking tea in the small hours after a night of dancing in celebration of the marriage of one of Edgeworth's sisters. When one of the lads slipped on a white coat someone said he looked like a clergyman in a surplice. Having just attended a wedding it was natural enough that one of the merrymakers should suggest a mock marriage —marrying Richard to the girl with whom he had been dancing. Edgeworth was a great lad for the ladies and very probably he had shown a marked partiality for his partner, a clergyman's daughter and a nice girl. Bridal costumes were improvised and a hilarious ceremony was performed.

The youngsters considered it a great lark, but Richard's father was in a taking when he heard of the affair. He had reason to be uneasy, for at this period marriages were often so casually contracted that many a man was astounded to find himself legally married when he hadn't intended it at all. You remember how Olivia, the older daughter of the Vicar of Wakefield, supposed herself married to the villain with whom she eloped until he told her that the priest was fraudulent. She was a dishonored female until it was discovered that a real priest had been substituted for the intended fake and that made her a respectable wife. Rules concerning licenses, rites, registration, parish habitation, and the calling of banns, were so ill-defined that unintentional slip-ups as well as planned fraud were all too frequent. In London the infamous Fleet-street marriages had only recently been suppressed and Gretna Green was flourishing in Scotland. Since Richard was the heir to the Edgeworth estate his father took no chances with the mock marriage. After some difficulty he had the contract dissolved in the ecclesiastical court. Richard was impatient with his father for he thought it was sufficient that everyone knew that neither he nor the girl were in earnest. One phase of the matter pleased him; so much attention was attracted to the young lady by the difficulties of the annulment that gentlemen appeared who *were* in earnest and she was "suitably married."

Edgeworth did not marry again—even in fun—until he was almost nineteen and this contract stood, for the bride was insistent although Richard wished to cry off. When the young man had gone to Oxford his father had taken the precaution of recommending him to a friend, Paul Elers, Esq., of Black Burton, to prevent his making unfortunate acquaintances among the ladies. Mr. Elers warned Father Edgeworth that he himself had some attractive but unportioned daughters who might be a danger, but Mr. Edgeworth took the risk. The Elers girls were young, handsome, and goodnatured. They danced and sang and entertained the son of their father's friend. Richard engaged himself to one of them. When he went to Bath he found other even more beguiling possibilities, but the lady of the first party held him to his promise and he considered himself in honor bound to marry her, although he was frank about his reluctance. His father refused consent, and the couple went to Gretna Green for a Scotch marriage. Father Edgeworth thereupon surrendered, but insisted on matters being made clearly legal; and after a few months the couple were remarried in England.

The alliance developed as unfortunately as it began. Husband and wife were uncomfortable with each other. Edgeworth, who was a fair man in summing up personalities, gave his wife credit for being an efficient housewife and an affectionate woman, but said she was of a despondent nature and a complaining habit. Edgeworth later developed to a high degree a talent for maintaining a large, heterogenious family in unity, harmony and exceptional happiness, but during this first discordant union he spent much of his time in Lichfield, London and on the continent. He was happy everywhere but at home.

When Edgeworth returned to Lichfield four years later, both his own situation and that of the group of young intellectuals centering around Anna Seward, had greatly changed. He had grown more completely away from his wife, and they on their part, had been getting themselves entangled in a web of complicated love affairs that finally caught and held him too.

CHAPTER VIII

The Saville-Seward Scandal

THE very special friendship between John Saville and Anna Seward was recognized as love by onlookers if not by themselves soon after a memorable Buxton holiday in 1769. The intimacy between John and Anna has been mistakenly thought a relationship of their later years and has been presented as affection rather than passion, but Anna was in her late twenties and John in his middle thirties when their absorption in each other could no longer be ignored by shocked and outraged neighbors in the Close.

It is difficult to calculate with certainty the ages of Anna and John. People had a strangely casual attitude toward dates. It was as if they said: "Want a date, do you? Well, catch this one," tossing out a haphazard month and year. Family Bibles, church records and tombstones are usually considered reliable authorities. When these differ we drift. Two circumstances partly explain discrepancies: a tombstone or an obituary may record as the age of the deceased the year toward which he was progressing. That is, the record may read "aged 68" when we would say "in the 68th year of his life." When John Saville died in 1803, his tombstone asserted that he was sixty-seven, while his obituary in *The Gentleman's Magazine* gave his age as sixty-eight. A variation of this sort makes it impossible to learn a person's exact birth date by calculating back from his death date, as was the custom when the birth record was not available. Other variations result from the confusion which followed England's shift from the Julian to the Gregorian calendar in 1752.

Neither of these confusions are sufficient to explain the Seward family's inaccuracy. Some person actually altered various birth and death dates in the family Bible. The dates do not agree with those in church registers. The register at Newton-in-the-Thistle gives the date of the Seward parents' marriage as October 27, 1741, while the family Bible gives it as 27 Oct., 1742. Anna's birth is recorded in the Bible as 1st Dec. 1744, while her baptism in the church register at Eyam, Warwickshire, where Mr. Seward was rector, is set down as Dec. 28, 1742. The true date of Anna's birth is almost certainly 1742.[1]

John Saville came to Lichfield from Ely in 1755 when he was about nineteen and served as Vicar Choral in the Cathedral until his death forty-eight years later. The Chapter Acts in the Cathedral Library (which are the minutes of the Dean and Chapter) contain the entry:

"2 May, 1755 before Rev. Thomas Smallbrooke, Canon Residentiary—Mr. John Saville the Younger was installed as Vicar Choral." [2]

A legend handed down in the Saville family has it that Saville's great-granddaughter destroyed family papers which showed that the Savilles had been connected with Oliver Cromwell. The only known fact that might substantiate this is that Saville came from Ely which is in the neighborhood of Oliver Cromwell's birthplace.[3]

Saville as a lay-vicar was not obliged to dress always in clerical black. His miniature painted in 1770, when he was in his early thirties, shows a handsome man in a bright blue coat, wearing a neat, snowy-powdered wig with a sausage curl over each ear. His nose is well-formed, his mouth full and curved, his eyebrows arched and heavy. The rather sleepy line of his upper lids gives a misleading expression of arrogance. He was not arrogant, but shy in the extreme. He shrank from meeting strangers, but once the initial shock was over, he became a devoted friend. He had a haunting fear of not being liked, a worry which had no basis in reality, and he suffered from stage nervousness even after he had been singing for years and taking principal roles in oratorios.

Saville's connection with the Cathedral gave him a higher social standing than the one usually accorded at that period to a musician who sang or played for pay. He was, in marked contrast to some of the Cathedral officers, a hard-working man. Beside fulfilling his church duties, he taught music and gave concerts. He conducted oratorios, in which he sang the principal parts, in Shrewsbury, Birmingham, Manchester and other cities, and was under contract at Covent Garden. He was in demand for both private and public concerts in various cities and had charge of Lichfield Race Week music.[4]

Most of our information about Saville comes from Anna Seward's letters, and even allowing for the fact that her tenderness for him in his lifetime and her grief after his death led her to portray him faultless, we are justified in believing him to have been a man of unusual talent, probity, and kindliness.

The Seward family was already settled in the Palace when Saville came to Lichfield, and Anna knew him from the time she was a little girl. When she began to take music lessons on her harpsichord it was probably from him, since he added teaching to his Cathedral duties. She did not become skilled enough to play in public, for she did not settle down to serious attention until too late, but she loved music and was always ready to play for friends.

Anna's first reference to Saville is in a letter dated February 1764. A group of amateur and professional musicians were gathered in the Palace drawing room, that large and hospitable room in which young Johnson and young Garrick had had early training in social amenities, and where Sally met her unknown betrothed in the middle of a card party. A gentleman considered a connoisseur maintained that Handel lacked delicacy and tenderness in his compositions. Anna opposed this judgment, mentioning some of her favorites— *Return, O God of Hosts, O Sleep why doest thou leave me?* and *Father of Heaven.* Saville, who was already making a reputation as a Handel singer, supported her contention by asserting that Handel had delicacy and pathos as well as spirit and sublimity. Saville and Anna were both passionate lovers of Handel's music.

The more intimate friendship began during the memorable holiday at Buxton aforementioned. Buxton was a favorite resort of the Sewards. Visitors went on the excuse of drinking the waters for their health, but also to meet congenial people and have a lively time. The spa was only twelve miles distant from Eyam where Dr. Seward as rector kept a two-month yearly residence, and the family liked to break their journey at the springs. Mr. Seward preferred to remain at Buxton during periods when the women of the family visited Mrs. Seward's sister, wife of the rector of Gotham, Nottinghamshire, the Reverend Samuel Martin. Martin was a man of violent temper given to snatching off the caps of his daughter and wife when annoyed. After such a duty visit Mrs. Seward and Anna were accustomed to join Dr. Seward at Buxton.

This particular sojourn at Buxton was especially delightful, for their social group was even more than usually congenial. John Saville was there, and though somewhat older than the other young people, contributed to the general entertainment with his beautiful voice. He was in love with Anna Seward, but had, most unfortunately, a wife and two children. We do not know whether his family was with him at Buxton. He and Anna were still at the stage when they could assure themselves that the feeling between them was simply an old, old friendship.

Another person who enhanced the charm of the visit was John André whose family was sojourning at the spa to raise its spirits after the recent death of the husband and father. The family consisted of John and William Lewis, and three daughters named respectively Louisa Catherine, Mary Hannah, and Anne. His sisters called John "cher Jean", and cher Jean he was to his Lichfield friends. Cher John proceeded to fall head-over-heels in love with Honora Sneyd who was, of course, one of the Seward party.

This happy time in Buxton was to be succeeded by a period of storm and stress for the Sewards, the Andrés, the Sneyds and the Savilles. The love affairs of Anna and Saville, and of Honora and André brought unhappiness to themselves and their families.

The young people explored the countryside on foot, on horseback and in light vehicles. The scenery of the Peak country was a magnificent tumble of crags and chasms and lofty outlooks; of giant trees and gentle woodlands; of swift streams, noisy waterfalls, and unexpected pools. The Seward family was passionately addicted to wild, rugged scenery. Admiring the beauties of nature was a part of the Romantic Revival taking place at this period, some nature-lovers carrying about with them pieces of different-colored glass through which to view the landscape. The Seward's delight in mountains, rivers, and forests was unforced, genuine; they did not need rose-colored glass.

In the evenings there were suppers and dancing and card-playing and impromptu concerts. Saville's fine voice was raised in song; Anna played the harpsichord well enough to please her friends; and there was talent among other Buxton visitors. Original poems were read to appreciative audiences, for nearly everyone wrote verse. Any unoccupied hours were filled in with reading aloud poetry, novels, history, and sermons on Sundays, but chiefly poetry. Saville had a vibrant and musical reading voice, and Anna's friends considered her Siddons' equal, but that was partiality. Young William Falconer, nephew of the Sewards' neighbor, Prebendary James Falconer, and frequent visitor to Lichfield, who was kicking up his heels a bit in Buxton before settling the next year in Bath to become a well-known physician, entertained by repeating by heart the whole of Mundy's recently published *Elegies to Laura,* as well as original verses. His voice was rough, but his memory was phenomenal, and though his recitations were not harmonious, they charmed the friendly audience.

The trip home was delightful, along a road running through Needwood Forest, lying between the rivers Dove, Trent and Blythe. This ten thousand acres of beautiful landscape was situated in the northern extremity of the Hundred of Offlow in four parishes with the delightful names of Tutbury, Hanbury, Tatenhill and Yoxall. Here in ancient times the nobility had eagerly pursued the cheerful sport of hunting. The oak land was estimated at a thousand acres and the giant of all trees had attained a name—Swilcar. Swilcar measured twenty-one feet around the trunk, was sixty-five feet tall, with a spread of forty-five feet. An even larger tree had been felled in the previous century in the village of Field, parish of Leigh, near Uttoxeter, an elm a hundred and twenty feet high and twenty-five and a half feet in circumference. It took three men on either end of the saw five days to bring down this giant. Sir Harvey Bagot, the proprietor, put his signature to the attestation and eye-witnesses added their crosses. The history of this section went back to the beginning of land records. Driving through it, one retraced the centuries. Manors on the outskirts of the forest were recorded in the Domesday book. Longcroft, near Yoxall, was still surrounded by a moat crossed by a stone bridge. Roman coins belonging to a yet earlier period had been found. The party must have had a fine time sight-seeing by the way.

From an eminence in the forest Lichfield could be seen, with the three slender red sandstone towers of the Cathedral rising from a bed of green trees. Honora told André that these light and elegant spires were called The Ladies of the Vale. That scene and that moment were forever imprinted on the memory of the young man fated to die soon and tragically far from home.

Saville lived from 1765 to 1772 with his wife and children in one of the charming half-timbered houses in Vicars' Close. Behind the house was a pretty garden which Saville's love for plants and flowers had made an exquisite spot. Anna and Honora were on visiting terms with Mrs. Saville and when-ever they entered this garden which Honora had named "Da-mon's Bower," they quoted a verse from Shenstone, another garden lover:

> How blithely pass'd the summer's day!
> How bright was every flow'r!
> While friends arriv'd, in circles gay,
> To visit Damon's bow'r![5]

Vicars' Close was (and is) a mediaeval huddle of half-timbered houses, built in two small quadrangles, in the west side of the Cathedral grounds between the handsome houses which face the west front of the Cathedral and those which face Beacon Street—one of the latter being Erasmus Darwin's house. Here was once the old large Vicars' Hall used for con-certs and assemblies, but long ago converted into small sep-

111

arate houses. The earliest house in the Vicars' Close was built in 1314. As a Vicar Choral Saville had the right to a dwelling in this Close.[6]

The friendship which had made the Buxton visit so pleasant to Anna grew yet warmer. Saville became a member of the blue-sittingroom group and Anna wrote to Mary Powys, cousin to both her and Honora, "a whole cluster of Beaux, one of them no *common Beau,* the lively, the sentimental, the accomplish'd, the scientific, the gallant, the learned, the celebrated, Mr. Edgeworth—he with young Mr. Hinckley [a Seward cousin], Mr. Robinson [one of the clergymen] & Mr. Saville came at 7 and stay'd till nine."

"The dear Quartette," she wrote to the same friend the following summer, "do not forget you. . . . Our rambles up on the Terrace have been *very* animated these last evenings, Mr. Edgeworth enlivening us by a wit, extensive as the light of the Sun & active as its heat, Dr. Darwin laughing with us, while we have felt the fine edge of elegant, ingenuous, & what is most rare, good humor'd irony . . . Il Penseroso Saville sighing & singing to us, sharing or imparting our enthusiasms . . . Mr. Day *improving* our minds while he delights our imaginations." [7]

This paean of joy was written July 13, 1771. A month later Mrs. Saville no longer received Miss Seward in her home. Anna's last visit to Damon's Garden was on the second day of August. Mrs. Saville's indignation at her husband's friendship with Anna had boiled over. She complained to Dr. Seward.

What Mrs. Saville was like we do not know. Anna said she was shrewish, vulgar, and in many ways an unamiable wife,[8] but Anna was prejudiced. Mrs. Saville's complaint to Anna's father did not stop the affair, for he had no influence over his daughter. He was an easy-going man, amiable unless annoyed. "When his sentiments are oppos'd, his way is to fall

PLATE VII

Mrs. Samuel Johnson

*From an undated portrait by an unknown painter. By
permission of Mr. Tennant, whose ancestor Rev. John
Batteridge Pearson inherited it from Lucy Porter*

PLATE VIII
Lucy Porter, Dr. Johnson's stepdaughter
By Permission of Mr. Tennant

PLATE IX
John Saville
From a miniature painted by John Smart, 1770.
By permission of James R. Beard, descendent of Saville

PLATE X

Anna Seward

From an engraving by A. Cardon, from a painting by Tilly Kettle, 1762

into a passion, and abuse the person or book who express contrary ideas," said his candid daughter.[9] She liked her mother better than her father during this period of strain, but not enough to be guided by her advice. The Seward household must have been worried and exasperated almost beyond endurance.

Mrs. Saville next carried her grievance to the Dean, Dr. John Addenbrooke.[10] It was the office of the Dean "to correct any irregularities of the members of the church." One looks in vain in the Chapter Acts of this time for any account of any action taken by the Chapter. The matter is not referred to. The Chapter clerk of those days kept only the most meager minutes, sometimes entering none at all, other times recording trifling admonitions for tardiness and the like.

Dr. Addenbrooke, the Dean, died three years later, having been unable to deal with the matter. The situation must have been embarrassing all round as Dr. Seward was a member of the Chapter which the Dean consulted in affairs of discipline. The succeeding Dean, Baptist Proby, S. T. P., Rector of Doddington, in the Isle of Ely and of Thornton, in Northhamptonshire, was equally helpless in the matter although a man of stronger will. Dr. Johnson in a letter to Mrs. Thrale, written from Lichfield, August 27, 1777, says: "We have a new dean whose name is Proby; he has the manners of a gentleman, and some spirit of discipline, which brings the Cathedral into better method. He has a lady that talks about Mrs. Montagu and Mrs. Carter. . . ."[11] The Probys had no more influence than the Addenbrookes, though Dean Proby's ladies showed their displeasures by refusing to call on Anna,[12] and Anna nicknamed the reverend Dean "Dr. Bamble-Bee" and scorned his "epicurism, his spleen, and his gullibility."[13] Prebendary James Falconer and Mrs. Falconer also became Anna's enemies, though their nephew, the William Falconer who had been one of the happy Buxton group with André and Saville and Honora and Anna, continued to call on Anna whenever he visited his uncle.

The Bishop was doubtless consulted in this crisis, but apparently took no official notice of the trouble although Henry Egerton who held the office from 1768 to 1771 was considered a skillful conciliator. His successor, Brownlow North, of a retiring disposition and amiable, had no more influence.

Anna's reply to the worried Dean, distressed friends and frantic parents was that she was "innocent." By this she meant that she had not committed adultery. She certainly was not innocent of having involved them all in a most distressing situation; of having, as it were, dropped a very big basket of eggs in the church dooryard. Her statement that they were not lovers in the full sense of the word is probably true. She was no hypocrite; it was her nature to blurt out whatever she felt. Like her father she talked too much to be secretive. She was not the sort of woman to fling her cap over the mill, being turbulent but not reckless, nor was she led off the beaten path by any free love theory. The general opinion at the time was that the relationship remained on the pardonable side of the line of demarcation. She was not, to borrow a Victorian phrase, Saville's "wife in the eyes of God." She referred to herself when she was elderly as a "celibaic cypher" and again as being thankful for her "celibastic exceptions" [14] from chaperoning young folks to races and balls, and spoke of her "stale maidenhood."

The scandal in the Close reached a climax when Mr. Saville, in 1773, left his wife and moved to an adjoining house, a very small house with only one bedroom and a place for a servant to sleep. His wife seems to have remained in the Saville home next door with the two little girls, and Mr. Saville appears to have financed both establishments. The husband and wife are said not to have been on speaking terms, though he shopped for her and she saw to his laundry. In later years there was a close bond between Saville and his daughter Elizabeth.

Young Richard Sykes, later rector at Foxholes, Yorkshire, who was apparently living at the Palace, made matters worse by taking up Anna's cause. He was the son of Joseph Sykes, a prosperous merchant in West-Ella, near Hull, and Dorothy Twigge Sykes of Blakewell, Derbyshire. As that is the country in which Anna lived before the Sewards moved to Lichfield, and where she spent two months every summer, it is probable that the close friendship between the two women began there. Anna was much younger than Mrs. Sykes but older than the Sykes children. Young Richard galloped into the fray, lance levelled, to defend Anna's fair fame and by so doing involved her in a subsidiary scandal. His parents thought Anna wished to recover her reputation by marrying Richard. A letter from Anna to Mrs. Sykes tells of the misunderstanding; though long, it is worth reading:

May 1773

I own it amazes me, when I reflect upon the unreserved freedom with which I laid my heart open to you, how the idea could for one moment be entertain'd, by either you or Mr. Sykes, that it was possible for me to act so vile and foolish a part as to draw in a youth, 12 years younger than myself, into a marriage with me, that cou'd produce nothing but misery to either of us—how utterly incompatible with such a scheme is my present conduct, situation, the turn of my mind, and above all my confidence in *you*, which has been unbounded. As little am I capable of such malevolence as the setting of a young man against his parents upon whom he is dependent.—To advise one, whom I professed a friendship for, and from whom I had received a thousand marks of kindness, to walk in the paths of misery and ruin.—Good God what possible purpose cou'd a conduct so diabolical answer to me? As to sentiments which, in the warmth of argument

115

I may have expressed concerning the frequent cruelty and injustice of arbitrary power, exerted in private families, let it be consider'd that misery, probably for life, had recently been inflicted on me by that very authority against which I cou'd not help inveighing when so barbarously exerted upon people advanc'd to the middle of life, who surely, if they are not fools, have, at such an age, a right to think, judge and act for themselves. . . .

I do not take your solicitations ill but it is not in my power to comply with them. The Dean did make an offer of continuing to Saville the income of his place in this church if he would remove from Lichfield but the Dean is extremely old and he can engage for this only during his life; but that is out of the question. Saville knew I cou'd not bear a total separation and sent an absolute refusal to listen to the proposal before I knew it had been made. It is true he has offer'd to leave Lichfield if I cou'd make my self easy—not for his own sake for he assures me it wou'd cost him his life—and I am sure it wou'd cost me mine. There is *no* evil can happen to me so heavy and insupportable as the knowledge that in all human probability I should never behold him more. I have thought deeply upon this subject and can never be persuaded that it is either my duty to renounce the sight of him and those little transient conversations we sometimes have or that there wou'd be any virtue in doing it—therefore I cou'd never expect the reward you mention of Heaven for bringing so much and such insupportable torture upon myself, even if I believ'd that Providence made all worthy people happy here which that it does not ev'ry days experience evinces.

. . . As to my Parents after having made me miserable to the utmost extent of their power after their deaf and inexorable cruelty to me last summer the part they took with my worst foes the stigma they fix'd upon me by the prohibition so disgraceful to my character they have very little right to expect that I shou'd inflict upon myself the additional torture to which their power does not extend. If they attempt further persecutions the consequences will be more desperate. I lov'd Saville for his

virtues. He is entangled in a connection with the vilest
of Women and the most brutally despicable. He cannot
be my husband but no law of earth or heaven forbids
that he should be my friend or debars us the liberty of
conversing together while that conversation is innocent.
The world has no right to suppose it otherwise—if it will
be so unjust we cannot help it—all its severest censures
we shou'd both look upon as a less misfortune than that
of seeing each other no more. . . ." [15]

Dr. Seward was a tactless father, impatient and unhelpful
when his daughter was in trouble. A letter he wrote her from
Eyam, November 12, 1771, where he had gone for his annual visitation shows that he was in a state of exasperation
with her, although he does not mention the Saville affair;

> Dear Nancy,
> . . . I desire you would write to me soon, as I hope
> you will send me a better account of your own health
> both of Body and Mind, for I have sometimes seen that
> one or both was a good deal hurt. It has certainly been a
> great misfortune to you that your agreeable and ingenious
> Friends both the Travellers and the pretty Quaker whom
> I left with you should all have been disaffected to the
> Established Church of which your Father is a Priest and
> your Mother a sincere Believer. From your ingenious
> Philosophers you will hear more subtle Objection to the
> Scriptures, etc. [16]

The letter contains seven pages of dreary, impersonal, religious advice, at a time when only sympathetic understanding of her plight might have inclined her toward taking any
advice.

Anna was able to defy the conventions which pressed so
heavily on other unmarried women by reason of her strong
will, her loyal family, and her financial position. Dr. Seward
held benefices in addition to his prebendaryship. Clergymen
were allowed to compensate for low salaries by holding sev-

eral offices. Unfortunately the extra appointments tended to fall to influential clergy rather than to the needy, so that one man sometimes held five or six preferments. So long as her father lived, Anna had an impressive home and when he died he left her a good income.

The love affair continued for over thirty years. The Close got used to it, but never approved. It was a story to tell to new-comers and a subject to point a moral for young girls. Mary Martha Sherwood, to whose disapproving pen we owe much information about Lichfield sinfulness, was properly shocked when at the age of thirteen she met Mr. Saville. When she and her mother, during a Lichfield visit, were invited to the Palace there was a long discussion about the propriety of their ac-cepting, although the Seward-Saville affair had been going on some fifteen years. It was finally decided that since they did not live in Lichfield, it was allowable for them to dine with Miss Seward.

The mother was small and plain of feature, but Mary Martha took after her large, handsome father. By the time she was twelve she was as tall as a woman and looked ridiculous in the pinafores her mother considered appropriate to her age. To keep her back straight during this period of rapid growth the mother fastened her to a backboard with an iron collar for hours every day, fed her on plain food like bread and milk, and never allowed her to sit in the mother's presence. The child was so blatantly healthy that her father called her Hygeia. She did not suffer from her mother's shyness. She had her father's self-confidence and more, but she lacked his charm. Mary Martha sat continuously in judgment on her fel-low men and never doubted that she was infallible. She re-called the circumstances of this Palace visit years later:

"At dinner Mr. Saville was present, a handsome, gentle-manlike man, with fine grey hair, but evidently very grave and sad. He had been putting out the wine, we remarked, like a man in his own home, and on some particular wine being wanted, he directed the servant where to find it. His spirits did not rise during the repast; he was still grave, and even sad, but she, in a little while made us forget every person but herself. . . . She was the first female, and perhaps I may almost say the last, who ever gave me the idea of overpowering fascination which is described as being independent of either youth or beauty. . . ." [17]

As to Saville's hair, we know from his portrait that he wore a wig in his earlier years, and Anna states that he powdered his hair until his death so that no gray showed. Mary Martha's mother regretted the depression which Saville displayed, for she recalled him a lively young man. He was older now and may have been bored. One really cannot like either Mary Martha or her mother.

It seems probable that Saville atoned for transgression which he never committed; that he carried the sense of guilt without the pleasure of sin. He was a faithful platonic lover to a tempestuous, domineering woman, often unreasonable, and in later years cantankerous. He loved her for the warmth of her nature, the passion of her heart, and for her charm—that compelling attribute of charm which takes a thousand forms in a thousand personalities. A man who could love Anna Seward must have had a high degree of both courage and pity.

A love affair with a woman of Anna's temperament under the happiest circumstances would have had its ups and downs; and under the strain of continuous outspoken disapprobation, it was far from serene. A letter to Mrs. Sykes, August 29, 1778, lifts the curtain on one of the periods of stress:

> That I did not mention to *you* the quarrel between Mr. S. and myself by no means arose from want of confidence, but from the same reason which keeps me silent upon the subject to my Mother, who possesses *all* my

confidence, affection, gratitude, and esteem. I know she wishes the connection broken off, I know also that *you* have that wish, and you are kind enough to interest yourself warmly in my destiny. I *believ'd*, it is true, and I *still* believe that Mr. S. and I are eternally separated— but as the disagreement between us was *recent* I was not *quite sure* it wou'd be *lasting,* and I was therefore unwilling to mention it till my resolutions upon the subject were more absolutely *confirm'd.* While I continue in my present persuasion that Mr. S. has lost his affection for me, and can bear without anguish an everlasting absence from *my* society I firmly am convinced my resolution of conversing with him no more will not falter—but shou'd he convince me these suspicions of extinguish'd tenderness are injurious, I have no power of inflicting misery on him—the idea of doing so wou'd make me more wretched than all the censures of a cruel and misjudging world. A little more time is necessary to determine our fate. . . .[18]

Yet in spite of all Anna's suffering and indignation, this career of mistress-in-name-only suited her temperament. She dramatized herself in the role of martyred innocence. She was not good wife-material according to the marital standard of the period and place, but in this unstandardized love affair she functioned nobly. She had the satisfaction of ardently loving and being loved in return, while she still kept the independence of an unmarried woman. Anna herself in her later years wrote an astonishingly keen analysis of her own temperament, inscribing it on the back of a silhouette drawn on a sheet of note paper and captioned, "Portrait of the Lady who wrote the following lines."

> Ah! poor old Lass. —and is she gone?
> Tell who she was, thou senseless stone.
> In her own words, the enquirer teach;—
> Nor very poor—nor very rich.
> Of Passions strong—of hasty Nature;
> Of graceless form; and dwarfish stature.

By few approved: and few approving
Extreme in Hating, and in Loving.
In forming Judgements never long,
And, for the most part, Judging wrong.
In Friendship firm. But still believing
Others are treacherous, and deceiving.
And Thinking in the present aera,
That friendship is a pure chimaera.
More passionate no creature living—
Proud, obstinate, and unforgiving—
But, yet for *those who kindness shew*
Ready through smoke and fire, to go.[19]

CHAPTER IX

Wife Trouble Among the Clergy

JOHN SAVILLE'S course in providing separate maintenance for his wife was not so unusual a proceeding as it seems at first thought. We have fallen into the way of assuming that when there were no divorces there were no broken families. At this time divorce was possible in England only by a special sitting of Parliament to free some nobleman of influence and wealth. No divorce could be obtained by any woman under any circumstances no matter how high her rank, how great her wealth, and how grievous her suffering. Legal separations, arrangements for separate maintenance, and elopements of spouses to the continent were not uncommon. They occurred even in clerical circles.

In the group of churchmen who especially interest us, six men holding ecclesiastical appointments lived apart from their wives and two of their female relatives were separated from husbands. The men were: John Saville, Vicar Choral; Dr. John Taylor, of near-by Ashbourne, holding five preferments; Rev. William Vyse, holding four preferments; Dr. John Sedgewick Whalley (not a resident of Lichfield, but a visitor), rector of Hagwortham, Lincolnshire; Samuel Jackson Pratt (married to a former Lichfield woman), briefly a curate; and some years later, William Sneyd, curate at Hanbury, who eloped to the continent with a married woman. Elizabeth Smith, Saville's daughter, left her husband; Fanny Sage, Dr. Whalley's niece, deserted her husband for a lover whom she later married.

Dr. Johnson's friend, Dr. John Taylor, attained eminence and property. In addition to being Rector of Market Bosworth, he was Prebendary of Westminster; Preacher of Broadway Chapel, Westminster; Rector of Lawford; Perpetual Curate of St. Botolph's, Aldersgate; and Rector of St. Margaret's, Westminster. In his leisure time he raised blooded cattle at his home in Ashbourne, where he was a justice of the peace, and because of his influence and his generosity to the poor, he was called the King of Ashbourne. He inherited from his father and from an only brother and his income was estimated at £9,000 a year.

His first wife whom he married in 1732 was Elizabeth, daughter of William Webb of Ashbourne. She died in 1745. His second wife, Mary, daughter of Roger Tuckfield of Fulford, Devon, left him to live with relatives, in August 1763, making scandalous, unproved accusations against her husband. Dr. Johnson was deeply concerned at his friend's marital trouble. Indeed one feels that Johnson attributed to Taylor a greater sensitivity than the latter possessed, although Dr. Taylor was perturbed in mind and disordered in body. The letters which Dr. Johnson wrote Dr. Taylor are wise, tactful, and sympathetic. He advised making whatever financial concessions the wife's relatives demanded, and counseled the abandoned husband to move from Ashbourne to some place among strangers where he would not be the object of gossip. Dr. Taylor did not, however, leave his commodious home, his park with a waterfall, his deer and his prize cattle, but made a satisfactory money settlement with his wife's relatives and got along very well without her.[1]

The case of Rev. William Vyse, L.L.D., Chancellor of the Diocese of Lichfield and Coventry, Canon-residentiary of Lichfield Cathedral, Archdeacon of Coventry, Rector of Lambeth and Sunridge, was unique. While his first wife was still living, Dr. Vyse engaged himself to marry (conditionally on his wife's death) Sophia Streatfield, a young lady with a lovely neck, a knowledge of Greek, the ability to weep easily and beautifully, and many admirers. This odd betrothal lasted many years, but after the wife finally died, Dr. Vyse jilted Sophia and married another.[2]

Among Sophia's several infatuates was Mr. Thrale, at whose home she was a frequent visitor. On one occasion Mr. Thrale had asked his wife, who was then pregnant, to sit in a draft so that Sophia could sit warm in her hostess's seat at the foot of the table. Mrs. Thrale left the room in tears and later reproached Johnson for not having spoken up in her behalf, but Johnson was lenient to male frailty although it must have been painful to see Thrale making a fool of himself over a pretty girl. Besides, Johnson had a tremendous respect for Thrale who could do two things which he could not: make money and rule his family. Johnson could flatter a woman or snap at her, but he never controlled any woman, from his wife to the ungrateful shrews to whom he gave a benevolent home. Johnson cared too much for his freedom to be a good ruler— for a ruler is not himself free.

Samuel Jackson Pratt, who wrote poetry under the romantic name of Courtney Melmouth, was a man of flickering talent, a mean disposition, and irresistible charm which he turned on when he wanted something, and off when he did not. It is difficult to follow his life, as he had a lying tongue and probably actually believed his own falsehoods. As well as can be determined, he was the child of respectable middle-class parents who stinted themselves to give him a university education. He took holy orders and obtained a curacy in a Lincolnshire parish, which we know only as P—, but decided he was not cut out for the church. He eloped from Birmingham to Scotland with an eighteen-year-old girl who had formerly lived in Lichfield and had been a childhood friend of Anna Seward. When his wife's fortune, said to have been fifteen hundred pounds, was exhausted, he wrote, 1771, a self-pitying letter to Dr. Johnson, dripping with fulsome flattery, offering Dr. Johnson in capitalized emphasis, a chance to Ameliorate the Anguish of one who was a Football of Fortune. His style makes Anna Seward's sound primer-simple by comparison. He wishes Dr. Johnson to defray his expenses to Ireland where he could get a job as an actor. "Cou'd I raise the *Pity* and *Confidence* of some *good Being* to indulge me with a *small Sum* to get my Things (I mean *the comforts of life*) about me, and convey me to Ireland, my *gratitude,* and *Honour* wou'd be *eternally engag'd* to him, and I wou'd return the Favor the first moment of my Power." [3] One trusts that if Dr. Johnson sent the money to his grateful and obedient servant, S. J. C. Pratt, lodging with Mr. Deals, Cheesemonger, corner of Berners Street, near Middlesex Hospital, London, he did it without expectation of return, for paying back money was something Pratt did least well of all. When Mrs. Siddons, the actress, immediately after her husband had lent him a hundred pounds, asked him to return ten pounds she had earlier lent him, he went into a tantrum and accused her of persecuting him. He made the trip to Ireland accompanied, gossip had it, by a married actress with whom he acted in touring companies, until he returned to England, deeply repentent and ready (he said) to do anything his friends advised, except rejoin his wife. He must have been an engaging rascal, for among his friends he counted, off and on, Mrs. Frances Moore Brooke, the writer; "Perdita" Robinson, the actress; Dr.

Walcot, the satirist who wrote as Peter Pindar; Angelica Kauffmann, the painter; Anna Seward's friend, Dr. Whalley; and Dr. Johnson's friend, Dr. Taylor.

Mrs. Pratt lived for a while with her husband's parents in St. Ives and later went to London where she supported herself and her little girl. She spent a day at the Palace while visiting in Lichfield and Anna was sympathetic, for she herself had been bamboozled by the engaging humbug into mending his verse, flouted when his need was passed, wheedled back when he again wanted help, and again dropped. Anna's resentment added lively color to her account of the miscreant's treatment of his wife. When emotionally moved (and when was she not?) Anna saw azure as deep-dyed indigo, and pastel pink as incarnadine.

Dr. Taylor, who considered Pratt a kind, benevolent, friendly man, was indignant at Anna's criticism. He said: "Miss Seward, however, was one of the last persons who should have assumed the office of a severe and moral censor, as it is well known that she suffered the attentions of a public singer, a married man, who resided with his family at Lichfield, and was in the habit of receiving him almost daily. Admitting also that the connection was innocent, and I have no reason to suppose it otherwise, surely it was acting in contempt of public opinion to withdraw a man from his duty to his wife and family." He seems to have forgotten that his own marital conduct had been subjected to criticism.

One more cleric may be added to the list, although his connection with Lichfield, through the Sneyd and Butt families, is indirect. We are again indebted to Mary Martha Sherwood for information, à propos of a visit in 1789 by the two Miss Sneyds. "The family at this time was in great trouble," reads Mary Martha's autobiography. "The history of Mrs. Cecil and Mr. William Sneyd is but too well known. . . . The ill-fated young man never looked up after the fatal step which he had been induced to take by the unprincipled woman. . . . William was a remarkably elegant and handsome young man; he was, for several years, curate at Hanbury. Mrs. Cecil (Miss Vernon), married for her splendid fortune, was a plain, ordinary woman, older than Mr. Sneyd by several years. Mr. Cecil always neglected her; he was cold and severe, and she was left much in the society of Mr. Sneyd . . . she became violently attached to him. He never liked her, but acting from a false view of honor, he yielded to her fascination; she left her husband with him." In viewing extra-marital relations Mrs. Sherwood always saw a seducing female pressing an apple upon a reluctant male.

The story of this affair is told with more detail and less moral deduction by Mrs. Charles Bagot in her *Links with the Past.* Thomas Vernon, of Hanbury, Worchestershire, desirous of uniting his riches with a title, over-persuaded his only daughter and heiress, Emma, to marry Henry Cecil, heir to the Ninth Earl of Essex and to the magnificent showplace, Burghley, near Stamford, Northampshire. The marriage was most unhappy, and after enduring it some twelve years, Emma fled to the continent with William Sneyd, curate in Hanbury where she had grown up. Accompanied by a faithful woman servant the eloping couple finally settled in Lisbon hoping that the climate would benefit Mr. Sneyd who had fallen into bad health. Mr. Cecil, being heir to an earldom, was able to obtain a divorce in 1791, whereupon Mrs. Cecil immediately married Mr. Sneyd. Mr. Sneyd did not live many years, and after his death his widow returned to England to take possession of her large inherited property which had remained legally hers. Later she married her estate manager. When it came her turn to die, she sent for her former servant who had married and settled in England, gave her certain instructions, and adjured her second husband not to interfere with whatever the woman might do. What the woman did was to wrap the corpse in the linen which had been William Sneyd's winding sheet, and to scatter on the coffin earth from William's Lisbon grave.

Mr. Cecil also made a love match under circumstances so unusual that Tennyson used the romantic theme in his poem *The Lord of Burleigh*. In recoil from his disastrous loveless marriage, Mr. Cecil left his home, took another name, and as an itinerant painter lived among the simple folk. In this guise he wooed and won Sarah Hoggins, daughter of Thomas Hoggins, a farmer of Bolas Magna, Salop, not revealing his identity until he led her through his stately halls between rows of bowing menials! Tennyson's poem is substantially correct except that Mr. Cecil did not inherit the earldom until two years later. Horace Walpole reports that the farmer's daughter won approval in high circles by her great humility and modesty. She did not live many years, but she left an heir to her fond husband. The Earl, having experienced marriage for money and for love, made his third match with rank, marrying Elizabeth, Dowager Duchess of Hamilton, widow of the Eighth Duke.[4]

If one includes in this informal, incomplete survey, men who visited their friends in the fair city of Lichfield, Dr. Whalley, a clergyman-poet, had three marriages with one separation. When Thomas Sedgewick Whalley left Oxford a friend of his father, the Bishop of Ely, presented him with the living of Hagwortham in Lincoln on the condition that he should never live there as the miasmic air of the fens was fatal to anyone not a native. For fifty years Dr. Whalley drew his stipend and kept his word to the bishop. As he had a talent for magnificent expenditure he eked out his salary by marrying three fortunes.

He was a tall, thin, handsome, sentimental man with close-set eyes, small mouth, and high cheekbones. He wore an unusual wig parted in the center and draped over his temples.

DeQuincey found him bilious, irritable and of a gloomy turn, but most people liked him, especially ladies. He had life-long friendships with Mrs. Siddons, Hannah More, her sister Martha, and Anna Seward, all of whom he visited. His poetry, fiction, and drama were popular. He had a taste for building and when he was not trying to economize by travel-ing in a princely manner on the continent, he was building or remodeling his houses in the Mendip Hills, in Bath, and in London. His crowning architectural achievement was an Ital-ian villa halfway up one of the Mendip Hills. The veranda across the front was wide enough for three to walk abreast, the floor was mosaic sailcloth, the back wall was mirrors, and the front arches contained twenty-four huge china jars kept filled with cut flowers. The kitchen was sixty steps down the mountain, a housekeeping arrangement that sets one wonder-ing. Delightful paths zigzagged up the mountain-side to a terrace with a view, with frequent rustic seats dedicated to friends. A project which has lived after him was his wide planting of trees on the Mendip Hills. One can see that a rec-tor's salary would be insufficient for his needs.

When his first wife died after more than twenty-five years of pleasant married life, he was left without resources, for he had generously insisted that his wife's fortune be settled on her relatives, excepting an annuity of two hundred pounds for himself. His second wife lived but a few happy years after their marriage. The third marriage was a calamity. He mar-ried the widow of General Charles Hornbeck under the im-pression that she had a fortune. She made the same mistake about him. Her fortune was a large allowance from the Court of Chancery for taking care of a lunatic brother who had to live with the Whalleys. After some indecisive separations and reunions, a legal separation was effected and the third Mrs. Whalley received a settlement and lived in Catherine Place, Bath. It is puzzling how members of the gentry-class who had no money and no earning power still managed to live comfortably. Dr. Whalley spent much of his later years on the continent with a niece who, born Fanny Sage, was married to William Townsend Mullins, heir to the first Lord Ventry. She eloped with a lover and the marriage was dissolved by act of Parliament, the husband being a member of the favored class who could obtain a divorce and permission to remarry. Since she was afterward called Mrs. Sullivan she evidently also married again. She was a silly, pretty little thing, with a bushel of curls, an arch expression and an eye for the gentlemen. Her uncle adored her and was always pulling her out of some scrape, usually financial.[5]

John Saville's daughter Elizabeth grew up, married, had two children, left her husband, returned to Lichfield, and was trained by her father to be a concert singer. She was shy, gentle, docile, and a favorite. She sang in concerts where her father was engaged, wearing frocks supplied by rich, kind, old Mr. Newton, and applauded by friends who bought "gold tickets"—special tickets for which purchasers paid extra according to their means and generosity. Her voice was true and tuneful rather than strong, and harmonized with her modest appealing manner. William Hayley, the poet, was interested in her. Mr. Hayley lived in Eartham, near Felpham, Sussex Downs. He was sentimental, handsome, and charming. His wavy hair, unpowdered, dipped in a widow's peak over a high, broad forehead; his face was long and the features perfect; the expression suggested ardor rather than strength. We know him now chiefly as the man who obtained a pension for Cowper and was a long-suffering friend to William Blake. His poetry was so popular during his lifetime that no one would have guessed his future obscurity. *The Triumphs of Temper* is his best-known poem.

Hayley's connection with Lichfield came through his friendship with Anna Seward, his "Sister in Parnassus," whom he visited in Lichfield and entertained in Eartham. The fervid admiration between the two evoked from Richard Porson, an English classical scholar, the following lines:

> *Miss Seward loquitur*
> Tuneful poet, Britain's glory,
> Mr. Hayley, that is you.
>
> *Mr. Hayley respondet*
> Ma'am, you carry all before you,
> Trust me, Lichfield Swan, you do.
>
> *Miss Seward*
> Ode, didactic, epic, sonnet,
> Mr. Hayley, you're divine.
>
> *Mr. Hayley*
> Ma'am, I'll take my oath upon it,
> You yourself are all the Nine.

Mr. Hayley married Eliza Ball in 1769. Her mind became affected and seventeen years later a separation was arranged. The same year that he separated from his wife he suggested to Anna Seward that it would be fine if Elizabeth Saville Smith— whom he called Eliza as he had his wife—would accompany him on a continental tour as governess for his little illegitimate but adopted son Thomas Adolphus. Elizabeth was a sweet singer like his demented wife. Anna's common sense squashed that daydream. She wrote Hayley a letter which tactfully began with the statement that so fascinating a man should not think of traveling with a young female. She went on in words dictated by her own experience:

"Nothing but a considerable independent fortune can enable an amiable female to look down, without misery upon the censures of many; and even in that situation, their arrows have the power to wound, if not to destroy peace. Surely no woman with a nice sense of honor,—and what is she worth who has not?—would voluntarily expose herself to their aim, except she has unwarily slid into a situation where the affections, making a silent, an unperceived progress, have rendered it a less evil to endure the consciousness of a dubious fame, provided there is no real guilt, than to renounce the society of him without whom creation seems a blank." [6]

Mrs. Elizabeth Smith soon had a continental trip under more conventional auspices, with the Burts, a glamorous visiting West Indies couple which was hypnotizing all Lichfield. They sound like a fairy tale. He was gay, thoughtless, impetuous, good-natured and of a princely spirit. He was also uxorious and jealous. She had perfect beauty in height, figure and a complexion delicate without bloom. She bore herself with pensive dignity and her air was foreign rather than English. Her jewels were set in the newest style. She was out of health being accustomed to a warm climate. These Burts took Mrs. Smith on what was to be a two-year tour of the continent. Mr. Burt settled an annuity of a hundred pounds a year on Mrs. Smith for life, the Burt estate being legally responsible, Anna Seward's cousin, Mr. Hinchly, making the deed. There was a new traveling coach, Mrs. Burt's maid accompanied them, and Anna Seward lent them her favorite man servant. Mrs. Smith was to share Mrs. Burt's singing lessons from famous masters.

The party left in February, 1791. September of the same year Mrs. Smith was on her way home. What broke up the arrangement is not clear. It had sounded too good to be true and it was too good to be true. Mrs. Smith, by leaving, forfeited the annuity. The Burts, too, returned sooner than they had intended; their magic gone, their spell broken.

CHAPTER X

John André Comes to Lichfield

WHEN the Seward family returned in 1769 from the memorable holiday in Buxton in the Peak country, they were accompanied by John André who had fallen deeply in love with Honora Sneyd.

Honora had grown from a lovely child into a beautiful, lovable woman. In reviving personalities of a past age it is difficult to get a sharp impression of charm that lies in gentleness and affection or to see in the mind's eye a face distinguished by delicate, conventional beauty. Honora does not come alive for us as do more aggressive women. She was now between sixteen and seventeen and bore herself with a self-possession resulting from her constant association with older persons. As a very little girl she had come to live with the Sewards after her mother's death and, though she made long visits to the sister who lived with their cousins, the Powyses, at the Abbey in Shrewsbury, and to others of the scattered family, the Palace was home to her.

Anna was passionately devoted to Honora. A few months before the Buxton visit, while Honora was on a long visit in

Shropshire, Anna wrote a poem gloomily entitled, *Honora, an Elegy*. Writing on the anniversary of Honora's coming to live with the Sewards, Anna recalled how she and Sally, returning from a walk that summer evening went carelessly to their mother's room to meet the little guest and instantly loved her. She was Sally's particular care until Sally's death, after which she became Anna's beloved charge. More and more she came to fill the place left vacant by Sally's death, and more and more she grew like Sally; beautiful, docile, intelligent, sensitive, loving and intuitive. The good fairy godmothers had clustered round her cradle and the wicked ones had been absent.

André, Honora and Anna formed an odd triangle. André loved Honora, deeply and forever. Anna loved both and worked for their marriage with all the zeal of her over-fervid nature. Neither now nor at any time later did Anna manifest the slightest jealousy of her lovely foster sister. Honora had a tenderness for cher Jean, but was not much in love, if at all. She was willing to marry him if her father approved, but the esteem she felt was mild in comparison with André's devotion. To go the rounds of the families, Mrs. André liked Honora and Mr. Sneyd liked André, but neither looked with fervor on his suit, because the young man had no way of supporting a wife and children except in the family importing house—a business for which he was obviously unfitted. The Sneyd family was wealthy and the Andrés were not poor people, but the two families together had nine daughters to dower or support for life. The parents on both sides were mild, but practical. They did not forbid the marriage, but they pointed out the imprudence of setting up a family without an income sufficient for comfortable maintenance. The uncertainty which hung over the outcome made André's visits to Lichfield periods of poignant happiness; ecstatic meetings under the shadow of eternal separation.

André's letters picture for us his delight in those visits. The letters are directed to Anna, but they were written for his beloved. No well-bred young woman at that time either wrote to a young man or accepted letters from him unless they were openly affianced. Honora occasionally put in a postscript ("very short, indeed" was André's reproach), but other times Honora excused herself from writing even a line, on the plea of a pain in her side which made writing troublesome and injurious. This explanation threw the lover into a frenzy of anxiety.

André called Anna "Julia." To bestow a fancy name on a friend was a way of circumventing formality of address without undue familiarity. John Saville was "Giovanni," but never John. Hayley, the poet, later on, called Anna his Sister in Parnassus and signed his letters "your Brother H." Thomas Whalley, also later on, was "Edwy" to Anna from the hero of one of his books.

André wrote:

> London, October 19, 1769
>
> From the midst of books, papers, bills and other implements of gain, let me lift up my drowsy head a while to converse with dear Julia.—And first as I know she has a fervent wish to see me a Quill-driver, I must tell her, that I begin, as people are wont to do, to look upon my profession with great partiality. . . . But, oh, my dear Honora!—it is for thy sake only that I wish for wealth.— You say she was somewhat better at the time you wrote last. I must flatter myself that she will soon be without any remains of this threat'ning disease.
>
> It is seven o'clock—You and Honora, with two or more select friends, are now probably encircling your dressing-room fire-place.—What would I not give to enlarge that circle! The idea of a clean hearth, and a snug circle around it, form'd by a few sincere friends, transports me. You seem combin'd together against the inclemency of the weather, the hurry, bustle, ceremony, curiousness, and envy of the World. . . .

Another time he wrote:

> The happy social circle, Julia [Anna], Honora, Miss
> S—n, Miss B—n, her brother, Mr. S[aville], Mr. R—n,
> etc. etc. are now perhaps enlivening your Dressing-room,
> the dear Blue Region, as Honora calls it, with the sensi-
> ble observation, the tasteful criticism, or the elegant song;
> dreading the iron-tongue of the Nine o'clock bell [the
> supper bell], which disperses the Beings, whom friend-
> ship and kindred virtues had drawn together.—[1]

Singing, reading, and discussion were occupations of the evenings which André so much enjoyed. Reading aloud went
well with the incessant sewing which occupied women many
hours a day. In those days, when every stitch set in a woman's
garment was a separate motion of the hand, dresses reached
a peak of elaboration; fashioned with darts, gussets, biases,
insets, panels, drapery; decorated with masses of embroidery
and quantities of pillow lace. Although spinning was still
largely a hand process (the spinning jenny was invented in
1764 and Arkwright's cotton spinning frame five years later),
this occupation was followed chiefly by the wives and children of laborers and weaving was done largely by cottagers
whose business it was. Doubtless some of the older women
in the Close still twirled their flax wheels and twisted wool
into yarn on spinning wheels, but the younger ones were more
skilled with knitting needles, crochet hooks, bobbins, tambor
frames, bodkins and needles and thimbles. Heavy work such
as hooking and braiding carpets and quilting coverlids had to
be performed at home, but lighter work went with the ladies
when they visited. Informal visits were sewing bees and ladies
listened with pleasure to some one reading aloud, while they
gathered, shirred, ruffled, scalloped, over-and-overed, felled,
rolled edges, overcast, couched and fagotted; but did not
scratch gathers with a needle because it would interrupt. A
sentence found in some of the novels brings before us a pic-

ture of evenings of sewing and reading; "She rang for working candles."

Reading aloud was a prized accomplishment and much attention was paid to training the voice. John Saville was not
the only good reader in the group. Honora's voice was con-
gruous with her personality, sweet and low, but not strong
enough for dramatic inflection, reminding listeners of the
murmur of an Eolian harp. Anna was a magnificent reader.
Every comment on Anna's appearance, voice and manner is
favorable, even from those who bitterly criticized her disposition. The advantage of possessing a pleasing voice had been
impressed upon her as a young girl when she was spending an
evening at the home of her friend Mary Howard, later Mrs.
Darwin, the daughter of Charles Howard, a lawyer for whom
Johnson had respect and recommended as a consultant to
both Lucy Porter and Dr. Taylor. After supper the Howards
and their guests sat in their grotto, looking down the slope of
the lawn set with shrubs and flowers to a pool which gleamed
in the moonlight. The guest of the evening was the moneyless,
orphaned daughter of a man who had been Mr. Howard's
friend. She was only twenty and she was on her way to take a
position as a governess. She had no beauty to aid in rescue
by marriage, but the listeners forgot her unprepossessing appearance when she began to sing from Handel's opera,
Athalia, the verses:

> Cease thy anguish, smile once more,
> Let thy tears no longer flow.

In the praise which followed the lovely song in a beautiful
voice, Mr. Howard advised her to sing that song if ever she
wished to subdue a heart. She followed his suggestion with
marked success. The story came back to Lichfield that no special attention was paid to her in her new home until she sang
this song and in so doing had sung the heart out of her em-

ployer's bosom. He, a widower, married her and her financial future was assured.

What did these young people read? Everything. They were omnivorous. English publications they read as they appeared. French books were Honora's share, for she had studied French at the Lattufiers' school in Derby to such advantage that when her eyes took in French, her tongue gave out English. There was by 1779 and probably earlier a group of readers who formed a Society which bought books and circulated them from house to house. Sterne's novels were coming out, and Goldsmith's *Vicar of Wakefield* and Walpole's *Castle of Otranto* were still new. *Rasselas* had been published. The English novel was getting on its feet. The young people could discuss Locke's *Essay on the Human Understanding,* Burke's Essay on the *Sublime and the Beautiful,* and Adam Smith's *Moral Sentiments.* For drama they read the Elizabethan plays and the Restoration drama. Poetry was their favorite literature and there were Shakespeare and Milton and Dryden to draw upon.

Along with the reading went discussion—endless discussion, on marriage, literature, Handel, Shakespeare, natural philosophy, friendship, diet, conduct, theology, mechanical inventions, and what the neighbors were up to. Most of all they discussed marriage.

André made another visit toward the end of October to see his beloved, plead with her father and draw courage from Anna's support. He wrote her, after his return to London:

> Ah, Julia! The cold hand of absence is heavy upon the heart of your poor *Cher Jean!* He is forced to hammer into it perpetually every consoling argument that the magic wand of Hope can conjure up; viz., that every moment of industrious absence advances his journey, you know whither. . . .
>
> . . . I know you will interest yourself in my destiny. I have now completely subdued my aversion to the pro-

fession of a merchant, and hope in time to acquire an
inclination for it. Yet God forbid I should ever love what
I am to make the object of my attention!—that vile trash,
which I care not for, but only as it may be the future
means of procuring the blessing of my soul. Thus all my
merchantile calculations go to the tune of *dear Honora*.
When an impertinent consciousness whispers in my ear,
that I am not the right stuff for a merchant, I draw my
Honora's picture from my bosom and the sight of that
dear Talisman so inspirits my industry that no toll
appears oppressive.

André probably visited Lichfield again before the engagement was definitely broken off. Richard Lovell Edgeworth
met him and was not impressed. He thought that Anna was
the object of André's regard, seeing no evidence of special interest in Honora until Anna explained to him how the affair
stood. Perhaps he did not wish to see André's love for Honora,
for his own excessive interest in her was soon to emerge.

The only indication of Honora's suffering when it was finally decided that the two should not marry, is the fact that
her father sent her to Bath in the autumn of 1770 for her
health. Her constitution was delicate and she was in recurrent
danger of tuberculosis, that scourge then fatal to so many
young women; but Honora was so homesick that after three
months of Bath gayeties she wrote Mrs. Seward secretly, begging her to represent to Mr. Sneyd that she needed Honora
with her because of her own bad health. The conspiracy succeeded and Honora started for home in such haste that she
was in peril from a spring freshet which swept over the Bath-
Lichfield roads. Two ladies who were traveling with their
own horses and servants took her into their coach and delivered her safely at the Palace.

André left the counting-house which he had endured only
in hope of earning enough to marry upon, and in March,
1771, he entered the army and rose rapidly. Shortly after

Honora's marriage, and before he was sent to America in 1773 or 1774, he again visited Lichfield. He saw again the lovely spires that Honora had taught him to call the Ladies of the Vale; he strolled under the lime trees of the Dean's Walk where he had courted Honora; he joined the evening reading in the Blue Region and was doubtless entertained at dinner by the Darwins and drank tea at the Deanery. He had come to Anna for the sympathy she always gave to those in trouble. The lad carried a sick heart with him to America.

Every school child knows André's tragic fate. He rose rapidly in the service of the English army and was made adjutant-general. He was detailed to carry on negotiation with Benedict Arnold for the betrayal of West Point in 1780, was captured, tried and hanged as a spy. André entered with zest into the social life of the pro-English American colonists, dancing with Miss Peggy Clews, writing poetry to Miss Peggy Clews, and inscribing to Miss Peggy Clews a pageant he wrote for a banquet given to Sir William Howe in Philadelphia. Inscriptions to the Townsend sisters, on a pane in the window of a bedroom André occupied at Raynham Hall, in Oyster Bay, L. I., can still be seen, and bear witness to his fatal flirtation with Sally Townsend. For she passed on her suspicions of his plans to brother Robert, one of Washington's under-cover officers, and this is said to have led to André's arrest as a British spy.

Although André found lovely ladies lovable, he could not forget Honora. He carried always with him a miniature of her which he had himself drawn in happier days, and on the eve of his execution he wrote a friend that he had been able to conceal the picture and, preserving that, felt himself fortunate. Honora was spared the knowledge of his execution. He was arrested in September of 1780 and hanged at Tappan, New Jersey, in October. Honora had already died in July of that same year.

Anna Seward's grief expressed itself in a *Monody on the Death of Major André* published in *The Monthly Review* of April, 1781, which attracted attention and won praise. André's family were offended at the poem, perhaps because Anna tore the veil of reticence too rashly, perhaps because she altered events for the sake of poetic logic. She stated that the disappointed lover enlisted after Honora's marriage, when in fact he enlisted previous to it. The mother and sisters, who lived for many years at No. 23 The Circus, Bath, were indignant. Anna's over-glib explanation of their resentment was, "They will never forgive me for the injuries I have received from them." [2]

General George Washington was pained by her portrayal of him as vindictive against the young British officer. After peace was made between the two countries he sent an American officer to Lichfield with copies of the papers and letters relating to the affair, papers which showed that Washington had done his best to save André so far as he was able within the code of war honor. Anna's regret at her injustice was as vehement as her accusation had been.

Among the commendatory letters received by Anna was one from Eliza Cottnam, a Canadian poetess in Halifax, who had also written lines on André. Sandwiched in between paragraphs of fulsome flattery for Anna, she writes:

". . . . I was indeed charmed with the letters of André . . . [I] have often lamented the Destiny that tore him from his Honora. May I ask why it was so? I think I should be more partial to her memory had she died single, could the happy maid distinguished by the Love of an André feel a second attachment? and while he lived, or could the adopted sister of a Miss Seward give a hand without a Heart—but I am opening the wounds of Friendship, which the lenient hand of Time is closing. Gratify not my curiosity at the expense of your own Peace." [3]

CHAPTER XI

Thomas Day Comes to Lichfield

EDGEWORTH'S first visit to Lichfield, which had been largely devoted to discussions with Dr. Darwin concerning the science of carriage-construction, was followed by a second visit four years later in 1770. The young people who had liked him on the earlier occasion, now took him to their hearts as one of themselves. They were not quite the same group any more, cocksure of happiness and success as a sort of inalienable right of their youth and station. Disturbing awareness of human limitations that applied to them as well as to the lower orders, had come to some of them. Edgeworth, with his gaiety and Irish optimism, no doubt strengthened their somewhat shaken self-confidence.

Moreover, Edgeworth brought along with him this time Thomas Day, whose stimulating eccentricities contributed a new and exciting flavor to the circle's gatherings, which had already been enlarged by Honora Sneyd's having grown from a child to an adorable, marriageable young woman, and by her sister, Elizabeth, who was also at this time living in Lichfield. Complicated love affairs ensued involving in intricate, intertwined pattern the two Sneyd sisters, Anna Seward, John

Saville, Edgeworth and Day. If anyone of the group was reticent about intimate concerns, it was John Saville; but he stood no chance against the volubility of his few confidants. In the cramped quarters of the Close, under the interested eyes of the residents, these young people pursued the tortuous, ecstatic paths of love.

Actually, Thomas Day, now best known as author of that edifying juvenile, *Sanford and Merton,* came to Lichfield to consult Dr. Darwin on the conduct of life. Day had met Darwin through Edgeworth two years earlier under circumstances calculated to impress each with the other's personality. When Edgeworth was living unhappily with his first wife and two children at Hare Hatch, between Reading and Maidenhead, in Berkshire, during one of his frequent absences from his father's estate in Ireland, he heard of young Day down on a vacation from Oxford, staying with his mother and step-father nearby at Bear Hill, Great Warley, Berkshire. Edgeworth looked him up and the two became lifelong friends, though they seem to have had little in common save passion for talking. Day accompanied Edgeworth and his little boy on their next trip to visit Father Edgeworth in Edgeworthstown in Ireland.

Day dressed according to the current idea of a philosopher by the simple method of paying little attention to his clothing, and not combing his hair. He was tall, heavy, stooped, and bore himself with awkward dignity. His face was marked with smallpox and his expression was gloomy until his interest was aroused, when his hazel eyes gleamed with intelligence. He was a very serious and worthy young man who lived up to his ideals of virtue, generosity and contempt of society. Edgeworth, though not handsome, was lively, lithe and well-bred.

Edgeworth, Day, and little Richard Lovell Edgeworth traveled toward Ireland in one of Edgeworth's trick carriages;

not the one in which the driver sat practically under the horse's tail, but a coach with two horses. As they approached Eccleshall, Staffordshire, Edgeworth suggested that Day pretend to be the master and the father of little Richard while he played the part of servant. Edgeworth drove up to the Eccleshall Inn with a flourish and by a hidden lever suddenly released the horses into the astonished arms of approaching hostlers. Day lolled in the coach and shouted orders. Little Richard, aged two, dressed not according to fashion as a little gentleman, but with the bare head, arms, and legs that Rousseau approved, showed off his agility in leaps and daring. Edgeworth took advantage of the joke to order dreary cold meat for the master, a tart for the child, and the best the house afforded for himself. They were in the full swing of the jest when Dr. Erasmus Darwin, accompanied by a friend, arrived and greeting Edgeworth by name, exposed the masquerade. Darwin and his scientific companion joined Edgeworth and Day for dinner. As long as the conversation ran on science and mechanics, Day was bored and silent, but toward the end of the evening he was able to shift the subject and woke up to talk so eloquently on philosophy that Darwin was charmed and invited him to come to Lichfield sometime, to continue the conversation.

Day's chief interest at this time was in getting himself married, a common enough concern for a youth of twenty, but he was having more difficulty than is usual for a well-born man with a good income. His requirements were excessive. He wished to retire to a hideaway with a Perfect Woman to live in Perfect Marriage. He demanded intelligence, congeniality and obedience. She was to love him enough to give up her fortune if she had one, disdain luxury, live in retirement, subordinate her tastes to his, and discuss every subject of every day's occurrence with logical accuracy. In return she would gain a devoted husband with much information, instructive

PLATE XI
John André
From a self-portrait

PLATE XII

Thomas Day

From a portrait by Joseph Wright, 1770. By permission of the National Gallery, London

conversation, unquestionable virtue, and an income, who would teach her to do good to the poor and oppressed. Unfortunately Day had a way of falling in love with beautiful women who enjoyed gaiety, dress and admiration. He thought he disdained beauty, but whenever a friend suggested a possible woman, his first question was, "Has she white and large arms?" He was a romantic who thought he was a realist.

The matrimonial engagements he achieved were tentative and soon broken. He was balked by his conflicting predispositions and by his inertia at crucial periods. His mind went one way and his desires another; the tug of war was inexplicable to him. It was painful to his friends also.

Twice before he came to Lichfield he had thought he held perfection within his grasp. Of one disappointment we have only the information afforded by his poem about Nature and Fancy and Philomel, beginning

> Thee, Laura, thee, by fount, or mazy stream,
> Or thicket rude, unpress'd by human feet,
> I sigh, unheeded, to the moon's pale beam;
> Thee, Laura, thee, the echoing hills repeat.

After many symbolic lines on storm and a shipwrecked mariner, comes the final verse:

> Yet let the tempest roar! . . . love scorns all harms,
> I plunge amid the storm, resolv'd to save;
> This hour, at least, I clasp thee in my arms,
> The next let ruin join us in the grave.

His second fiasco was as lover-on-probation to Edgeworth's sister Margaret, whom he met in Ireland. She overcame a violent initial prejudice to the extent of accepting his hand on the condition he would mend his manners, she on her part agreeing to study metaphysics. After he left Ireland she changed her mind, influenced perhaps by her father who could not abide Day's table habits. Day suffered, but recovered to engage in a bizarre scheme.

The project was this: as soon as he came of age Day adopted two little girls to educate according to his theories, the more worthy of whom he would choose to be his wife. Day ignored the unhappy experience of a young man named Milton who married a girl to train into wifehood, and he disregarded Sir Thomas More's equal failure with his child wife who, hard-pressed, evaded education by throwing herself on the floor and beating her head on the stone flagging. Or perhaps scrutiny of these disappointments was responsible for Day's cautious decision to educate first and marry the result only if satisfactory.

John Bicknell, a barrister in The Temple with whom Day had kept his terms, was his confidant in the experiment. Bicknell was a young barrister with a ready tongue, of whom people thought well. He accompanied Day to the foundling hospital in Shrewsbury where they chose a little girl whom Day named Sabrina Sidney, from the river Severn and the Irish patriot Algernon Sidney. She had a clear auburn-brunette complexion, dark eyes, a glowing bloom and chestnut hair. As it was necessary to bind her to a married man, they bound her to Edgeworth, without waiting to inform him. Mr. Day promised that he would educate Sabrina, would not violate her innocence, and would maintain her in a respectable family. If he chose not to marry Sabrina, he would apprentice her to a respectable tradeswoman with one hundred pounds down and four hundred when she went into business for herself or, if she married, a five hundred pound dowry. The terms were liberal as one would expect from this generous man, but no provision was made for the contingency of Sabrina refusing to marry Day. Such a contingency occurred to none of them.

After the papers were signed the two young men traveled

to the famous London Foundling Hospital where Day adopted a blond on the same terms. He called this flaxen-haired child Lucretia.

Day placed his two wards with a widow in a house near Chauncery Lane and began their course of instruction. He undertook to teach them simplicity, innocence, and attachment to himself, as well as reading and writing. He talked to them against fine dress, fine people, fine living and all forms of luxury. He talked in praise of humanity, benevolent generosity and pure reason.

The curiosity of acquaintances and the well-meant advice of friends annoyed him so much that he took the girls to France, without an English servant, and did not allow them to learn French, that no influence but his should reach them. The homesick girls acted like Sancho. They were seriously ill and would have no one but him attend them. They screamed if he left them and compelled him to perform all the offices of a nurse.

At the end of eight months Day brought them back to England. His next step was to travel to Lichfield to consult Dr. Darwin. He thought that, because Darwin was informed on science, metaphysics, philosophy, botany, medicine, and literature, he would also understand Woman. Oddly enough he was right; Dr. Darwin understood people and was able to give good advice to those who asked for it. Day stayed at the Darwin's house for a time and then rented Stowe House, owned by Mrs. Elizabeth Aston who herself lived in Stowe Hill a little higher up. Day's temporary home had a view, high ceilings and a room full of books. Day could afford to indulge his whims as well as his generosities, for he was now of age, with an income of about 1200 pounds a year.

Lichfield young people liked Day and took him into their group. One can't understand how they endured his ponderous expositions, but young people attempting to dig reassuring

certainties out of life's insecurity can stand a vast deal of spec-
ulation, reiteration and dogmatic assertion. Day believed that
what was pleasant to an individual was bad for him, and that
there was virtue in going against one's nature. He had compassion for those who suffered from poverty and was generous
in succoring them, though Anna found him callous to anguish
caused by over-refinement of spirit.

Thanks probably to Dr. Darwin's common sense, Day began
to extricate himself from his matrimonial tangle. He apprenticed Lucretia—whom he considered stupid—to a milliner, and
when she later married a London linen-draper, gave her her
dowry. Sabrina he boarded with Bicknell's mother. After he
leased Stowe House he brought her there to live with him.
She was about thirteen, good-humored and obedient, and,
apart from Lucretia, she was well-behaved. She had beautiful
hair, long eyelashes, and an unusually pleasant voice. Lichfield
ladies spoke well of her. Everyone from now on approved of
Sabrina—except her proposed husband. Nothing Sabrina did
satisfied him.

One of Day's black marks against Sabrina was that she
screamed with terror when, to teach her self-control, he fired
blank cartridges at her petticoat, and flinched from pain
when he dropped hot sealing wax on her arms. This last
alleged black mark is, at any rate, disputed by Rev. Richard
George Robinson in the unpublished letter which we quoted
apropos of Darwin's odd vehicle. He wrote:

"What Miss Seward says respecting Sabrina's not bearing
pain heroically is not true. I have seen her drop melted sealing wax voluntarily on her arm, and bear it heroically without flinching. Mr. Day told me he could not conquer her
dread of a horse; and that no persuasion or bribe could prevail upon her to stroke its neck, though it was held by the
bridle." [1]

Day's pedagogical principles allowed him to deceive

Sabrina. She believed that the blank cartridges contained bullets and he tested her discretion by telling her a fantastic tale of danger to himself which he warned must be kept a secret. The thirteen-year-old Sabrina told the other little girls and got a terrible black mark from her guide. He lied to inculcate truthfulness.

The general impression was that Sabrina loved and feared her guardian, although she was unable to please him. She did not like books, and she had a longing for pretty clothes. Day made no attempt to win her affection. In fact he never tried to win the love of any woman he courted. It seems as if he were afraid of love. It seems also as if it may have been an effort for him to be so very, very good, since he tried to reform everyone with whom he came in contact. His discontent with others may have been at bottom discontent with himself.

In spite of Day's complaints about Sabrina, his friends expected him to marry her as soon as she was old enough. She was already, they pointed out, too old to be living in his household. The misdemeanor which brought about the dissolution of the engagement had something to do with her arms. Her guardian told her to wear certain long sleeves or not to wear them; the story is vague; her arms were to be covered or not to be covered. At any rate, through carelessness or misunderstanding, she did the opposite to what she was instructed. That proved to Day that she had no strength of mind or, too much strength of mind, or else it proved to him that she was not attached to him; there is confusion here. He banished her to boarding school at Sutton-Colefield where she was to be taught reading, writing and arithmetic, but not music or dancing.

Sabrina passed out of Lichfield annals save for visits to Dr. Darwin and to her other friends there. She stayed in boarding school three years, growing more beautiful and always pleasing her teachers. Day saw her seldom and never without witnesses.

One reason that Day was so dissatisfied with Sabrina was that he was falling in love with Honora. Or maybe he was falling in love with Honora because he couldn't force his heart to concentrate on Sabrina. Day's driving desire for marriage was blocked and turned into devious bypaths by an impediment which he thought was intelligence. According to our present way of thinking he was struggling between contrary emotions, one instinctive and one acquired. He now considered marrying Honora Sneyd. This time he seemed to have a good chance of winning an ideal wife, but he messed up his wooing with more of those clumsy gyrations which he called reasoning.

Day fitted into the social life of Lichfield. He was especially adept at the favorite recreation of talking, discussing, arguing on every subject under the sun; eager, unforced play with ideas. This group of young and serious thinkers contained diverse personalities. Edgeworth had an agile mind and original slants on every subject. Day was a plodder, terribly, terribly in earnest, but with a sweep of learning and a depth of compassion. Anna had the gift of lifting a party and setting others to capping her quips and jests. Honora was an appreciator of others' talents and, with so many show-offs in the running, an intelligent listener was an asset. She did not write verses and she was not a great reader, but she had a natural bent toward mathematics and mechanics. When Darwin proposed a mathematical problem, Honora was eager to solve it; she listened intelligently to Darwin's instructions, when Anna and Day were weary and inattentive. Honora could hold her own in discussions on politics or metaphysics, though she never harangued. Her conversation was easy, amusing and sensible.

Day did not for some time realize that he was in love with Honora. He did not recognize the symptoms, because he disapproved of her graceful dancing and her fashionable attire. Her arms, he told Edgeworth, were not sufficiently round and white.

Edgeworth, arriving to spend Christmas in Lichfield, fell immediately in love with Honora. Edgeworth differed from Day by knowing when he was in love; he could name the day the emotion began and give the reasons why. Recalling the circumstances in his memoirs, he tells us about Honora:

"Her memory was not copiously stored with poetry; and though no way deficient, her knowledge had not been much enlarged by books; but her sentiments were on all subjects so just, and delivered with such blushing modesty (though not without an air of conscious worth) as to command attention from everyone capable of appreciating female excellence. Her person was graceful, her features beautiful, and their expression such as to heighten the eloquence of everything she said. I was 6 and 20; and now, for the first time in my life, I saw a woman that equalled the picture of perfection, which existed in my imagination. I had long suffered much from the want of that cheerfulness in a wife, without which marriage could not be agreeable to a man of such temper as mine."

Roused by Edgeworth's admiration of Honora, Day observed her more carefully and decided that he could forgive her grace and fashionableness when he had made over her personality. Her apparent docility misled him. He began his courtship by explaining to her his plan of marriage. Honora listened. If she advanced any views of her own it was in a gentle voice, respectful to man's greater knowledge of the world and keener understanding of life's problem, and she was so attentive to instruction that Day dreamed not she had ideas of her own.

As Day advanced Honora in his esteem, he began to worry about Edgeworth's infatuation with her and reproached him. Edgeworth, being an honorable man, returned to his family.

Day feared to marry Honora lest it should divide him from his friend. He wrote to Edgeworth a letter which the recipient considered "one of the most eloquent letters I ever read, to point out to me the folly and meanness of indulging a hopeless passion for any woman, let her merit be what it might; declaring at the same time, that he 'never would marry so as to divide himself from his chosen friend.'" Day asked if Edgeworth had sufficient strength of mind totally to subdue love which could not be indulged compatibly with peace, honor, or virtue.

Edgeworth, deeply moved, replied that nothing but trial could make him acquainted with the influence which reason might have over his feelings. He announced that he would bring his family with him to Lichfield where he would be constantly in company with the dangerous object, and he promised faithfully to acquaint Day with all his thoughts and feelings. Mr. Edgeworth, his depressed wife and their three children moved into Stowe House with Day, so that Edgeworth could expose himself daily to temptation and report his reactions. He found that Day and Honora were invited out together and everyone looked forward to their marriage as a fixed conclusion. Says Edgeworth in his *Memoirs:* "When I saw this I can affirm with truth that I felt pleasure, and even exultation. . . . I was the depositary of every thought that passed in the mind of Mr. Day; and from everything he told me and from my own observation I was persuaded that nothing was now wanting but a declaration on his part and compliance on the part of the lady."

Edgeworth, conscious of his own noble unselfishness, spoke to Honora of the intended match. Honora expressed doubts as to its conclusion. Edgeworth, assuming she was doubtful as to Day's state of mind, warmly assured her that it was all settled. Honora shook her head.

The morning after this conversation, Day handed Edgeworth a packet of papers to give to Honora, telling him that it was a resume of their conversations and a reasonable, sincere description of a calm, secluded life which, once undertaken, she would enjoy more than gay splendid scenes and public admiration. Day was not a cozy lover. His proposal of marriage had no more warmth than a table of vital statistics. Edgeworth took the packet to the Palace with conscious satisfaction and was told to come the following day for an answer. Honora's tone indicated that all was not settled. When Day, after a night of suspense, read the answer which Edgeworth obediently fetched back, he felt pretty sick. It was a clear, dispassionate statement of Honora's idea of the rights of women. Written, her opinions carried a weight which her gentle voice and downcast eyes had denied them. Edgeworth summarizes them for us. Honora would not admit the unqualified control of a husband over a wife's actions: ". . . she did not feel that seclusion from society was necessary to preserve female virtue, or secure domestic happiness. On terms of reasonable equality she supposed that mutual confidence might best subsist; she said that as Mr. Day had decidedly declared his determination to live in perfect seclusion from what is generally called the world, it was fit that she should decidedly declare that she would not change her present mode of life, with which she had no reason to be dissatisfied, for any dark and untried system that could be proposed to her." Honora was so gentle and lovely, she looked up at a man with such soft eyes and spoke in so respectful a voice, that one did not fully realize her intelligence, her courage, and her clear understanding of where she stood and where she was going. She was not going with Mr. Day.

Day went to bed with shock and a fever. Dr. Darwin was called and bled him, but after a few days the disconsolate one was able again to take his part in Lichfield social life.

He now met Elizabeth Sneyd, Honora's sister. Edward

Sneyd, Honora's father, came back from London to Lichfield to gather his daughters under his own wing. Honora moved from the Sewards' where she had been so long a member of the family. Her sister Elizabeth came from Shrewsbury where she had lived with her cousins at the Abbey, the Edward Powys family.

Elizabeth had visited enough in Lichfield to be at home there. Day met her for the first time at an archery party. Edgeworth had introduced archery. The butts were set up on the bowling green and the prize was a silver arrow. There was also music and dancing, and the gentlemen fenced and showed how high they could vault. It was a merry party.

Mr. Sneyd brought his daughter Elizabeth just as a country dance was ending. Honora who had come early with Anna, introduced Edgeworth to Elizabeth, requesting him to be Elizabeth's partner so that she would not be exposed to the danger of being squired by a stranger. Edgeworth was a graceful dancer and had attained some fame as a choreographer at Oxford. He later gave up dancing lest his skill distract attention from his intellectual prowess, but at this time he had not begun to worry lest he be thought a faun.

Elizabeth, a year younger than Honora, was generally considered handsomer. Her eyes were beautiful and expressive and she had a healthy clear brown complexion. She was better educated, more fashionable in appearance, had more vivacity and more humor, less energy and decision. She did not have her sister's interest in science.

Day was immediately intrigued by her appearance, not because of these excellencies, he said, but because he thought she had less personal grace than Honora. She walked heavily and danced without enjoyment. This in Day's eyes offset her fashionable appearance. He noted also that her arms were large and white; Day was obsessed by ladies' arms. Like Honora, Elizabeth listened while Day talked, without contradicting. Elizabeth on her side found him a romantic figure and when he talked of love, theoretically and impersonally, she was impressed and felt that she too was capable of such an idealistic union. The Lichfieldians during the next few weeks gave the two every opportunity to meet for better acquaintance, just as they had done for her sister.

Day proposed marriage and Elizabeth accepted provisionally. She made it a condition that he go to France to learn manners, for, she told him, it was illogical for him to scorn accomplishments in which he was so strikingly deficient. She on her part promised not to visit Bath or London during his absence or resort to any public place. He laid out a course of reading for her to pursue.

Day made to Elizabeth concessions of principle which Miss Edgeworth, Sabrina, and Honora had not succeeded in forcing from him. In Paris he took lessons in dancing and fencing to improve his co-ordination and stood an hour a day in a wooden frame designed to correct his posture. He learned to talk like a soldier and bow like a macaroni. He patronized the tailor and the hairdresser. He wrote Anna from Lyons, 18 Dec., 1771:

" . . . I am a lac'd coat, a bag, a sword, and nothing else. I am become a Type, a Parable, a Symbol. Eyes have I which see nothing but Absurdity, ears which hear nothing but Nonsense, a mind which thinks not, etc. etc. But in return I speak French very prettily, I bully, I vapour, la, la, cut capers and am what a Gentleman should be. . . ."

Curled, perfumed, gaudily dressed, he bowed before his lady love on his return to Lichfield. He strutted, he struck attitudes, he said la, la, and other phrases considered French. Elizabeth burst out laughing. The awkward dignity of a sincere man was gone. A clown postured before her. Elizabeth was lost to Thomas.

Day returned to Paris.

155

In a letter which he wrote Anna from Lyons, dated "The New Year, 1772" a postscript to Honora indicates that he had loved her more than Elizabeth all along. The clumsy jocosity suggests that his pride was still hurt:

> Miss H.S.
>
> Dear Madam   May I die, if it didn't give me an inconceivable Pleasure, to see that so accomplish'd a Personage as Yourself, did me the honour to remember me—May I perish if I don't wish I had it in my power this very moment, to kiss your fair hand and to assure you in person, of the Sentiments you inspire me with—Could you prevail upon yourself to cross the Seas, and venture as far as Lyons?—We shall have Balls masque and Balls pare all the carnival—And if you will do me the honour of trusting yourself to my Protection—You will look charmingly en Bergere and if you'll put on a little Rouge, let me die if you won't look charmingly—where'er I am, wherever I may be,
>
> My heart untravell'd still returns to thee.
>
> T.D.

A long letter to Anna, March 14, 1772, shows him having a rather bad time with himself. One is sorry for the poor blundering, well-intentioned lover:

> . . . I do not believe I ever was much in Love, and I scarcely believe I shall ever be again. A Knowledge of the world tends to make a Man very much a Philosopher, or very much a Libertine and it is very unfortunate that we generally acquire the Power of doing hurt, in Proportion as we lose the Inclination to do good. The reason which makes me give so disadvantageous a character of myself in that Respect, is the ease with which I have borne so many disappointments, and the Promptitude with which they are entirely obliterated from my mind. In respect to my fair Lichfield Friend, I have forgotten the very feelings of Passion: it is to my mind as a thing which never has existed: but in return I have not forgotten the Opinion I had of Goodness, and Sincerity in

her mind, of Virtue in her character, and a disposition of tender concern for her Welfare, unmix'd with Anger, Passion, or Regret, whenever I recollect her Idea. Had I married as last Summer I doubted not but I should, I doubt not but that she would have made me happy, in a tender Friendship and domestic Life; that I am disengag'd with honor to myself, and without Prejudice to her Happiness, I rejoice, for I confess I see no good in the holy State of Matrimony proportionable to the Sacrifice we make. How different are the Sentiments I retain for E.S. [Elizabeth Sneyd], from those I have constantly felt for my first Mistress—I have never recollected Miss Edge[worth] without contempt mix'd with Detestation; I see her as I should a Toad, which I would not injure, but I cannot help beholding with abhorrence.

Day had more common sense in dealing with Anna's unhappiness over the Saville situation than in meeting his own troubles.

> . . . if I might advise you my dear Friend, for what appears to be your Interest, even upon your own Ideas, avoid all actions of Violence and eclat as much as possible; you ought to endeavor as much as possible to make everybody cease to talk or think of these unhappy circumstances. . . . I think the people of your Town equally ill-natured and foolish, to shew markt contempt to S[aville]; but you cannot brave them with Impunity; therefore you ought to temporize as much as possible— In respect to your father and mother, I think both from Good-nature and Prudence, you ought as much as possible to avoid dispute. . . .
>
> . . . Pray remember me to poor dear Honora, with the greatest Tenderness; everything I say to her, she is to interpret literally; when I tell her how sincerely I interest myself in her preservation, how much I lament her sickness, how sincerely I love her, and all her family. Tell Miss Betsy that she is very good to remember a discarded Lover; but yet she has the Merit, except in a few Moments' Anger, to have thought and felt and spoken

as she—[erasure]—the sincerest of her Friends. Tell her
if you see her that I am not at all in Love with her, but
that I have a higher opinion of her, and more Affection
for her than ever.

In a postscript he adds:

As I have talk'd to you in a manner that may hereafter
be very dangerous to myself, (which is a great proof of
my generosity) if I should ever make Love again, I must
desire that you will commit my Letter to the Flames,
when you have read it. I have been studying the Minuet
step, all the winter, and under the Tuition, of fair French
Philosophers, and am not yet five and twenty. Therefore I
cannot answer before I sink into an old Batchelor, that
I may not have one more epanchment du coeur—And I
am sensible that this is not exactly the style which is
necessary upon such occasions: therefore I trust "that
you will purify me by fire"—And not expose me hereafter, to have all these wicked Sentiments come staring
me in the face, like so many little Devils, the Accom-
plices of my former crimes, when I would fain amend
and live honestly—[2]

CHAPTER XII

Two Marriages

WHEN Day resigned all claims to Honora's attention, Edgeworth fell deeper and deeper in love with her, until Day's shocked protests and his own conscience compelled him to flee from Lichfield. Making beautiful gestures of renunciation, he accompanied Day abroad, taking his young son Richard to be inspected by Rousseau and leaving the two other children with their melancholy mother in England.

Before he left, Edgeworth had serious talks with Honora in the course of which he told her that young women who had not large fortunes should not disdain to marry even if their romantic dreams were not realized. Honora listened and, according to her custom, agreed. Cheered by the thought of a loveless marriage for the woman he could not himself have, Edgeworth said goodby, smugly certain that no one in the Close suspected his love for Honora, and that she herself had not guessed it.

Edgeworth's volatile spirit found interests in France. He concerned himself with marine engineering in Lyons and sent for Mrs. Edgeworth and the children. When she became pregnant he returned her to England in charge of Day who was going back to propose to Honora's sister Elizabeth. Mrs. Edgeworth died at home, in childbirth. Day notified Edgeworth. Edgeworth crossed the channel and hot-footed it to Lichfield. He went directly to Dr. Darwin's house where he was received by the doctor's sister, Mrs. Darwin having died. Said Miss Darwin, "You will excuse me for not making tea for you this evening, as I am engaged to the Miss Sneyds; but perhaps you will accompany me, as I am sure you will be welcome."

The Sneyds' drawing room was filled with acquaintances and friends who had "without concert among themselves, assembled as if to witness the meeting of two persons whose sentiments could scarcely be known even to the two parties themselves," says Ostrich-Edgeworth in his memoirs. Perhaps the Close was deceived by his greeting Honora the last of all the gathering, but probably the Close whispered, "Didn't I tell you?"

The courtship was brief. Less than four months after the death of the first Mrs. Edgeworth the two were married by special license in the Lady Chapel of the Cathedral, the ceremony being performed by Dr. Seward. Honora's father was reluctant to give his consent to this hasty marriage. Anna vehemently defended it. Reviewing the matter in a letter to Mary Powys, who also approved, she said: "Everybody except about a half a dozen rail at Mr. Edgeworth, & prognosticate misery to my Honora. . . . They call her behavior undutiful, & spare her not for presuming to judge for herself, & for being too wise to sacrifice her felicity to her Father's & Mr. Grove's [Honora's brother-in-law], & the world's idle prejudices." [1]

Honora had a resolute spirit under her quiet loveliness. She did not give up Edgeworth as she had given up André. It is probable that each knew of the other's love long before Edgeworth was able to ask for her hand. Certainly her rush into his newly widowed arms suggests a previous consciousness of mutual love. Edgeworth, in his memoirs, states that though Honora admired André, she failed to find in him the reasoning mind she required. We assume therefore it was Edgeworth's reasoning mind which swept her off her feet.

The wedding is described in a letter from Anna to Mrs. Sykes:

July 27, 1773

Your son wou'd tell you, my dear Mrs. Sykes, why I have thus long delay'd answering your kind and obliging letter, that my thoughts were taken up by my Honora's nuptials. Saturday seven-night she became a bride in our Choir. My Father married her and her own gave her away, not with the best grace in the world, Mr. Sneyd and Mr. Edgeworth are too different to like each other. The former gave Honora a thousand pounds, and articled for another at his death. Mr. E. has made his first children independent of himself at the age of 21, and settled upon Honora four hundred a year in case she survives him, and six hundred till her own children receive their fortunes. His estate is a clear 15 hundred pounds a year. The joy of united hands and hearts, esteem, friendship, and congenial talents shone in the lovely faces of the charming Pair. The late Mrs. Edgeworth's brother, a worthy agreeable young gentleman came down from London on purpose to the wedding, and spoke most warmly in the praise of Mr. Edgeworth. We were a smart cavalcade, and behold Mr. Grove [Honora's brother-in-law] graciously condescended to come over to accompany his sister Honora to Church. He look'd a little grave but said nothing disobliging. I was Brides Maid. The knot was tied at nine o'clock. We then adjourn'd to Mr. Sneyd's to breakfast, and at 12 o'clock Mr. Edgeworth put the fair sweet Bride into his Phaeton, and drove off triumphantly. Well may he triumph, for he has obtain'd a matchless prize! . . . I had a letter from Mrs. Edgeworth yesterday, dated Chester. She has been very ill, the fatigue and hurry of the journey, and the weeks of business that preceded it were too much for her health, but she was better when she wrote to me, and expresses the utmost happiness, declaring that Mr. Edgeworth's tender care, and the delight of his society made even the hours of sickness and pain more blessed than words can paint. . . .[2]

The Victorian three-volume novelist, having finally deposited the heroine at the marriage altar after a devious and risky journey, usually added a brief chapter of what-happened-last. Following that pattern, here is the rest of the Edgeworth and Day story, so far as it is connected with Lichfield.

During the following years Anna came to hate Edgeworth vehemently. The explanation sometimes given, that Anna wished herself to marry Edgeworth, cannot be correct, for her passionate preoccupation with Saville was at its height. Edgeworth says in his memoirs that Anna never showed any of the mean jealousy common among young women when one of their companions is preferred. She disliked him because they both had dominating natures, and she hated him because he crowded her out of the chief place in Honora's heart.

The course of Anna's disaffection can be traced in her verse. While Honora was making one of her usual visits to relatives in Shrewsbury, in 1772, Anna wrote a plaintive but not resentful *Epistle to Miss Honora Sneyd, written in a summer evening, from the grave of a suicide*. Bessie Banks had hanged herself from a tree and was buried beneath its branches, which made it a romantic spot fit for lonely meditation. Seated on "the tumulus," beneath the fatal tree, Anna wrote:

> It suits the temper of my soul to pour
> Fond fruitless plaints beneath the lonely bower,
> Here in this silent glade, that childhood fears . . .
>
> . . . . . .
>
> Ah! dear Honora, summer sheds again
> Music, fragrance, light, and bloom, in vain,
> While my sick heart thy smiles no longer cheer,
> Nor melt thine accents on my listening ear.

This was enjoyable romantic sadness, but sonnets written the following year when Edgeworth, free to marry, had returned from France to court Honora, breathe a sense of personal injury. Sonnet X, dated April, probably soon after his arrival, reads:

> Honora, should that cruel time arrive
> When 'gainst my truth thou should'st mine errors poise,
> Scorning remembrance of our vanish'd joys;
> When for the love-warm looks, in which I live,
> But cold respect must greet me, that shall give
> No tender glance, no soft regretful sighs;
>
> When thou shalt pass me with averted eyes,
> Feigning thou see'st me not, to sting, and grieve,
> And sicken my sad heart, I cou'd not bear
> Such dire eclipse of thy soul-cheering rays;
> I cou'd not learn my struggling heart to tear
> From thy lov'd form, that throu my memory strays;
> Nor, in the pale horizon of Despair,
> Endure the wintry, and the darken'd days.

Sonnets XII, XIII, and XIV, written in July, the month of Honora's marriage, record poignant suffering. The first begins:

> Chill'd by unkind Honora's alter'd eye,
> Why droops my heart with pining woe forlorn,

The next is on insomnia:

> Thou child of Night and Silence, balmy Sleep,
> Shed thy soft poppies on my aching brow!

The third:

> Ingratitude, how deadly is thy smart
> Proceeding from the form we fondly love!

However irrational Anna's unexplained anguish, it was genuine.

The Edgeworths went to Ireland where they remained for

three years. Honora enjoyed her life in Ireland, although she carried heavy domestic burdens, being stepmother to three children and soon bearing two of her own. Edgeworth in all his marriages except the first one, showed talent for pleasant family life. He was demanding, but he made it pleasant for others to fall in with his wishes. He had an affectionate nature, gaiety and love of living. It was necessary to his happiness that those around him be happy also. His twenty-two children admired him and were docile; his second, third and fourth wives adored him—perhaps the first did also.

Edgeworth brought his family back to England after three years, taking a house near Great Berkhamstead in Hertfordshire. The meetings of Anna and the Edgeworths were strained. A letter to Mrs. Sykes describes one encounter:

June 16, 1776

. . . last Monday evening I was sitting in my dressing Room with a silly Coxcomb of an Officer who had call'd upon me. John open'd the door and said—"Madam, Mr. and Mrs. Edgeworth are below stairs."—Oh my Friend! I had not the least expectation of such an event—Good God! I exclaim'd and sunk back in my chair more dead than alive—I desir'd he wou'd say I was out. A violent flood of tears reliev'd me. The Macaroni was astonish'd, but if a thousand Fops had been present I cou'd not have conceal'd my emotion. I did not intend to see them at all.—it was an hour before my Aunt cou'd prevail upon me to go down, she and my Mother were out when they came. I will reserve a particular description of this, to me, heartrending scene for the first tête-à-tête I have the pleasure to share with you, since my paper will not allow me to be circumstantial now. They staid only two days in Lichfield are now in London. The time of their return thro' here is uncertain.[3]

Mary Martha Sherwood tells in her autobiography of meeting Edgeworth at the Palace the following year; although as she was only two, she could not have recalled the episode from her own memory. Dr. Darwin and Anna were present as well as Mary Martha's parents. Edgeworth took up little three-year-old John—Mary Martha's brother—by the leg like a frog, exclaiming, "What a fine animal! What a noble animal!" Looking at Mary Martha he complimented her father on her physical well-being, adding, "But you may depend upon it,———,you may depend upon it she wants it here," tapping his own brow. This worried Mary Martha's mother.

The alienation between the Sewards and the Edgeworths was never complete so long as Honora lived, but as Honora's illness increased, Anna's antagonism to Edgeworth became intense. When she heard that the husband went to dances during his wife's illness, her anger burst forth in Sonnets XXXI and XXXII: *To the Departing Spirit of an Alienated Friend:*

> O, ever dear! thy precious, vital powers
> Sink rapidly!—the long and dreary night
> Brings scarce a hope that morn's returning light
> Shall dawn for thee!—In such terrific hours,
> When yearning fondness eagerly devours
> Each moment of protracted life, his flight
> The rashly chosen of thy heart has ta'en
> Where dances, songs, and theatres invite.
> Expiring Sweetness! with indignant pain
> I see him in the scenes where laughing glide
> Pleasure's light forms;—see his eyes gaily glow,
> Regardless of thy life's fast ebbing flow;
> I hear him, who should droop in silent woe,
> Declaim on actors, and on taste decide.
>
> Behold him now his genuine colors wear,
> That specious false-one, by whose cruel wiles
> I lost thy amity; saw thy dear smiles
> Eclips'd; those smiles, that used my heart to cheer
> Wak'd by thy grateful sense of many a year
> When rose thy youth, by Friendship's pleasing toils
> Cultur'd;—but Dying!—O! forever fade
> The Angry fires.—Each thought, that might upbraid

Thy broken faith, which yet my soul deplores,
Now as eternally is past and gone
As are the interesting, the happy hours,
Days, years, we shared together. They are flown!
Yet long must I lament thy hopeless doom,
Thy lavish'd life and early-hasten'd tomb.

In a letter to Mrs. Sykes in 1779 Anna wrote:

Mr. Edgeworth was in Lichfd last week, very sprightly and happy with a fine picture of Honora by Smart, drawn near two years ago, but finish'd lately, and sent down to him only Thursday was seven-night. The day it came he flew over to Lichfield to shew it us all. The exaltation of his vanity to have possess'd the original of so beautiful a portrait absorb'd all shadow of regret for her danger, and it was with the utmost *force* that he drew a transient veil over the sunshine of his vivacity, on being ask'd if she was not a little better. I heard of his being in Lichfd with the picture before I *saw* him, and burnt with impatience to behold the semblance of a face so dear.

When we met he had the cruelty to keep it some minutes in his hand before he would open the case, gaily trifling with my too tender curiosity. The picture is beautiful, but my disappointment was extreme, for it gives me very little idea of Honora.—Oh! That it had been a striking likeness! since, when she is no more, I might perhaps have procur'd a copy! As it *is*, it wou'd scarsely be an object of sufficient importance to make me ask a *favor* of a man who has so deeply injur'd me. In a fortnight he takes Honora to Bristol. If she had gone there last spring I firmly believe it wou'd have sav'd her. Oh! That the gay heart of this man cou'd have been persuaded to have fear'd *in time* for the life of *her*, whom he. . . . [the rest is missing] [4]

Anna could not bear to admit that Honora was happy in Ireland, but she was. The Edgeworths were an unusually co-operative family and they enjoyed each other. The father had the ability to interest them all in his projects and to utilize their delighted assistance. Honora, for instance, took down verbatim the young children's conversation, and from the study of their prattle Edgeworth deduced their mental development in relation to age and other important matters which had not been sufficiently considered in teaching.

Honora died in Ireland. If she wore out her frail body in the service of the Edgeworth household, the service was voluntary and not imposed. Edgeworth was guilty of no greater fault than accepting his wife's selfless devotion. Honora found happiness in performing domestic duties that made life pleasant for herself as well as for others.

A touching incident accompanied her death. On her arrival at Edgeworthstown as a bride, her wedding ring slipped unnoticed from her finger. She realized its absence at the dinner-table and starting up she instantly returned to where she had been most of the morning watching some thirty laborers leveling a large tract of ground. She promised them a reward for finding the ring. They quartered the ground and walked in formation across it. They even sifted dirt. When the ring was found Honora slipped it back on her finger saying that she would never lose it again but with her life. When she died, supported on pillows, her husband and a sister bending over her, her arm slipped over the side of the bed and the wedding ring which she had held on her wasted finger to the last, dropped tinkling to the floor.

To shift our attention to Thomas Day: he who carried always the awful responsibility of being perfect, actually won a Perfect Wife. After his refusal by Elizabeth Sneyd, he returned to France and spent the winter in Paris. Following what was now a habit, he proposed marriage to a charming, witty, penniless young French woman who refused to marry him on account of the foggy English weather. After this, his sixth disappointment, Day gave up his search for a wife.

His friend Dr. William Small, a Scotchman living in Birmingham, a physician, a mathematician, a philosopher and a member of the Lunar Society, took over the task. Dr. Small was a kind and a wise man. He was fond of Day who, he knew, would never be at ease in life until he married. Dr. Small decided that Miss Esther Milnes was the correct answer to the problem. She was lovely, she was an heiress, she was so wise that she was called Minerva, and she was widely known for her charitable activities. When Dr. Small mentioned her to Day as a possibility, that side of Day's nature which impelled him to choose women who would not have him, or by his behavior to alienate those who might, this defensive mechanism which had so far protected him against marriage, sprang into action.

"But has she white and large arms?" inquired Day.

"She has," replied Dr. Small.

"Does she wear long petticoats?"

"Uncommonly long."

"I hope she is tall, strong, and healthy."

"Remarkably tall and not robust. My good friend, can you possibly expect that a woman of charming temper, benevolent mind, and cultivated understanding, with a distinguished character, with views of life congenial with your own, with an agreeable person and a large fortune, should be formed exactly according to a picture that exists in your imagination? This lady is two or three and twenty, has had some twenty admirers; some of them admirers of herself, some, perhaps, of her fortune; yet in spite of all these admirers and lovers, she is disengaged. If you are not satisfied, determine at once never to marry."

"My dear doctor, the only serious objection which I have to Miss M. is her large fortune. It was always my wish to give to any woman whom I married the most unequivocal proof of my attachment to herself by despising her fortune."

"Well, my friend, what prevents you from despising the fortune and taking the lady?"

Day went to Yorkshire to inspect Miss Milnes and found her wholly desirable. He explained to her his ideals of marriage. Miss Milnes listened and agreed. For months they talked and talked and talked until they talked themselves into marriage. Day insisted that Miss Milnes's whole fortune be settled on herself, contrary to the custom of the time. She on her side gave up music, her friends, and her family and moved with him onto a farm which he had bought because it was so undesirable that he wished to bring it into good condition. They never ran out of conversation; Day always found a subject and Mrs. Day held up her end with spirit and originality. She was obedient, admiring and loving. Sometimes she wept, but she never repined.

Thomas Day died as curiously as he had lived. He was not a good horseman, but he had theories on horse training based on man's kindliness and on the intelligence of animals. He perhaps over-estimated the intelligence. One morning he saddled, bridled, and mounted a favorite colt which had never before been ridden and the theory worked until the colt, startled and shying, accidentally struck one of Day's spurs. Day was thrown and so seriously injured that he died without recovering consciousness. Mrs. Day survived him by two years, dying, it was thought, of a broken heart.

Sabrina Sidney, who failed to pass Day's tests for wifehood, lived in boardinghouses after she left school, sometimes visiting in Lichfield, until she married John Bicknell, the friend who had been with Day when he took her from the orphans's home. Day, as her guardian, rather grudgingly gave his permission and paid the promised dowry of five hundred pounds. When Bicknell died, leaving her with two little boys, it came out that he was a whited sepulcher. Neither his money nor his good name survived, and Sabrina was left in straitened circumstances. Day made her an allowance of thirty pounds, and George Hardinge, Attorney to the King, raised eight hundred pounds among Bicknell's fellow members at the Bar. Edgeworth with his usual generosity helped her with remittances until his death. Day did not bequeath her anything, but his widow continued her allowance. Sabrina was finally settled in a pleasant position as housekeeper and assistant to Charles Burney, Fanny Burney's brother, at his boys' school in Greenwich. Everyone liked and admired and spoke well of Sabrina. Everyone except Day.

CHAPTER XIII

Dr. Erasmus Darwin

DR. ERASMUS DARWIN came to Lichfield in 1756, seven years after the Sewards, when he was twenty-five. He was the youngest son of Robert Darwin of Elston, in Nottinghamshire, and Elizabeth Hill of Sleaford, Lincolnshire. His father could trace his lineage back two hundred years. There must have been money in the family, for Erasmus's grandmother, Anne Waring, was an heiress who brought Elston Hall into the family; but there was a raft of children and, when Erasmus was being educated with two brothers at St. John's College, Cambridge, they had to be so economical that Erasmus learned to reheel his worn stockings without dropping a stitch from the knitting needles. After taking a medical degree at Cambridge, he spent two years studying at Edinburgh. By the time he settled in Lichfield the economic strain seems to have lessened; he must have had help from home, as he almost immediately married, bought a house, began raising a family and entertained a good deal.

Upon his arrival in Lichfield, with letters of introduction, he had the good fortune to save his first patient, who had been given up by another physician. It was a triumph for the young doctor and a calamity for the older one who had been so rash as to state there was no hope.

The year after his arrival in Lichfield, Dr. Darwin married Mary Howard. The bride was talented, witty, young and charming, and Erasmus was very much in love. In a letter which he wrote her when he was called away four days before their marriage, he suggested that the ceremony take place on his return at eight o'clock in the morning before anyone knew of his arrival; Mr. Howard could get the license the previous evening, and Nellie White, the bridesmaid, need not be told until the last moment. Nellie White was Helen, the beautiful chatterbox who ran about spreading the news when Joseph Porter seemed inclined to jilt Sally Seward.

The young doctor's practice grew rapidly, sparing him the dreary novitiate endured by most new practitioners. An account book gives his income, which must be judged in relation to the high purchasing power of a shilling at that time: the first year he made £192. 10. 6.; the second, £305. 2. 0.; by his sixth year his income was £726. 0. 0. He took no fees from clerical families.

Dr. Darwin bought an old, half-timbered house in the Cathedral Vicarage, fronting on Beacon Street, and remodeled it with a handsome front and Venetian windows. It was separated from the street by a deep narrow dingle which had been a part of the moat in the days when the Cathedral was circled by water. He planted it with roses and lilacs and spanned it with a bridge in the form of a flight of shallow steps leading up to the entrance door and guarded by a Chinese-style paling, a touch of fashionable *Chinoiserie*. An opening between the houses across the street afforded a pleasing outlook from the windows. The Darwins lived here comfortably, keeping four horses and a groom, as was necessary to a country doctor's far-flung practice, and a gardener, beside a number of house servants.

The favorable reception accorded the young doctor did not exempt him from struggle, judging from the warning which he gave to the friends of another young doctor who asked advice about settling in Lichfield. Darwin pointed out that the youth would occupy a subordinate position in Lichfield society, for surgeons, though admitted to dancing assemblies, were not invited to card parties. He must make friends with farmers by dining with them at the inn on market days, and must have a panel of blue and red glass in his windows to attract attention to his office. Dr. Darwin mentioned that Mr. Richard Greene who in addition to being a surgeon-apothecary, was proprietor of a museum at which Dr. Johnson marvelled, received through his retail trade in drugs "by means of his show-shop and many-colored window" a hundred pounds a year. The bitter tone of his counsel suggests that even Dr. Darwin had suffered humiliations from his calling. About the only cheery note was his comment à propos of the young man's stammer, that a little impediment in his speech would not at all injure him, but rather the contrary, by attracting notice.

Dr. Darwin's humor slipped easily into irony, and his friendship did not preclude a critical attitude. He had a surface irritability and could be extraordinarily rude when displeased. On the other hand, he was hospitable and generous. His political views were radical and his religious beliefs unorthodox. He was learned, brilliant, talented and dogmatic. Anna Seward said that he warmly defended human liberty but was himself a tyrant.

Dr. Johnson and Dr. Erasmus Darwin never met socially if the hostess could prevent. Both men had heavy, unwieldy bodies, shockingly overweight; both were gourmands and both had a zest for life which did not lessen with the years. While both were tender-hearted toward troubles like illness, poverty and the grief that death brings, they were scornful of the romantic attitude toward life and the suffering which comes from a thin skin. Both had Gargantuan brains and a tendency to outtalk the rest of the company. Perhaps the friction between them rose from their being rival conversationalists. Each said what he thought when he thought it, regardless of the feelings of his listener. Dr. Johnson had a tongue that was a cudgel, while Dr. Darwin's was a rapier. When they competed for an audience the advantage lay with Dr. Johnson because he could bellow louder—and did. Dr. Darwin was handicapped by his conversation technique. He utilized a natural stammer to heighten the effect of his remarks, building to the climax by hesitations partly natural and partly intentional. When the rival panjandrums competed for applause, Dr. Darwin's delicate vocal maneuvering was lost in the boom of Dr. Johnson's sonorous sentences.

Nothing shows Darwin's broad, unconventional sympathy better than the letter he wrote to a gentleman who was looking into the matter of the murder of an infant thought to be the illegitimate offspring of a lady of position. He told the shocked investigator that he would give him no aid, for, he said, women who commit this most unnatural crime should be the objects of pity because their education had induced a distorted viewpoint; an artificial passion of shame had been inculcated so strong that it fought the instinct of nature and set up an agonizing struggle which resulted in a horrid crime. He would have no part in hunting down the unhappy mother.[1]

Fresh air and a light diet with little or no alcohol was the basis of Darwin's treatments, although he did not abandon blood-letting. His passion for fresh air is illustrated by a story often told in Lichfield of how when he first came he was invited by John Sneyd, then of Bishton, later of Belmont, to join a group of men in a rowing expedition on the River Trent, from Burton to Nottingham to Newark. It was a summer day, warm and sultry. The men were young and vigorous and carefree. They had excellent appetites for the good food and drink they brought along. As the tale was told and retold in after years, the glass went gaily round until the travelers' spirits were in a high state of vinous exhilaration. This vinous exhilaration inspired young Darwin, as they approached Nottingham, to step over the side of the boat, swim to shore and set off across the fields. His startled friends bent to their oars and reaching the town by water went in search of him. They found him in the market place, dripping wet, standing on a tub, making a speech to a crowd on the need of opening bedroom windows in the morning. Note that he did not go so far as to advise sleeping with open windows; to air bedrooms in the daytime and workshops at night was as radical a doctrine as his listeners could comprehend. Smiling and waving his hand he stepped from the tub, rejoined his comrades and continued the journey. The memory of this incident must have helped two-bottle patients later on when the doctor tried to cut down their drinking.

Though the doctor was adventurous in medical theory he was cautious in the treatment of his patients. When he had been in Lichfield some twenty-odd years and had a reputation for curing desperate illnesses, he received into his house the beautiful Lady Northesk, wife of the Sixth Earl of Northesk, and her thirteen-year-old daughter Mary Anne Carnegie, known as Marianne to her friends. Lady Northesk was tubercular. Dr. Darwin consulted with her about reviving an ancient practice of injecting into the veins blood from a healthy human being or a calf or a sheep, a technique which had been forbidden as impious before experience had determined its possible value. The doctor thought that a skilful watchmaker of his acquaintance could construct a syringe for the purpose. Lady Northesk was willing to give him authority to make the experiment and Anna Seward who was present offered to supply the blood. Dr. Darwin said he would consult his pillow. The pillow counseled against the experiment, and Dr. Darwin continued the milk, vegetable and fruit diet accompanied by much rest and much fresh air. This treatment was so successful that Lady Northesk lived seven years longer, when she died from having set fire to her cap, the sort of accident all too common in those days of muslin caps and reading candles, open hearths and billowing skirts.

The doctor designed a carriage which was more comfortable though less picturesque than his early one which had a probosis instead of thills. This improved vehicle was a two-wheeled chaise for one person, drawn by two horses, and fitted up as a living room, a library, an office and a pantry. It carried books, pen, paper, and a writing arrangement, and had a skylight with a shade in the roof, as well as a hamper for fruit and sweetmeats, with knife, fork, and spoon. Oats, hay, and a water bucket were lashed on for the horses. A saddle horse named "Doctor" followed this chaise without being hitched, ready to take over transportation when a road was so bad that the team could not get through. "Doctor," the horse, lived to a great age. Darwin spent so much time on his rounds that a friend once addressed a letter to him, "Dr. Darwin upon the road."

The well-fitted-up chaise was the doctor's workroom. He wrote both poetry and prose during the long hours he spent on the road, but he published nothing till toward the end of his years of active practice, because he feared that his patients would lose confidence in a doctor who was also a poet.

When the amazing Dr. Erasmus was not relaxing from professional duties by writing poetry or tinkering with a machine which could articulate words made up of the letters p., b., m., and a.,—like mama and papa—he might be attending the Lunar Society. This was an association of scientists, living in

View of Mr Greene's Museum at Lichfield.

PLATE XIII
View of Mr. Greene's Museum at Lichfield

PLATE XIV
Dr. Erasmus Darwin

and around Birmingham, who met for dinner on the Monday nearest the full moon. They gathered at two in the afternoon and dispersed at eight in the evening, to ride home by moonlight—if the moon favored them with its countenance.

Among the members of the Lunar Society—naturally dubbed Lunatics—was Dr. William Small, a physician, chemist and machinist. How wise and tactful his nature may be judged by his finally finding a satisfactory wife for the choosey Thomas Day. Matthew Boulton, tall, dignified, and cordial, took the lead in conversation; and he must have been good to get the lead away from Dr. Darwin. He had position, wealth, and the habit of command. Boulton's partner in the manufacturing of steam engines, James Watt, with whom he lived at Heathfield, was a different type; stoop-shouldered, lanky and sallow, calm, low-voiced and gentle. He was always ready to help his friends' wives when the chimney smoked or dresses faded in the wash, and once he made a dulcimer for the little daughter of one of his hosts. Josiah Wedgewood was another member, the kind and generous King of the Staffordshire Potteries, living at Etruria. Less well known were Capt. James Keir, proprietor of chemical works at West Bromwich, John Baskerville, inventor of the type which bears his name, and other men of many interests. It was a noble company.

The range of the dinner discussions was wide: new books on all subjects and in many languages, theories of propulsion, heat, and engineering problems. The men were interested in canal digging and all forms of transportation. They invited as their guests naturalists, geologists, lighthouse and bridge builders, astronomers, and their ilk who lived in England or came visiting. When Richard Edgeworth and Thomas Day attended with Dr. Darwin they were entranced by the men and the talk.

Though the group was not political, the members were all sympathetic with the struggle for liberty in the colonies and in France. They were theists and admirers of Rousseau. Dr. Darwin had to his credit the triumph of once having inveigled Rousseau into conversation against his will. The suspicious philosopher sojourned for a time at Wootten Hall, the beautiful residence of Richard Davenport in the parish of Ellaston, Derbyshire. Rousseau had for some unknown reason taken a prejudice against Darwin and refused to meet him. Darwin set himself to circumvent this. Learning that the Frenchman traversed a certain terrace to reach a favorite grotto, the doctor placed himself in the way and conspicuously studied an interesting plant. Rousseau fell into the trap and entered into a discussion on botany.

Erasmus Darwin had four children by his first marriage and six more by his marriage to a widow with three children. During the eleven years between the two alliances, he begot two illegitimate daughters. The legitimate children make an impressive showing, listed in Burke's *Landed Gentry of Great Britain*. The boys when they grew up lived as leisured gentlemen or went into the army or the church, while the girls made the approved kind of marriages or died spinsters. The second Mrs. Darwin had a florid taste in names for her girls: Elizabeth Anne, Millicent, Frances Anne Violetta, Emma George Elizabeth, and Harriot. In the third generation, the famous Charles Darwin was the son of Robert. When following the lines of descent in Burke's great tomes of high-born families, one is struck by the number of sons and daughters whose names are followed by the letters *d. unm.*—died unmarried. So it was in the Darwin family.

The two illegitimate daughters were not eligible for mention in Burke. Anna Seward speaks of them as the Miss Parkers, Dr. Darwin's relations, good and ingenuous young women. Their father educated them to be school teachers, sending them to different seminaries for instruction, after which they gained experience by teaching in various schools and in private families. When he felt that they were qualified to conduct a boarding school he set them up in one on the outskirts of Ashbourne in a pleasant and healthy situation. The house had a walled garden with a stream of water flowing through it, for outdoor bathing. The school accommodated thirty girls, each of whom brought two sheets, two towels, a knife and fork and a silver spoon.

To further the success of the school he wrote *A Plan for the Conduct of Female Education in Boarding Schools*,[2] recommending a technique far in advance of that of most contemporary establishments. He advised playing ball, shuttlecock, swinging, dancing in the open air, pulling weights over a pulley, skating and swimming. He warned against weights on the head, lead soles on the shoes, corsets, and underfeeding. So modern was his outlook that it is a surprise to find him dubious about play-acting, lest bold action and louder voices should injure the modesty and blushing embarrassment which was one of a young lady's charms.

Dr. Darwin courted his second wife with unabashed enthusiasm while her first husband was still living, although that husband was a wealthy and important man, Col. Edward Sacheverel Chandos-Pole of Radburn in Derbyshire. Mrs. Pole brought her children, Sacheverel, Anne Eliza, and Millicent, to stay in Dr. Darwin's home under his care when they were so sick that their lives were despaired of, having been injured by severe medicines given them for whooping cough. Mrs. Pole was young, beautiful, tall, and graceful. She was merry and kind and devoted to her children. Dr. Darwin fell in love with her as enthusiastically as he did everything. After she returned home with her saved children, he wrote to Matthew Boulton in Birmingham to have a tea-vase made for her inscribed "To the Fairest." He wrote his instructions in verse:

> Let wreaths of myrtle round the brim,
> With rosebuds twisting shade the rim;
> Each side let woodbine stalks descend,
> And form the branches as they bend;
> While on the foot a Cupid stands
> And twines the wreath with both his hands.
>
> Perch'd on the rising lid above,
> O place a lovelorn turtle dove,
> With hanging wing and ruffl'd plume,
> With gasping beak, and eye of gloom.

When Mrs. Pole was taken ill of a violent fever, Dr. Darwin was sent for. When night came Dr. Darwin was not invited to remain, although the patient was seriously ill. The doctor spent the night outside, under a tree, watching her window and writing verses about her. One wonders if the Colonel put him out. Upon her recovery he wrote *An Ode to the River Derwent* which closes with the lines:

> And tell her Derwent, as you murmur by,
> How in these wilds with hopeless love I burn,
> Teach your lone vales and echoing caves to sigh,
> And mix my briney sorrows with your urn.

Two years after Dr. Darwin first saw and loved Mrs. Pole, the Colonel died, leaving her a very beautiful and very wealthy widow. Her suitors were many, young, attractive, and moneyed. Dr. Darwin was in the forefront, though he lacked his rivals' qualification. She is reported to have replied to someone who asked if she would accept the doctor, "He is too old for me." "Nay, madam," she was told, "what are fifteen years on the right side?" "I've had so much of that right side," she protested. Yet within a year she consented on condition that he leave Lichfield, for she disliked the city. They compromised on Derby, where they lived with their children, his, hers, and theirs. Dr. Darwin raised a fine family with the help of Mary Howard Darwin, his first wife; Elizabeth Collier Chandos-Pole Darwin, his second wife; and Mrs. Parker, interim wife without legal status.

CHAPTER XIV

Lichfield Gardens

THE later part of the eighteenth century was a period of adventure in landscape design and in flower development. Tudor gardens, walled, clipt, and as geometric as a patterned coverlid, were plowed under and replaced by informal arrangements. Landscape architects went to landscape painters for design and coerced nature into copying art. Small rivers were taught to meander, brooks were damned into ponds. A form of sunken fence called a ha-ha was invented to reveal vistas, paths were curved, green mounts were raised, and trees were planted in groups. Deer, sheep and even cows cropped broad meadows into lawns. High balustraded terraces were utilized to keep these cattle away from the windows of country mansions.

Some estate owners showed a tendency to clutter up their grounds with sham Gothic ruins leering around dead trees, hermitages complete with effigies of hermits, Greek temples of Friendship, rock grottos and Chinese pagodas. Waterfalls were sometimes framed in stone arches. There was a liking for cenotaphs, obelisks, urns and thatch-canopied seats-of-remembrance, with a heavy sprinkling of odes lettered on tablets nailed to trees. The passion for rustic bridges and summer houses developed later.

Lichfield, like the rest of the country, was influenced by the vogue for remodeling geometric parks and gardens into a semblance of natural growth; that is, nature with her hair combed. Anna Seward gave the movement an impetus when she returned from a London trip where she had been impressed by the charming effect attained by serpentining a muddy rivulet into The Serpentine, in Hyde Park. The problem in Lichfield was the treatment of untidy Minster Pool and Stowe Pool, left after the draining of the Cathedral moat. Since it was not the designated duty of anyone in particular to care for the two ponds, they were continually filling up with silt and overflowing their marshy banks. Owners of gardens which ran down to the waters dredged the pools and used the muck to extend their grounds. The Bailiffs fumed but had no remedy. Anna proposed a plan of wavy borders and a shaded walk along the southern bank of Minster Pool. Thus the present Minster Walk came into existence. The scheme was not wholly satisfactory, however, for "two gormandizing aldermen" filled Stowe pond with water plants and secured the scummy surface so loved by fish. From an angler's point of view the result was admirable, for trout grew to fabulous size. A fifteen pound trout, variety undesignated, has gone down in history with the name of his captor—T. W. Greene—not the museum Greene.

Anna was passionately devoted to trees and no dryad perishing with the destruction of her habitation sent up a louder lamentation than Anna when an axe approached a tree. When, during her absence, her father once had two trees felled, she went into such hysterics on her return that he heartily regretted his action. When the Dean and Chapter thinned the trees during André's time, André tried in vain to console her with the thought that time would repair the mischief, and when in later years the order went forth that every other tree should be felled because so much foliage made the houses dark and gloomy and shaded the gardens over-much, she cried out that the Dean's Walk would look like a mouth with every alternate tooth extracted and there would be no refuge from the sun upon a summer's day. She felt that a horrid spirit of renovation was abroad; the west entrance to the Close was widened, the Close reservoir was replaced by a pump, and the Cathedral was closed for restoration. Anna's cries of protest beat often upon the skies. She did, however, under the influence of Humphrey Repton, the landscape gardener, cut a vista through the Palace shrubbery to afford a view of Stowe Pool, Stowe Vale and the Stowe villas and gardens. Mr. Repton sketched the view from the Palace drawing room window, and Anna in return wrote verses about the outlook.

Lovely country places in the neighborhood, closely connected with Lichfield through the social life of their owners, were developed in conformity with the new standards. John Sneyd (the one who was not allowed to marry Sarah Seward, but did marry for his third wife her friend, Polly Adey) made a lovely spot of his manor, Belmont, situated in the wild and hilly moorlands in the north of Staffordshire. He cleared the glen of underbrush and skillfully widened a brook into a long, narrow lake of a glassy smoothness which suddenly ended in a waterfall of forty feet. A narrow path encircled this five-acre lake. Other country gentlemen were equally successful in arranging "landskips." Calwich, the Granville family seat, where Mrs. Patrick Delany, née Mary Granville, visited her brother and later her nephew, had the popular arrangement of open land gently sloping to a spread of water, to form a sweetly smiling picture. Sir Brooke Boothby's place in Ashbourne was similarly graded. Johnson's friend, Dr. Taylor, had a park with deer and a waterfall back of his house on the main street of Ashbourne.

184

Ilam was the most beautiful estate in Staffordshire and the only one which called forth Dr. Johnson's hearty commendation. He took the Thrales there when they left Lichfield to proceed toward Wales. Though his entry in his journal is lukewarm ("I was less pleased with Ilam than when I saw it first, but my friends were delighted") yet he thought Roland Hill's showplace inferior and had the same feeling about William Shenstone's estate, The Leasowes, near Halesowen, although it was rich with fourteen waterfalls. "It is the next place to Ilam gardens," Johnson admitted. Dr. Johnson evidently liked to visit Ilam, for according to a notation, July 11, 1777, in a memorandum book at Ilam,[1] Dr. Johnson was there that day, and we know that he took Boswell there in September of that same year.

Mrs. Patrick Delany, best known to-day from having been in her youth a correspondent of Jonathan Swift and in her age a favored friend of King George III and his Queen, used to visit Ilam when it was the home of her niece Mary Dewes Port. She must have visited Lichfield and been acquainted with Lichfield people, but there is no mention of the city nor of its inhabitants in her letters. Perhaps they did not come up to her standard, for though she was a kind lady she had firm ideas about caste and formal manners. Indeed rumor has it that this very correct gentlewoman refused to meet Dr. Johnson or his friends, the Thrales, whose money came from a brewery.

This was a period of gardening and botanical adventure. England had always been gardening country; early pictures show flowers, herbs and shrubs, and early manuscripts record the development of wild flowers into cultivated specimens. Strange plants arrived with the Romans, and later the Crusaders brought back seeds and roots and slips from far countries. Roses came to England from Holland, Provence, the Pyrenees and China. This plant immigration had been going on from the dawn of history, and now toward the end of the eighteenth century botanists went on long journeys to study plant life. They traveled with Captain Cook to the South Seas, made expeditions to South Africa, and were especially enthusiastic about trophies from North America. They wrote up their discoveries in books illustrated by colored plates. Ladies embroidered roses and tulips with exquisite fidelity and reproduced bouquets and specimens in accurate water colors. Mrs. Delany in her old age originated a method of reproducing flowers in cut paper so precisely that her paper mosaics are preserved in the British Museum.

Lichfield flower gardens must have been lovely, varying from the usual fruit and flower patch to Dr. Darwin's marvelous water garden. References to these plots in letters give personality to the different plantings. It was when sitting in Charles Howard's grotto, gazing at the moonlight reflected on the water and listening to music, that Anna first realized the beauty of the human voice. Lucy Porter bought extra land for a garden at Redcourt where she left the best gooseberries on the bushes for Dr. Johnson to pick for himself. Mrs. Aston had strawberries and currants and cherries for him. Boswell walked with Miss Mary Adey and Richard [Museum] Greene in the garden of Mrs. Docksey, née Garrick. Mrs. Thrale, calling on the Darwins with Dr. Johnson, was entranced by a marvelous climbing rose on which she counted eighty-four blossoms within reach of her hand. This was probably a musk rose which Dr. Darwin had improved to an unusual degree.

The three best known Lichfield gardens had each a character of its own, although all three were floral experimental stations. Sir Brooke Boothby built a conservatory, alongside of his villa, where he could raise tropical blooms. John Saville in his plot by Stowe Pool collected and developed rare specimen plants. Dr. Darwin's woodland water garden a mile and a half from his home, was devoted to native and acclimatized trees, shrubs, herbs, and flowers. None of these gardens was made in a year and a day but each was developed over a period of time and the older the three men grew, the handsomer were their plantations.

Sir Brooke Boothby, the Sixth Baronet, was the nephew of Dr. Johnson's friend, Hill Boothby. Boothby's early years before he inherited the title were spent largely in London, and his name appears in lists of guests at important events but in the also-present class. He associated with Lord St. Helens who was the little Alleyne Fitzherbert in the days when Boothby's Aunt, Hill Boothby, lived with the Fitzherbert family at Tissington. Other friends were Edward Tighe who read Robert Jephson's tragedies aloud at Mrs. Vesey's *bas bleu* parties, and George Hardinge, attorney-general, who read Milton aloud to Anna Seward in the Dear Blue Region, the upstairs sitting room in the Palace. Boothby was a poet in his own right of some reputation, as well as a writer of political pamphlets. He had the dubious honor of being blackballed in company with the eccentric Lord March, when they were put up for membership in a Female Gambling Club at Almack's, made up of the crème de la crème. (Lady Marlborough was also blackballed but later admitted. Horace Walpole was voted in unanimously.)

Brooke Boothby began spending more time in Litchfield than in London about 1772, when his name appears as a city householder on the list of houses with oil street lamps. His great uncle, Sir William (of whom Walpole thought highly) was getting along in years and, since he was unmarried, the line of inheritance ended up eventually with our Brooke Boothby. Indeed he inherited the title in 1789 when he was about forty-five. He is best known as the one who obtained the glass now in the Lady Chapel of the Lichfield Cathedral from the Cistercian Abbey of Herckenrode in Belgium after it had been suppressed by order of Napoleon. He bought the glass, which was in three hundred and forty panels, for two hundred pounds, and gave the Dean and Chapter the opportunity of buying it from him at the same price.

He was a man of kindliness, elegance, charm and education. He was also a spendthrift, with an extravagant taste for rare plants, wine, poetry, politics, and ladies. From his great uncle, Sir William, he inherited fifteen hundred pounds a year, his own patrimony was twelve hundred pounds a year, and his wife's dowry was twenty thousand pounds in money, besides eight hundred a year. Yet he died in debt. Sir Brooke Boothby had holes in all his pockets.

Part of his wealth went for horticultural experimentation, for he was an ardent botanist, like Saville and Darwin. On inheriting Ashbourne Hall he spent a great deal re-scaping the grounds and, as he had taste as well as money, it became one of the show places. He was clever in remodeling the mansion. He enlarged the drawing room, to make it suitable for entertaining, by throwing together two rooms of different heights, a discrepancy which he concealed by building in place of the wall a large chimney with horizontal flues forming arches on either side and two fireplaces facing in opposite directions. Along the side of this room he ran a conservatory which could be shut off with sash windows, and here he raised tropical plants at vast expense. We have no description of his exotics beyond Anna Seward's statement that the conservatory was filled with a prodigious collection of rare and splendid shrubs and flowers of every climate, and was one of the many graves in which his three fortunes were interred.

John Saville's first garden, which Honora named "Damon's Bower," was attached to the house in Vicar's Close where he lived with his wife and children. It must have been small but very lovely. Sometime after he separated from his wife, moving into a tiny house next door, he leased a tract in Stowe

Parish, beside Stowe Pool, near the houses of Mrs. Gastrell and Mrs. Aston, in the section once occupied by Michael Johnson's ill-fated parchment works, where grew the famous Johnson willow. He had no fortune to lavish on rarities, but through exchanges, gifts, careful purchase, and horticultural skill, he assembled a collection mentioned as a "curious garden" in Rev. Stebbing Shaw's *History of Staffordshire*.[2] Here he worked in his free hours. ". . . we seldom see him through these long warm days," Anna wrote their mutual friend, Dr. Whalley, "except to take a hasty dinner, a dish of tea, or to make us wait supper for him till ten." She stated that he had some two thousand plants; Shaw says seven hundred; let us compromise on thirteen hundred.

Dr. Darwin and Anna were walking one day in Saville's garden. They were a striking couple, the doctor a shambling bear of a man and the lady a mature goddess who limped slightly. Anna herself once said of the two of them that though they were two poets, he looked like a butcher and she like a fat cook maid, but Anna was so handsome that she could afford to joke about her overweight. Even in her later years strangers commented on her resemblance to Mrs. Siddons. The hulk of a man and the majestic lady strolled in happy companionship among the greenery and flowers. One likes to think that the ever-handsome Saville, in a bright blue coat and flour-white hair, accompanied them to point out new acquisitions for Darwin's stuttering appreciation.

Darwin inquired of Anna if she had ever seen the *Calmia*, commenting:

"It is a flower of such exquisite beauty that it would make you waste the summer day examining it. You would forget the hour of dinner; all your senses would be absorbed in *one;* you would be all eye."

"What is its color?" asked Anna.

"Precisely that of a seraph's plume," replied the doctor.

Later he confessed that he had never seen the flower. It was the American mountain laurel *(kalmia latifolia)* named for Peter Kalm, a Finn who published a book on his travels in North America from 1775-61.

As Darwin's dingle, the dry moat in front of his residence, did not offer scope for his experiments, Darwin purchased an eight-acre tract of brook, springs, woods, and rocks in a section called Abenalls. An earlier scientist, Sir John Floyer, had once been interested in the strange water formations of this section. Sir John had been a Fellow of the Royal Society, a physician, a medical writer, and a Lichfield Justice of the Peace. It was he who recommended Mrs. Johnson to take little Sam to be touched by Queen Anne. Michael Johnson had been connected with the publication of some of his medical works and the books had been on sale at Johnson's stores at Lichfield, and his stalls at Uttoxeter and Ashby de la Zouche. Sir John's medical practice in general was not as quaint as his belief in the curative power of the queenly touch might suggest. He was the first to count the number of a patient's pulse beats to the minute, and he held advanced ideas about cold bathing. He persuaded Lichfieldians to construct a cold bath to be fed by a spring that was called Unite's Well, the temperature of which was several degrees colder than that of any other spring in the neighborhood. Three drops a minute trickled from a rock—never more, never less—all the year around. It did not freeze in winter nor moderate in summer. Another oddity was a wall-spring, that is a thin sheet of water sliding out between two strata of silicious sandstone, separated by a stratum of clay.[3]

After Dr. Darwin had cleared the underbrush with discretion, he set out many varieties of trees, shrubs and other plants and widened the brook into pools that reflected the surrounding loveliness.

He put up an inscription supposed to be spoken to visitors by a guardian water nymph:

> If the meek flower of bashful dye,
> Attract not thy incurious eye;
> If the soft, murmuring rill, to rest
> Encharm not thy tumultuous breast,
> Go, where Ambition lures the vain,
> Or avarice barters peace for gain.

When all was prepared, Anna Seward was invited for a formal visit of inspection, because during planting time she had not been allowed in this, one of her favorite walks. The two poets, Erasmus and Anna, enjoyed each other's poetry and projects, although the doctor was often impatient with her romantic susceptibility, while she resented his corrosive sarcasms. This first visit to the new garden was a ceremony to which they both looked forward, but at the last moment Dr. Darwin was called to a sickroom and Anna went on ahead. She was enchanted, and pulling out her tablet and pencil, sat down to write a poem to the water nymph:

> O, come not here, ye Proud, whose breasts infold
> Th' insatiate wish of glory, or of gold;
> O come not ye, whose brand'd forehead wear
> Th' eternal frown of envy, or of care;
> For you no Dryad decks her fragrant bowers,
> For you her sparkling urn no Naiad pours;
> Unmark'd by you light Graces skim the green,
> And hovering Cupids aim their shafts unseen.
> But, thou! whose mind the well-attemper'd ray
> Of Taste and Virtue, lights with purer day;
> Whose finer sense each soft vibration owns,
> Mute and unfeeling to discord tones;
> Like the fair flower that spreads its lucid form
> To meet the sun, but shuts it to the storm;
> For thee my borders nurse the glowing wreath,

My fountains murmur, and my zephyrs breathe;
My painted birds their vivid plumes unfold,
And insect armies wave their wings of gold.

Anna's poem went on in the same pleasant fashion, praising the Vale and the Genius who planted it to loveliness. Dr. Darwin was so pleased that he sent the verses to *The Gentleman's Magazine,* where they were published in 1783, over Anna's signature and copied into *The Annual Register.* She was slightly annoyed that he had replaced the last six lines of the poem with eight of his own, but that was a liberty versemakers often took with each other's work.

Dr. Darwin suggested that Anna use her verses as the introduction to a long poem in which flowers, plants and trees should be personified; Ovid's Metamorphoses in reverse. The poem would show the likeness between humans and plants in life habits of impregnation, birth, nourishment, and habitats. He wanted Anna to write the poem, while he supplied scientific notes of explanation. Though the-bees-and-the-flowers data were not then taught in kindergarten, Anna knew enough of the facts of botany life to shy off, observing that "beside her want of botanical knowledge, the plan was not strictly proper for a female pen." She begged him to undertake the plan himself, and he soon began the long task of *The Botanic Garden.*

Dr. Darwin worked for ten years on this vast compendium of science and imagination, composing it in his chaise on the road. On each page some lines of poetry float above a sea of fine-type notes; botanical, chemical, geographical, mythological, philosophical, and biographical. Each plant is identified by its common and its botanical name, is described, classified, placed in its habitat, and accompanied by its history of practical use and its place in mythology. Inserted between Part I and Part II are thirty-nine essays on such varied subjects as meteors and other sky phenomena, rock formation, the Portland Vase, shellfish, theories of growth, and other wide-ranging investigations.

The poem itself is a series of pictures, a delicate, stylized mural of plants, goddesses, landscapes, compliments to personal friends, salt mines, the slave trade, Lot's wife, the steam engine, Iceland, and so on, and through all subjects dance and float zephyrs, naiads, dryads, fawns, mermaids, salamanders, and their ilk. The printed volume is exquisitely illustrated with flower drawings, charts, and pictures, a combination of accurate observation and unrestrained imagination.

The allegory of the flowers was startling in its novelty. For instance, after toying with the description of a spring morning, the poet goes on:

> So shall from high the bursting *Anther* trust
> To the mild breezes the prolific dust;
> Or bow his waxen head with graceful pride,
> Watch the first blushes of his waking bride,
> Give to her hand the honey'd cup, or sip
> Celestial nectar from her sweeter lip;
> Hang in soft rapture o'er the yielding Fair,
> Love out his hour, and leave his life in air.

The note on the last line is sprightlier than is usual in botanical information:

> Darwin, *The Botanic Garden,* V I, Canto IV, II, 465-472. *Love out his hour.* 1. 472. The vegetable passion of love is agreeably seen in the flower of the *parnessia,* in which the males alternately approach and recede from the female; and in the flower of the *nigella,* or devil in the bush, in which the tall females bend down to their dwarf husbands. But I was this morning surprised to observe amongst Sir Brooke Boothby's valuable collection of plants at Ashbourne, the manifest adultery of several females of the plant *collinsonia,* who had bent themselves into contact with the males of other flowers of the same plant in the vicinity. Sept. 16.

When the book was finally published, Anna was outraged to discover her verses, altered and interpolated, used as the introduction, without credit being given to her. She did what she could to assert her right by sending them in their original form to be printed in Shaw's *History of Staffordshire*.[4]

The statement sometimes made that Anna was angry because the doctor did not wish to marry her, is open to the same objection as the similar allegation in the case of Edgeworth. The first Mrs. Darwin died in 1770, when the Saville-Seward affair was well started and it continued its stormy vigor for years. Comparing the published letters printed by Mr. Constable with her confidential outpourings to Mrs. Sykes, one suspects that the editor drew a discreet pen through much that related to Saville, Anna's lover, while he saw no reason for deleting her exuberant expressions of regard for Dr. Darwin.

Darwin formed The Lichfield Botanical Club of three members only: himself, Sir Brooke Boothby, and a Mr. Jackson. John Saville was invited to join, but he refused because he knew that he would have to do all the paper work, Darwin being too busy and Boothby too lazy. So Rev. Joseph Jackson was invited in his place. He was a proctor of the Cathedral jurisdiction. He had educated himself in French and Latin, and by sheer force of ability had achieved a place in the ecclesiastical hierarchy. Under the supervision of the two better educated men he was able to turn out translations and feature articles, signed "Lichfield Botanic Society," which attracted scientific attention. The Society published at least two important works: *A System of Vegetation* and *The Families of Plants*. Learned men who interested themselves in such matters, when passing through Lichfield sometimes paused to consult with the writers and were astonished to discover that the erudite society was only a threesome.

CHAPTER XV

Dr. Johnson's Visits

AFTER Dr. Johnson received his pension in 1762 he could afford to take time off from writing and he had money for traveling. From this time on until his death he came every few years to Lichfield. He spent six months there in 1767. In 1770, 1771 and 1772 the lengths of his visits varied from a month to six weeks. His tour through North Wales with the Thrales was inaugurated by a few days in Lichfield. He made a short stay in 1775, brought Boswell in 1776, spent two months there in 1777, and made a longer visit in 1779. He came in 1781, and his final visit in 1784 was not long before his death.

Dr. Johnson was of two minds about the town in which he had grown up. He swung from praise to scorn to praise, according to his mood. He told Boswell that the inhabitants were the most sober, decent people in England, the genteelest in proportion to their wealth, and spoke the purest English. He saw it as a city of philosphers. In this same mood of filial affection he assured John Nichols, writer and editor, that the inhabitants of Lichfield were more orthodox in their religion, more pure in their language and more polite in their manners than those of any other town in the kingdom.

When he was in Lichfield, however, he was often bored and despondent. Letters written to Mrs. Thrale during his visits there sometimes disparage the place. He wrote her once that he was afraid his dear townsmen would be mentioned in future days as the last part of the nation to become civilized. He wrote again: "I have felt in this place something like the shackles of destiny. There has not been a day of pleasure, yet I cannot get away." Another year, "At Lichfield I found little to please me. One more of my old school friends is dead." Dr. Johnson was like the Book of Proverbs in that his aphorisms were always striking but often contradictory.

His emotional attitude depended on his mood and his mood was greatly influenced by physical comfort. When he over-praised Lichfield dialect, he was comfortable after a tiresome journey, eating supper with Boswell at Lichfield's Three Crowns Inn.[1] When he boasted to John Wilkes that he had in Lichfield shown Boswell genuine civilized life, he was dining at the excellent table of the publishers, Charles and Edward Dilly, feeding on veal with a little of the stuffing please, some gravy, and a squeeze of lemon. One surmises that when he extolled Lichfield to John Nichols, whom we know best as compiler of *Literary Anecdotes of the Eighteenth Century,* it was over the table of the Essex Club, of which they were fellow members.

The doctor must have enjoyed his Lichfield visits since he came so often and stayed so long, but he could not reconcile himself to the changes he found. In the period between 1740 and 1770 Lichfield, like all the rest of England, changed greatly. The improvement of the streets was noticeable; raised footwalks were provided and cobblestones were used to pave the market place and damp areas, like the approaches to the reservoirs and the public laundry stations. The causeway across Minster Pool in Bird and Dam Streets, which had accommodated only pedestrains and saddle horses, was widened for carriages, and buildings which encroached on roadways were removed or altered. A street scavenger was employed. The cesspools into which drained the water from the street gutters were enlarged.[2] Lichfield streets on the whole stood well in comparison with other towns and even London. Lichfield was on the direct route between Liverpool and London. Coaches left the Swan Inn at the great port of Liverpool, and proceeded through Lad Lane, Prescot, Warrington, Knutsford, Congleton, New Castle-under-Lyme, and Stone, to Lichfield. The towns between there and London were: Meriden, Coventry, Dunchurch, Daventry, Towcester, Foster's Booth, Stony Stratford, Fenney Stratford, Brickhill, and then the great city itself.

The many civic improvements did not impress Dr. Johnson. He wrote Guiseppe Baretti, the Thrales' Italian tutor: "Last winter I went down to my native town, when I found the streets much narrower and shorter than when I had left them." Humorously but regretfully he informed Mrs. Thrale: "They have cut down the trees in George Lane. . . . As an impartial traveller I must however tell, that in Stowe Street where I left a draw-well, I have found a pump; but that the landing-well in this ill-fated George Lane lies shamefully neglected!"

Anticipated pleasure and subsequent disappointment is a sequence often experienced by a native son home on a visit. A great man returning to his boyhood locale is not always comfortable. However cordial the handshakes, however loud the band on his arrival, the next morning he is uneasy. The past and the present conflict. Not only has the place actually changed during his absence, but his recollection of it has acquired a dream-like quality. He tries to find a town which not only is not, but which never was.

197

During his Lichfield visits Dr. Johnson did his best to bring back the past. He left town in the morning on one occasion without telling Lucy Porter, his stepdaughter with whom he was staying, where he was going, and he did not return until evening. He made a penitential journey that day to Uttoxeter where his father had had a weekly bookstall. On the spot where the counter had been set up, the famous Dr. Johnson, spectacular in his bulk and eccentric appearance, stood bareheaded in the rain regardless of astonished passers-by, in expiation for a boyhood refusal to accompany his father there one market day, a day long past and forgotten by everyone save the repentant son.

Other scenes recalled pleasanter memories. The Johnson willow had now grown to a tree with a circumference of twenty-two feet, and a height of seventy-five. Visitors wondered at its size and Johnson inspected it proudly. He walked in John Levett's field which had been the schoolboys' playground; he climbed Mrs. Aston's five-barred gate to prove to himself that he could still accomplish the feat. Nevertheless Dr. Johnson was bored. In Lichfield there was no saucy Mrs. Thrale to tease him with provocative retorts; no Hannah More to sparkle bright eyes at him till he peppered her with return compliments; no socially skilful Mrs. Montagu to gather for him an audience that would stir his spirits; no harum-scarum Mrs. Vesey to steer him, like a busy tug convoying a rich merchant ship, at her lively, chattering parties. Lichfield social life was tranquil, and Dr. Johnson associated chiefly with elderly ladies whose chitchat was uninspiring even when spiced with malice.

Dr. Johnson's letters to Mrs. Thrale are a source of information as to how he spent his Lichfield days. They are in a different vein from those he wrote to other correspondents; full of quiet affection, sly amusement, and gentle humor. No outbursts of spleen mar their gentle confiding tone. They have the same easy confidence as had those he wrote years before to Hill Boothby. He reports on local matters. Lady Catherine Smith, daughter of Archbishop Vyse and widow of Sir George Smith, 1st Baronet of Stoke, afforded him quiet amusement. Lady Smith, calling at Mrs. Aston's, took tea before her mother. Was that correct, he solemnly asks Mrs. Thrale. Mrs. Thrale assures him that it was not right, because Lady Smith, in losing her husband lost also his rank and should not take precedence of her mother. Perhaps, Mrs. Thrale suggests, she has been corrupted by dear Mr. Johnson's odd speeches against parental authority. When Lady Smith's new post chaise rouses comment, Mrs. Thrale is duly informed.

Little Miss Queeney Thrale, aged eight, was a good correspondent when sufficiently nagged by her mother. Her letters, which the doctor read aloud to the Lichfield ladies, have not been saved for us, but we have some of those which he wrote to the little girl. He announces the death of Lucy Porter's fine black cat: "So things go. Generations, as Homer says, are but leaves, and you now see the leaves falling about you." Lucy had an old deaf dog named Brill which came to her, along with her fortune, from her brother. Dr. Johnson reports on Brill's health in his Thrale letters. Pets were people in Lichfield circles. When Mrs. Aston's parrot nipped Dr. Johnson's leg, the news traveled through the town and came back to the doctor when he was calling on Mrs. Cobb. When Mrs. Cobb gave the doctor sweetmeats for breakfast, that news made the grapevine circuit in the opposite direction and met him at Mrs. Aston's. The pet population of Lichfield at one time included John Saville's two dogs, two birds, and one green frog. Dr. Darwin's cat, Snow, proud of long white whiskers and topaz eyes, courted Miss Seward's Miss Po Filina, a short-haired tiger-marked pussy which had a beautiful round face, elegant ears, and a sinuous tail. In an exchange of letters and verse— much more amusing than the generality of such fancies—

199

Snow offered Miss Po Filina his heart, his paw, and a fresh-slaughtered Norway rat. Miss Po refused to have aught to do with a cat that caught birds as well as rats, for Miss Po had learned to live with an uncaged dove, a lark, and a redbreast that flew about the room and ate from her own dish. Another Seward pet was Sappho, a small dog that left a big vacant space when she suddenly died. These little animals have gained immortality in their owners' letters.

Sometimes the doctor brought to Lichfield with him his Negro servant Francis Barber. The two attracted attention; the small, delicate, pock-marked colored man was a contrast to the great rolling bulk of Dr. Johnson. Slavery, abolished in England, was still legal in British possessions in the West Indies, where English planters owned hundreds of slaves. Frank had been brought to England by one of these planters who came home to live in Lincoln Cathedral Close. Although Negroes were fairly common around London, Frank did not fit into life in the Cathedral Close. His master educated him and passed him about a bit, until finally the lad came to rest in Doctor Johnson's service where he remained until the doctor's death.

Barber was employed in household duties: marketing, answering the door knocker, waiting on table, serving coffee, and in personal service for the doctor. Since the latter was not the type to keep a gentleman's gentleman, and as the lad was likable, sensitive and affectionate, Dr. Johnson continued his education, and after a couple of unsuccessful attempts to place him in a trade, accepted him as a humble companion. Barber traveled with the doctor, attended him at his friends' tables, knelt with him in prayer, partook of the sacrament with him, and listened to spiritual advice. A few of Dr. Johnson's friends spoke harshly of the lad, but most of them had a kindly feeling for him and he was popular in the servants' halls.[3]

The events of Dr. Johnson's visits ran in the same general

course each time. A record of his 1779 sojourn will serve as an example. He arrived at Lucy's Saturday night and walked to Stowe Hill, but Mrs. Aston had gone to bed. Sunday she entertained him at dinner. That night he saw his old playfellow, Brodhurst, and gave him a guinea. Monday he went with Dr. Taylor and Mrs. Cobb to Greenhill Bower which he had not seen for fifty years, but found it degenerated: "Everything grows old." Mr. Greene of the museum called. Dr. Johnson ordered medicine. Tuesday he took the medicine. He had dinner with Lucy. Wednesday and Thursday he made visits, including one to Peter Garrick. He took medicine. Friday he dined at Stowe Hill. He took medicine. Saturday Mrs. Aston took him out in her chaise, he dined with Mrs. Cobb at the Friary, and returning to Lucy's found there Lady Smith and her sister, Mary Vyse.

One of the occasions which Dr. Johnson enjoyed in Lichfield was the annual walk of the Ladies' Amiable Society. This was a "box club," a sort of mutual benefit society, named from the coffer into which the members dropped their assessments. It was modeled after the men's "box clubs" which were springing up all over England. These precursors of savings banks and insurance companies were of financial help to the poor, but they had disadvantages, for an unusual number of deaths and illnesses during a short period depleted the treasury, and there was also danger of dishonesty on the part of the steward. The clubs became safer after 1793, when a law was passed compelling registration of a society's rules with a justice of the peace. Although the societies were more common in manufacturing than in agricultural districts, yet by the middle of the nineties Staffordshire, which was largely a farming community with the pottery industry still in infancy, had seventy-nine registered beneficiary societies.[4]

The women's clubs were more informal than the men's, and less money was dropped into The Box. Lichfield women paid in twopence a week and were entitled to six shillings a week in time of need. Upon the death of a member, five pounds was divided among her children.

The clubs held an annual outing, the women's usually celebrating separately, as the men's affairs were sometimes noisy. The members made a pretty picture, dressed in white or light colors with ribbons and gay bonnets, carrying wands topped with nosegays. The sunshine, the flowers, the pealing church bells, the music of drums and flutes, and the children capering alongside, made it a joyous occasion. Clergymen, the society physician, and other important men of the town led the procession.

Several descriptions of these decorous celebrations in Lichfield are recorded: On the Thursday before July 5th, 1773, some ninety ladies walked from Vicars' Hall in the Close to St. Mary's Church in the City, where they were edified by a sermon. They enjoyed an elegant dinner at the George Inn, where they voted for their society apothecary, Mr. Charles Salt being elected with twenty-seven votes, Mr. Richard Greene—he who had the famous museum—coming close with twenty-five.

The following year a hundred young women dressed in white, carrying shepherdess's crooks, preceded by Mr. Salt, two clergymen, and the Clerk of the Society, also carrying crooks, walked from the Guildhall in the City to the Cathedral to listen to a sermon by Rev. Thomas White. In like order they returned to the Guildhall to dinner where they entertained the Chief Magistrates, and spent the evening in the most harmonious manner. "In short," runs the record, "this Society, one of the first of its Kind, for Regularity, Decency, and good Order, may serve as a Pattern to all others." [5]

Dr. Johnson, visiting in Lichfield in 1775, wrote Mrs. Thrale that the box-club ladies walked from the townhall to the Cathedral in linen gowns, carrying sticks with acorns.

Why an acorn on a stick they knew not, until he told them that the Romans had given an oakland garland to anyone who served his country well, and that same symbol had later been adopted in England. The sermon this year was preached by Rev. John Betteridge Pearson, Perpetual Curate of St. Michael's Church, a friend of Lucy Porter, to whom she left her fortune. A dinner followed the sermon, and a ball followed the dinner.

A poem written by an unknown friend, presents a picture of one such an occasion:

WEDNESDAY IN WHITSUN WEEK OR THE CLUB FEAST
In Imitation of CYMON and IPHEGENIA

Recitative: The Day is come. Behold the Social Band
             In Gay attire with each his peaceful wand
             By Friendship led, While Music's softest Lay
             Inspires each Heart, and gladdens all the Way
             To Church. In Solemn Pomp, They move along
             The admiration of the Gazing Throng.

Air: When there with Cheerful Pious Awe
             They hear Religion's sacred Law
                 Their friendly Care approve (repeat)
             By whose example influenc'd
                 Of Comfort, Joy, and Love (repeat)

Recitative: The Sermon done. In the same Order Gay
             Back they return, In Mirth to spend the Day.
             The Cheerful Bells, Their coming do proclaim
             And the throng'd Streets reecho with their Fame.
             To Wilkins's with Joy they straight repair
             Fam'd for food Ale and plenty of good Cheer
             The Dinner ended, While they Drink and Smoke
             At Friendship's Shrine They thus the Power
                 Invoke.
Air: Come friendship. tc. Etc.[6]

Without doubt it was the gentlemen guests who smoked, but the ladies shared the famous Lichfield ale.

203

Another colorful annual holiday was Greenhill Bower. This carnival, held on Whit-Monday (the Monday following the seventh Sunday after Easter), was enjoyed by the citizens in general, but was too uproarious to please the older people. A court meeting in the Guild-Hall was immediately adjourned to Green Hill, for the Court of Array, or View of Men and Arms. The names of all the householders of the twenty-one wards were there called by the Dozeners (constables) and a fine was imposed on any man who was absent. This custom originated as an inspection of military resources. The assembly took its name from Bowers erected on Green Hill where beef, prunes, and cake were served free, along with plenty of wine and ale. Lichfield ale was always famous. Farquhar mentions it in the *The Beaux Stratagem,* and Mrs. Garrick served it in London at that first dinner she gave after David Garrick's death, when David's friends, including Dr. Johnson, gathered about her.

The great feature of Greenhill Bower was the picturesque, tumultuous procession marching at eight in the morning from the market place to Greenhill and returning at night to St. Mary's Church by way of Bore and Sadler Streets. Merrymakers marched through the city's streets by craft companies and wards and military units, carrying their Posies. Posies were originally figures of saints which later became decorations of flowers and greenery, symbolizing the craft companies which exhibited them, or simply puppets with garlands. Some of the craft companies displayed mechanical sets, somewhat after the manner of a Punch and Judy show. The procession marched to the music of pipe and tabor and fiddle. Morris dancers, gaudy in scarves and ribbons, danced sarabands and clashed their staves. The military men marched with their captains, accompanied by the Constables, the Gaoler, the Sheriff, the Serjeants at Mace, the Town Clerk, and the Bailiffs. The roughnecks of the crowd fired volleys from their guns over the roofs of the houses, and the roistering was displeasing to the more staid dwellers in Close and City. The procession broke up at St. Mary's Church where banners and Posies were deposited, as the images of saints had been in early years. The Town Clerk made an address recommending a peaceable demeanor and watchful attention to duty, and a final volley was fired. The holiday which began in a slight preparatory fashion on Sunday, dribbled over into Tuesday.[7]

The incompatibility existing between Dr. Johnson and the families domiciled in the Close made his relationship with the prebendaries and their households too formal to be satisfying. He was invited constantly and entertained courteously, but beneath the urbanity there was strain. This was the more unfortunate because the ecclesiastical atmosphere suited Johnson's tastes. The place was redolent of Greek and Latin; many of the clergy were talented, witty men, skilled in argument; and the young people were well grounded in English literature. Here, in a similar milieu, under the patronage of Gilbert Walmesley, brash young Johnson had awakened to his own genius. Now in his later life he was not at ease there.

Several reasons account for the disaffection. The clergy were accustomed to deference and so was the doctor; neither side was in the habit of taking second place. Johnson, being oversensitive to slights, probably suspected that the prebendaries did not forget, any more than he forgot, his off-the-Close origin and his youthful bumptiousness.

Again, Dr. Johnson was a passionate Tory and the clergy were mostly Whigs since, as ecclesiastical officers, they held their appointments by favor of a Whig government. Political partisanship was strong, and the Whig bias which Johnson could forgive in Molly Aston and Gilbert Walmesley and some other friends, was in general an offense to him. "I do not much like to see a Whig in any dress," quoth Dr. Johnson, "but I hate to see a Whig in a parson's gown."

On the part of the Close the early enmity between the important, pompous, brutal grammar-school headmaster, Dr. Hunter, and his loutish, obstinate pupil, would probably have disappeared had Johnson had a conciliatory nature. It was kept alive and increased by the doctor's tendency to suspect slights and disrespect. Attack was his form of defense. His compulsion to dominate any group of which he was a part came from the realization that if people were not awed, they would find him ridiculous.[8] Their attention must be continuously diverted from his grotesque appearance, untidy dress, and uncouth gestures, to his marvelous brain power. He must conquer every time and all the time. He was a superb conversationalist; he must always be supreme. As a result of this obsession he sometimes attacked when he was not menaced.

The discourtesy, even insolence, resulting from this technique pained his friends and offended his critics. He trampled on a certain inoffensive Mr. Wickins in this fashion, and Mr. Wickins, after Johnson's death, wrote out the episode for Mrs. Thrale. Mr. Wickins was a man of good standing, a Lichfield mercer who lived in Dam Street. He was sworn High Constable at St. George's Court in 1770 for a year of office, was Church Warden of St. Mary's Church, and his signature as witness appears on the wills of Dr. Seward and Charles Howard. He was always referred to as *Mr.* James Wickins, which indicates a highly respectable position in the city. He had a taste for gardening and collected statuary, pictures and books. Anna Seward called his place a "little temple of the Arts." He paid marked attentions at one time to Sophia Weston, niece of Dr. Whalley's first wife and intimate friend of Anna Seward and Mrs. Thrale. Anna refers to him as "the gentle Wickins." He gave up the idea of marrying Miss Weston because he thought she was too far above him socially. At least that is the excuse he gave her friends who were longing to see her released from a dreary life of skimping in order to pay a brother's debts and nursing an unsatisfactory mother who had lost her wits but lived to the age of ninety-seven. It may have been Sophia's encumbrances rather than her social superiority which convinced Mr. Wickins that it was safer to sigh than to kiss. One is glad to report that Sophia later made an excellent marriage, and was rescued from the domestic trap in which she had been caught.

When Dr. Johnson called on Mr. Wickins the host made the mistake of showing his guest through his pleasure grounds, ignoring or not knowing that the doctor detested prospects and views and terraces. Johnson's interest in a garden was vegetables, and a lake was known to him by its fish. Luckless Mr. Wickins rushed upon his fate when he said:

"This vista promises a larger extent of grounds than there is. You might conceive that you are entering an extensive labyrinth, but that would prove a deception, though I hope not an unpardonable one."

"Sir," replied the doctor, "don't tell me of deception; a lie, Sir, is a lie, whether it be a lie to the eye or a lie to the ear."

The host turned the conversation to an urn erected, after the custom of the time, to a deceased friend.

"How do you like that urn, Dr. Johnson?" he asked. "It is of the true Truscan order."

"Sir," returned the guest, "I hate urns; they *are* nothing, they *mean* nothing, convey no ideas but ideas of horror— would they were beaten to pieces to pave our streets!"

The two came to a cold bath and the host expatiated on its salubrity.

"Sir," said the doctor, "how do you do?"

"Very well, I thank you, doctor."

"Then, Sir, let well enough alone, and be content. I hate immersion."

Mr. Wickins deduced from this that the doctor could not swim, but he was an excellent swimmer, having been taught as a boy by his father.

Upon the margin of the pool stood a statue of the Venus De Medici.

"Throw her," growled the guest, "into the pool to hide her nakedness, and to cool her lasciviousness."

He was not interested in a summer house built of roots, perhaps because it was too small for his bulk, but he cheered up when with great exertion he succeeded in extracting a nail from the bark of a plum tree.

"There, Sir," he exclaimed, "I have done some good to-day; the tree might have festered. I make it a rule, Sir, to do some good every day of my life," said boy-scout Johnson.

Back in the house the doctor's mood grew more amiable; he had conquered the defiant nail. The study full of books attracted him. The first book he picked up was unfortunately Dr. Edward Harwood's *Liberal Translation of the New Testament*, an early attempt to bring the Bible closer to the reader by use of colloquial English. The book opened at the passage on the raising of Lazarus, where the phrase "Jesus wept" was translated, "And Jesus, the Saviour of the world, burst into a flood of tears." Dr. Johnson, with his feeling for rhetoric, can hardly be blamed for throwing the book aside with the exclamation, "Puppy." The second choice was almost as unfortunate, being the sermons of Laurence Sterne. Sterne's name was anathema to Johnson, and he considered the sermons worth reading only in a stage coach, and not good enough for that. But the doctor controlled himself, only asking,

"Sir, do you ever read any others?"

"Yes, doctor," replied Mr. Wickins, "I read Sherlock, Tillotson, Beveridge, and others."

At last the two had found something to admire in unison.

PLATE XV
Rev. Thomas Seward

PLATE XVI

The House where Dr. Johnson was born

Johnson's Willow

From *A short Account of the Ancient
and Modern State of the City and Close
of Lichfield (1819)*

"Ay, Sir," cried the mollified guest, "there you drink the cup of salvation to the bottom; here you have merely the froth from the surface."

This was really tolerant of the doctor, for he thought the style of Bishop Thomas Sherlock too elegant, and that of John Tillotson, Archbishop of Canterbury, not a style to be imitated by young preachers. It is to be regretted that Wickins did not hand him South, whom the doctor considered one of the best (though sometimes violent) and Jortin (very elegant) and Smallridge.

Safe from the garden within a book-lined room, the doctor's mood softened. Observing a Shakespeare mulberry vase on a pedestal, inscribed:

> Sacred to Shakespeare
> and in honour of
> David Garrick, Esq.
> The Ornament—the Reformer
> of the British stage

the doctor approved:

"Ay, Sir; Davy, Davy loves flattery; but here indeed you have flattered him as he deserves, paying a just tribute to his memory." [9]

CHAPTER XVI

Some Lichfield Ladies

ANNA SEWARD was all that Dr. Johnson detested in a
woman; domineering, argumentative, tactless, imagina-
tive, romantic, flouting the conventions by her shameless attachment to a married man. It was not her second-rate verse
which condemned her in Johnson's eyes, for a man who could
call Hannah More "the most powerful versificatrix in the
English language" was in no position to be critical of Anna's
output. He simply did not like her personality. He confessed
that he could tremble at the sight of Miss Seward, she was
so like her grandfather, Dr. Hunter, that pompous headmaster
of the Lichfield Grammar School who never entered the school-
room without his gown and cassock, and his full-dressed wig,
and his cane. On the other hand Anna possessed a quality
to which he was susceptible—social charm. She was handsome,
intelligent, warm-hearted and genuinely interested in people.
She was a good talker and good talk was irresistible to him.

Anna also had mixed feelings. She resented Johnson's personal rudeness (so different from her father's universal courtesy), and was indignant at his harsh criticism of minor poets
in his *Lives of the Poets* (the ugliest duckling of a poet was

a swan to her), but she passionately appreciated his intellect, his poetry, his essays, and his conversation. Her vilification of his personality after his death is widely known, while her equally intense admiration for some of his achievements has been ignored. Her acrimony was the reverse of a feeling which, under different treatment, would have bloomed as hero worship. If she could have brought herself to laud the sage, or if he had taken the trouble to make himself agreeable to her, they would have got on better together, but though both were egregious flatterers on occasion, such occasion did not arise when they were together. She was delighted when it was reported to her that he had spoken handsomely of her writings in the presence of a large company at Lucy Porter's, and again when Boswell relayed to her the information that Johnson had approved her verses on Lichfield. The one compliment he ever paid her to her face pleased her more than all of Hayley's raptures over everything she wrote. He was speaking favorably in her presence of Madame du Bocage's epic, *Colombiade,* when he turned to Anna, saying, "Madame, there is not any thing equal to your description of the sea round the North Pole, in your elegy on the death of Captain Cook." "I blushed, curtesied, and instantly turned the conversation into a different channel," comments the flattered lady. If only this great man who did that sort of thing so gracefully had done it oftener to Anna Seward!

When they met face to face the antagonism sometimes vanished in the irresistible charm of good talk; neither could resist angling for the other's approval and neither could escape being pleased with the other's response. They met often at Redcourt, Lucy's house, for Anna and Lucy were friends from childhood, and we have the record of one encounter between Anna and the doctor which was delightful to both of them. During his last stay at Lichfield when he was sick, depressed and brooding on death, he seems to have laid aside his distaste for Anna, since he asked her to come often to see him at his stepdaughter's.[1]

One day she found him asleep in an armchair and was loathe to wake him he looked so sick and miserable. He was finally aroused by a servant coming in to announce callers. These were Rev. Henry White, a cousin of Anna and a connection of Johnson's wife by her first marriage, who was bringing an Oxford gentleman to meet Dr. Johnson. The Whites were one of those clerical families toward whom ecclesiastical offices gravitated. Henry was Sacrist of the Cathedral, Vicar of Chebsy and Dilhorne, and Perpetual Curate of St. Chad. He had a social talent, a happy manner with visitors, and a taste for collecting ancient books and pamphlets. He had a way of going off into a brown study in company and awakening, rubbing his eyes, and joining the conversation. (His brother Thomas, one of the Proctors of the Ecclesiastical Court of the Cathedral, was, according to his tombstone, a singer and famous for the suavity of his manners and the probity of his profession.) Dr. Johnson was especially fond of Henry and once said that he was the rising strength of Lichfield. The presence of his favorite and the visitor from the university cheered the sick old man. Rising, he said to Anna:

"Come, my dear lady, let you and I attend these gentlemen in the study."

In the study he made them welcome and seated himself oddly astride a chair with his face to the back, keeping up a trotting motion as if on horse back, and talked as only he could talk, with wit and humor and good-nature. The others seconded him. Anna told about an educated pig, a wonderful educated pig which she had seen at Nottingham. Dr. Johnson was amused.

"Then," said he, "the pigs are a race unjustly calumniated. *Pig* has, it seems, not been wanting to *man*, but *man* to *pig*.

We do not allow him time for his education, we kill him at a year old."

"If this instance had happened in or before Pope's time," observed Henry White, "he would not have been justified in instancing the swine as the lowest degree of grovelling instinct," referring to the lines in the *Essay on Man;*

> How instinct varies in the grovelling swine,
> Compared, half-reasoning elephant, with thine.

"Much torture must have been employed to subdue the indocility of the animal," continued Mr. White.

"Certainly," agreed the doctor, "How old was your pig?" he asked Anna.

"Three years," she told him.

"Then," said he, "the pig has no cause to complain; he would have been killed the first year if he had not been *educated,* and protracted existence is a good recompence for a very considerable degree of torture."

Dr. Johnson could be charming when he chose, but in Lichfield he did not always choose. His friends must have sometimes said after a delightful call like this one, "Oh, why can't he always be like this!"

Dr. Johnson stayed with Lucy at Redcourt except on the occasion when he brought Boswell with him, and again when he accompanied the Thrales. Lucy, who had been pretty as a girl, with blue eyes, blond hair, and a fresh complexion, was now a faded woman with an odd taste in dress. She had always had a strong sense of duty and she had taken over as her own responsibility Dr. Johnson's mother from the time of his marriage to her own mother. One might say that she exchanged mothers with Samuel Johnson. On market days when trade was brisk she took "Granny's" place behind the counter, "nor," says Anna Seward, "nor thought it a disgrace to thank a poor person who purchased from her a penny battledore," a battledore being in this case a hornbook, or primer, shaped like a racquet. Anna thought Lucy's shrewdness, piquant humor, truth, and cheerfulness offset her mulish obstinacy and slipshod speech. In spite of Lucy's years of poverty and in spite of her working-class habit of serving at times behind the shop counter, the socially elect were her friends and were only amused at her odd ways. She was thrifty to a fault, and honest to the last farthing. When Dr. Johnson sent her from London material for a gown like Mrs. Thrale's, she was pleased with his thoughtfulness and the kindness of Miss Thrale who chose the pattern, but she was decidedly upset because she suspected that the carrier had overcharged for the transportation. In her letter of thanks she told him that she had just broken a very fine china cup and was always breaking her cups because she took her beer and ale warm, and asked if he would give or lend her a little half-pint silver cup which she remembered he had, and would he please send it to her if he had a chance [she thus avoided the over-charging carrier route], or bring it when he came.[2] One assumes that this was the silver cup marked "Sam" which little Samuel's mother bought for him when they made the trip to London for the child to be touched by the Queen to cure his scrofula. Tetty had had to sell this cup at the time of their dire poverty.

Lucy venerated her stepfather. She thought him almost next to the Deity, and Boswell was delighted to hear Lucy and some other ladies speak with affection as well as respect of the doctor when he was out of the room. The doctor seems to have been in awe of his sharp-tongued stepdaughter. It was reported that he meekly endured her scolding him like a schoolboy for tracking mud over her clean floor. This is significant, for one of the matters on which he and his wife had had words was her passionate love of cleanliness. She had, he told Mrs. Thrale, "a peculiar reverence for cleanliness . . . like those ladies who only sigh for the hour of sweeping their husbands out of the house as dirt and useless lumber: 'A clean floor is *so* comfortable,' she would say sometimes, by way of twitting; till at last I told her, that I thought we had had talk enough about the floor, we would now have a touch at the *ceiling*." There is no record of his putting up a defense against Lucy.

Indeed he was astonishingly meek before her. He wrote Mrs. Thrale during one visit when Lucy was ill: "Poor Lucy mends but slowly, but she is very good humored, while I do just as she would have me." Again, toward the end of a visit, "I behaved myself so well at Lichfield, that Lucy says I am grown better."

She spoke her mind, did Lucy. Said she in Johnson's presence to her friend, Rev. John Batteridge Pearson, Perpetual Curate of St. Michael's: "Why, Mr. Pearson, you are just like Dr. Johnson, I think; I do not mean that you are a man of greatest capacity in all the world, like Dr. Johnson, but that you contradict one every word one speaks, just like him." She evidently liked that type of man, for she left her fortune to this same Rev. Pearson.

Dr. Johnson was attached to his stepdaughter. In letters written from her house he complained about her lack of affection, just as he complained about other people's indifference. He was seldom sure that she wished him to prolong his visits, but there again one cannot be sure that this was not a fancy bred of home-sickness for London and London friends. He was very conscious of her failings and mentioned them in letters, but he was often frank about flaws in the personalities of those whom he dearly loved. He could write: "Miss Lucy is more kind and civil than I expected, and has raised my esteem by many excellencies very noble and resplendent, though a little discoloured by hoary virginity." That was rather cruel, but the phrase was too felicitous for the coiner to resist putting it on paper; it is one of the jewels in the Johnsonian treasury.

A kindlier and probably a truer summing up appears in a letter to Mrs. Thrale in 1771: "Lucy is a philosopher, and considers me as one of the external and accidental things that are to be taken and left without emotion. If I could learn of Lucy, would it be better? Will you teach me?"

"I hope we may long continue to gain friends," wrote Johnson to Boswell, "but the friends which merit or usefulness can procure us, are not able to supply the place of old acquaintance, with whom the days of youth may be retraced, and those images revived which gave the earliest delight." This was à propos of the death of Harry Jackson, an old schoolmate linked to Johnson only by the past and by Johnson's benevolent attitude toward men whom others disdained and avoided as tiresome failures.

Two friends with whom the days of youth were happily retraced were Elizabeth Aston and Mrs. Jane Gastrell, sisters of the beauteous Molly Aston, now deceased, who had briefly cheered the winter of his discontent when he was prowling after fame and finding only failure. Although Elizabeth Aston—with the courtesy title Mrs.—was elderly and an invalid, her house was a social gathering place. During Dr. Johnson's Lichfield visits he was always happy when he was there. He enjoyed being pampered, and these sisters petted and admired him to their hearts' content. Yet when Anna Seward tempted Dr. Johnson into an analysis of Mrs. Aston's personality, he did not resist picking the lady to pieces in a way in which he would not have spoken had she been present. His letters from Lichfield bear witness to his unceasing enjoyment of Mrs. Aston's companionship and when he was destroying personal documents during his last days, he said that Aston's letters would be the last papers he burned. Dr. Johnson blew hot and blew cold, and was seldom temperate in expressing the mood which had him temporarily in its grip. Even taking Anna's inaccuracy and exaggeration into account, his attitude toward his friend was critical.

"I have often heard my mother say, Doctor," said Anna, "that Mrs. Elizabeth Aston was, in her youth, a very beautiful woman; and that, with all the censoriousness and spiteful spleen of a very bad temper, she had great power of pleasing; that she was lively, insinuating, and intelligent. I knew her not till the vivacity of her youth had long been extinguished, and I confess I looked in vain for the traces of former ability. I wish to have *your* opinion, Sir, of what she was, *you* who knew her so well in her *best* days."

"My dear," replied the Doctor, according to Anna, "when thy mother told thee Aston was handsome, thy mother told thee the truth: she was very handsome. When thy mother told thee that Aston loved to abuse her neighbors, she told thee the truth; but when thy mother told thee that Aston had any marked ability in that same abusive business, that wit gave it zest, or imagination colour, thy mother did not tell thee the truth. No, no, Madam, Aston's understanding was not of any strength, either native or acquired."

"But, Sir, I have heard you say, that her sister's [Magdalen] husband, Mr. Walmesley, was a man of bright parts, and extensive knowledge; that he was also a man of strong passions, and, though benevolent in a thousand instances, yet irascible in as many. It is well known, that Mr. Walmesley was considerably governed by this lady [Elizabeth Aston], as witness Mr. Hinton's [Curate of the Parish of St. Chad] constant visits, and his presence at his table, in despite of its master's avowed aversion. Could it be, that, without some marked intellectual powers, she could obtain absolute intellectual dominion over such a man?"

Dr. Johnson leaped to Walmesley's defence:

"Madam, I have said, truly, that Walmesley had bright and

extensive powers of mind; that they had been cultivated by familiarity with the best authors, and by connections with the learned and polite. It is a fact, that Aston obtained nearly absolute domination over his will; it is no less a fact, that his disposition was irritable and violent. But Walmesley was a man; and there is no man who can resist the repeated attacks of a furious woman. Walmesley had no alternative but to submit, or turn her out of doors."

The circumstances which occasioned Mrs. Gastrell's taking up her abode in Lichfield were curious. Her husband, Rev. Francis Gastrell, Vicar of Frodsham in Chester, a man of property, bought, in 1753, New Place, in Stratford, the house in which Shakespeare spent the last nineteen years of his life. In the garden of this place grew the famous mulberry tree supposedly planted by Shakespeare, which Rev. Gastrell cut down because it shaded the house. The irate villagers showed their displeasure by breaking his windows, and the overseers taxed his property more heavily than the clergyman thought fit. Angrily he removed his house from the tax list by razing it, selling the timbers, and moving to Lichfield where he was already accustomed to spend a part of each year. This at any rate is the story which has come down to us.

Mrs. Elizabeth Aston built her house, Stowe Hill, in 1754. She bought for her sister, Mrs. Gastrell, the neighboring house, nearer Stowe Pool, called Stowe House which had been built in 1750 by Rev. Thomas Hinton, Canon of the Royal Free Chapel of St. George at Windsor and Curate of the Parish of St. Chad. This was the Mr. Hinton whom, according to the foregoing conversation, Mrs. Aston bullied reluctant Mr. Walmesley into receiving as a guest, and it was this house which Edgeworth subleased for himself and Day in 1770.

An unsubstantiated reputation of a shrewish disposition

218

hovers over Mrs. Gastrell as well as over Mrs. Aston, but we have the testimony of her tombstone that she was constantly engaged in acts of secret and extensive charity, and bequeathed a considerable part of her property to benevolent institutions. Twenty-eight lines of poetry tell of her "silent aid, by soothing pity giv'n" to orphans, debtors, slaves, and missionary societies. This statement is substantiated by her will dividing the large property, which, as last of the sisters, she inherited, into a large number of bequests to relatives, friends, and the needy of Lichfield.

The secret of Dr. Johnson's contentment in the company of two ladies who were not noted for the placidity of their dispositions may lie in the fact that bad temper does not alienate those on whom it is not turned. Indeed, one feels an amused complacency in being immune to the barbs directed at others. Moreover, fractious individuals commonly exempt certain persons from their ill humor to prove to themselves that they are really kind and long-suffering. Johnson found the asperity of these ladies amusing. When the races were on in August 1777, he wrote Mrs. Thrale that he and the sisters had been to neither race nor ball. "Mrs. Gastrell wraps her head in a towel and is very angry at the present mode of dress and feathers."

Dr. Johnson spent many hours at Mrs. Aston's. Dinner in Lichfield was customarily served at two, and dinner guests were expected to stay late, sometimes till after supper which was served at nine. In 1779 Johnson writes that he had made six visits to Stowe in eight days. The story that Johnson wrote much of his *Lives of the Poets* at a table by the window of the room where the sisters and their friends worked and talked, has been doubted, but certainly he had time enough to do a good bit of work between meals. Here it was that the doctor climbed with difficulty over the high gate because he had done it as a boy; and on the gravel walk in front of the house he ran a race with a Miss Innes, winning in spite of his bulk because the lady laughed so hard.

The doctor was at his ease and therefore at his best with the sisters. He was not on his guard against real or imaginary slights, nor was he under the strain of competing with other guests, as was the case in other drawing rooms. He relaxed in the atmosphere of admiration and affection. This gentleness is brought out in a series of anecdotes by Rev. Samuel Hay Parker, chaplain to the Corporation of Stratford-on-Avon and Curate of Bishopton, whose mother was brought up in the family of Sir Thomas and Lady Aston.

Mrs. Gastrell thought to amuse the doctor by setting a little girl to recite Cato's soliloquy. The child showed off to perfection, not missing a word. The pundit was not amused.

"What brought Cato to his end?" asked the doctor after a pause.

"A knife," replied the child.

"No, my dear, it was not so."

"My Aunt Polly said it was a knife," protested the child loyally.

"Why, Aunt Polly's knife *may do*, but it was a *dagger*, my dear. Now, what is the meaning of bane and antidote?" he inquired.

The little girl could not answer that one, and Mrs. Gastrell interposed, protesting,

"You cannot expect so young a child to know the meaning of such words."

"My dear, how many pence are there in a sixpence?"

The child by this time was confused. Not so had Aunt Polly conducted lessons. She was afraid of this large, strange man who did not applaud her recitation.

"I cannot tell, Sir," she replied.

"Now, my dear lady," said he to Mrs. Gastrell, "can anything be more ridiculous than to teach a child Cato's soliloquy, who does not know how many pence there are in a sixpence?"

One hopes the little girl got a sugar-plum to console her.

We do not know whether it was Mrs. Gastrell or Mrs. Aston who reproved Dr. Johnson for giving to the unworthy as well as to the worthy poor.

"There was that woman," said one of them, "to whom you gave a half-a-crown. Why, she was at church today in long sleeves and ribands!"

"Well, my dear," replied Johnson, "and if it gave the woman pleasure, why should she not wear them?"

At Stowe Hill the great man lived on the affectionate side of his nature. Although he wearied of the elderly chitchat and missed the exhilaration of whetting his wit on the sharp brains of London, yet he enjoyed the relaxation of the gentle ladies' society. He was secure in their admiration and happy in their love. It was the nearest he could come to being again a Lichfield boy in the loving shelter of his parents' home.

Mrs. Mary Cobb, widow of Thomas Cobb, a Lichfield mercer, was another elderly lady with whom Dr. Johnson spent much time when he was visiting in his home town. She lived at the Friary with her niece, Mary Adey. Mary Adey was the friend to whom Sally Seward wrote the brave letter about her happiness in her coming marriage, and Mary was later the third wife of John Sneyd. The Friary building was formerly an ancient monastery belonging to that branch of the Franciscans who were called Grey Friars, from their costume, a long grey habit, a hood, and a rope girdle, worn in memory of St. Francis. Later they were called Friars-minor because they were the lowest branch of their order, vowed to poverty. They were also called Mendicants because they begged from door to door, being thus distinguished from Monks who were confined to their monasteries. After the dissolution of the order by Henry the Eighth and the sale of ecclesiastical property, The Friary, built in 1545, came into private hands and was leased as a dwelling place.

In the case of Mrs. Cobb, as in the case of Mrs. Aston, Dr. Johnson, again egged on by Anna Seward who incited him to pick flaws, analysed Mrs. Cobb's personality with more acumen than kindness.

"How should Moll Cobb be a wit!" Anna reports him to have said in company. "Cobb has read nothing, Cobb knows nothing; and where nothing has been put into the brain, nothing can come out of it to any purpose of rational entertainment."

"Then why is Dr. Johnson so often her visitor?" someone asked.

"O! I love Cobb—I love Cobb for her impudence."

Miss Seward's own summing up, after Mrs. Cobb's death, was not unlike this portrait. She said that Mrs. Cobb had a strong understanding, quick perceptions, and wit that was shrewd, comic, sarcastic and original.

There is a likeness in the personalities of the women whose society Dr. Johnson enjoyed. This comes out clearly if one adds to the Lichfield ones the London ladies whom he found congenial. The list includes two young writers; one, Fanny Burney, the novelist, friend and protégée of Mrs. Thrale, and like Johnson a visitor who was almost a member of the Thrale family, and the other Hannah More, at that time a popular dramatist. Among the older London women were Mrs. Elizabeth Montagu and Mrs. Elizabeth Vesey whose evening gatherings he enjoyed; a third Elizabeth, the learned Mrs. Carter; and the blind poetess Anna Williams to whom he gave a home in his own house.

The women friends of Lichfield and London had a noticeable number of traits in common. Each was a woman of moral rectitude, honesty, veracity and reliability. The doctor could tolerate in men drunkenness, lying, dishonesty, and adultery, forgiving what was bad for the sake of what was fine in their characters, but for women he had a high standard. There never was a shadow on the fair fame of his women friends.

"A man should marry first, for virtue," said Dr. Johnson; "Secondly for wit, thirdly, for beauty, and fourthly, for money."

The first and second of these qualities he demanded in friendship as well as in marriage, but beauty was not important to him personally. Only two of his women friends have left a reputation for loveliness: the long-remembered Molly Aston and gracious, austere Hill Boothby.

He did not require a sweet disposition. The dear Lichfield ladies were gossips, and their tongues were frequently malicious. Learning, though not mentioned in the above list, he esteemed highly. All but three—his wife, Lucy, and Mrs. Cobb —had book-learning, and the natural intelligence of these three nonscholarly ones compensated for their lack of formal education. The acquirements of the others varied along a wide range: Latin; Latin and Greek; Latin, Greek and Hebrew; up to the prodigious scholarship of Elizabeth Carter who, in addition to the dead languages, toyed with Arabic, spoke modern languages, and was at home in the sciences.

Most women who studied in a serious way read Latin by stealth and concealed their interest like a secret sin; an attitude which perchance gave a fillip to dreary conjugations. But these women admitted their scholarship and even preened themselves on their learning, while their friends boasted of their achievements. A small amount of manuscript from a female pen was rewarded with rich praise. Mrs. Montagu won the title of "Our Aspasia" on the strength of one essay defending Shakespeare from Voltaire's criticism. Literary gems were passed about in script or printed (without payment) in *The Gentleman's Magazine*.

All of the ladies beloved by Dr. Johnson were sharp-witted.

The doctor delighted in women whose wits were as trigger-quick as his own. This does not mean that he liked a chatter-box whose tongue was hung in the middle. He once reproved a rattle who accused him of not liking ladies, with the words: "I am very fond of the company of ladies; I like their beauty, I like their delicacy, I like their vivacity, and I like their *silence.*" This was not accurate, for he liked them to talk cleverly but respectfully to him in such a manner as to draw out his own conversation. Giuseppe Barretti, who was a tutor at the Thrales and a travel-writer, said that Dr. Johnson always talked best to the ladies.

A trait which was *sine qua non* was rationality. Not one of the women lacked common sense. Dr. Johnson was not attracted by capriciousness, irresponsibility, and whimsy. He preferred the prudence which avoids risks.

The greater number of the women he liked were either spinsters or widows of long standing. Lucy Porter, Hill Boothby, Elizabeth Aston, Hannah More, and Elizabeth Carter died unwed, and Fanny Burney married rather late in life. Mrs. Gastrell, Mrs. Montagu, and Mrs. Cobb did not remarry after their husbands' deaths. These women seem not to have been tormented by love. Molly Aston married and moved from Lichfield so soon that we know nothing definite of her temperament. Three, in contrast, were warm-hearted women each of whom was swept off her feet by love. Mrs. Vesey went mad after the death of her second husband, who in the eyes of her women friends was nothing to grieve about, though men liked him. The remaining two, Johnson's wife and Mrs. Thrale, each of whom Johnson loved with all his heart, made passionate marriages after the deaths of their first husbands.

CHAPTER XVII

Dr. Johnson Brings Friends

TWO of Dr. Johnson's visits to Lichfield were enjoyable beyond all the other visits. Each was a holiday without a shadow. The first was in 1774 when he stopped for three days with Mr. and Mrs. Thrale on the way to Mrs. Thrale's birthplace in Wales, and the second was when three years later he showed the town to Boswell.

The Thrale party arrived in Lichfield Wednesday, July 6, traveling in the Thrale carriage with post horses hired at two shillings a mile, and put up at the Swan Inn. When Mrs. Thrale came down to breakfast the Thursday morning, dressed in the riding habit which, according to the custom of the time, she wore for traveling even though she was not riding horseback, Dr. Johnson insisted on her returning to her room and dressing formally for the round of visits.

The party called first of all on Lucy Porter who had now been living nearly ten years in her handsome house, Redcourt. They then went to the beautiful Cathedral which the Thrales had never seen. A call on Mrs. Aston at Stowe Hill came next, and then Johnson took them to Greene's Museum. This collection of antiques and curiosities was the pride of the town, and its owner, Richard Greene, was a man of standing, holding in turn the offices of Sheriff, Junior Bailiff, Senior Bailiff, and Alderman. According to Boswell he claimed kinship to Johnson, but the relationship has not been traced.

As a young man Greene was apprenticed to an apothecary-surgeon in Shrewsbury. He came to Lichfield in 1741 or 1742 and established himself as a surgeon-apothecary in Market Street in a house which is now a shop and is marked by a plaque. He is sometimes given the title of doctor and at other times is referred to as Mr. The titles Dr., Mr., Surgeon, and Apothecary were loosely applied. A physician like Dr. Darwin had a degree from a university; a surgeon served an apprenticeship in his profession and might or might not have a degree. A barber-surgeon was not attached to a hospital. An apothecary made up and sold medicine but could not charge for the advice he gave. An unlicensed practitioner, like Dr. Johnson's friend and housemate, Robert Levett, was one who had picked up his skill where and when he could; chiefly he learned by experience. The training was so unstandardized that it is frequently difficult to determine in which grade a medical practitioner belonged.

Richard Greene started collecting rarities early. It is not known when he first opened his celebrated museum, but the *Universal Magazine* for 1748 contains a letter from a Lichfield friend giving a description of a curious clock in Greene's possession. The Museum soon had a brave showing of "Curossitees." Greene's 1777 catalogue lists: Animals (preserved) viz., birds, etc.; Shells, corals, etc.; Stones, fossils, etc.; Woods, seeds and fruits; Roman and other coins; Dresses and ornaments of the natives of Otaheite; Remains of antiquity, urns, etc.; A Roman Breviary, a musical altar clock, etc.[1]

Greene's brother, Rev. Joseph Greene, head-master of the Free School at Stratford, who often rode over to Lichfield to visit his brother and enjoy the company of his friends, wrote him as early as Dec. 21, 1757:

"You desire I would not laugh at you for procuring a Magick Lanthorn, etc: but why my dear Brother should you imagine I should deal so ludicrously with You? Are you yet to be told that I have and always had a sameness of thinking with you in almost every respect? And let me tell you if I had as many Curossities (as ye Shew-men call them) as you have, viz. uncommon Clocks, Antiquities, Lanthornes, Monsters, etc., I would not be laugh'd out of them by ever a prig in England." [2]

After Mr. Greene's death the museum passed into the hands of his son-in-law, Dr. Wright, who exhibited the contents in a house in the Close. After Dr. Wright's death the exhibits were sold. The fossils and minerals were bought by Sir John St. Aubyn for a hundred pounds. The arms and armour were exhibited in the Egyptian Hall in London and later added to the collection in the Tower of London. Some of the articles came back to Lichfield and are in the present museum. One of these is "an organ, built originally by Father Smith, for the use of the Cathedral Church of Lichfield, after its destruction by the fanatics during the Oliverian usurpation when no part of that goodly fabric, fit for the celebration of Divine Service was left, but the Chapter House. This instrument was given to Mr. John Alcock, the then organist, by Dean Penny, in 1750, who sold it to Richard Greene in 1760."

When Dr. Johnson's party left the museum they went to see Mr. Andrew Newton's china. Mr. Newton's residence came near being a museum. Andrew and his brother Thomas were the sons of John Newton who had made a fortune in the brandy and cider trade. Thomas was not much in Lichfield after he left the grammar school, for he entered the Church and was rapidly advanced from honor to honor until he was the Bishop of Bristol. But Andrew lived in Lichfield and was a benefactor to the town. He financed repairs to the cathedral, provided books for its library, and did many minor deeds which showed a kindly nature, like providing suitable frocks for Elizabeth Saville Smith's concert singing. His great benefaction was the building of a substantial edifice at the West Entrance to the Close for the residence of twenty aged and necessitous widows or unmarried daughters of clergymen preferably of the Cathedral. They must needs be at least fifty years of age and have no income above thirty pounds a year. By his will he made bequests to public charities, to the Free School, and to the home which he had established.

This generous and kindly gentleman was passionately proslavery. He explained to Anna Seward that the British Empire could not be maintained without slavery and that severe discipline was necessary to rule sordid and insensible natures. When she demurred, he reminded her of the brutal murder of Ashwell, a West India planter, whose nieces lived in Lichfield, and the mutilation of his young nephew who had been left for dead. This crippled youth told Anna that his uncle had been soft and indulgent even to weakness in his relation to the treacherous, ungrateful, bloody-tempered slaves. When Josiah Wedgewood, of pottery fame, assured Anna by letter and pamphlet that the national interests would not be ruined by the abolition of slavery, Anna was relieved that she did not have to uphold an institution so abhorrent to her own spirit.

Mr. Newton's pro-slavery views and his political convictions alienated him from his nephew and heir, Henry Barry, later Colonel Barry, prominent in the war in America. Young Mr. Barry was a member of the Lichfield coterie and was in love with Honora. He was accustomed in later years to give as explanation of his never marrying, his inability to find her equal. Mr. Barry was said to have studied politeness from Chesterfield, poetry from the best critics, moral philosophy and style from Johnson. When he lost his uncle's immense fortune by arguing with him on politics, Anna Seward admired him for his manly avowal of his convictions. A man who would rather give up a fortune than hold his tongue was qualified to shine in the Lichfield group.

The large house of The Nabob, as Mr. Newton was locally called, was crammed with pictures, objects of art, curiosities, and Chinese oddities. One room was fitted up with sea shells and glistening minerals to represent a grotto. Mr. Newton lived with two elderly, oddly dressed sisters, and a great number of cats—a tabby, a tortoise, and a Persian among them. Miss Mary, one of the sisters, a cheery, industrious old lady who was ears to her deaf sister, was charitable to the poor and was cordial to all, died when seventy-nine from a tragic mistake. As a relief for a slight illness her brother Andrew gave her some pills which he had had made up for himself, of a harmless "extract of bark." She was taken violently ill, lapsed into insensibility and died. An apothecary examining the pills, found that they contained morphine, and Dr. Darwin confirmed the statement.

Dr. Johnson took his London friends to call also on Mrs. Cobb at the Friary, the Darwins in Beacon Street and, for a second time, on his very particular friend, Mrs. Aston. Saturday, their last day, they breakfasted with Peter Garrick and called on Miss Vyse. Dr. Johnson did not allow Mrs. Thrale to accompany him when he called on Anna Seward. Anna and Lucy had had a falling-out and when Anna finally made Mrs. Thrale's acquaintance, after the doctor's death, she expressed regret that "a slight shyness" between her and her cousin Lucy had prevented an earlier meeting.

Even more satisfactory was Johnson's visit to Lichfield with Boswell, from Friday evening, March 22nd, 1776, to the following Monday evening. The doctor did not fall into his

229

frequent state of Lichfield boredom. Each of the three days was crowded with entertainment and, cushioned by Boswell's excessive admiration and continual approval, Johnson was not so sensitive as sometimes to fancied disapprobation. Perhaps his own good humor encouraged increased cordiality in his fellow townsmen.

The travelers arrived after dark when the new street lights had been lit. "Now," quoth the doctor, "we are getting out of a state of death." These oil lamps were a fairly recent improvement. Not till 1750 did any residents have lights before their doors, and for this convenience they paid an annual rental of 5s. 10d. A 1772 list of private lamp renters shows twenty-five subscribers. Among those in the Close were Dr. Darwin, Dean Addenbrooke at the Deanery, Canon Seward at the Palace, and three lamps for the Cathedral. In the City were Mrs. Cobb at the Friary, William Inge in Market Street, and Brooke Boothby. For this same year it is recorded: "For putting up lamp at Mr. Garrick's [Peter] . . . 9. 8." [3]

Johnson and Boswell went to the Three Crowns Inn, next door to the house where Johnson was born. It was not a smart inn, but an old-fashioned house kept by Mr. Wilkins whom Johnson especially liked. The two men had a comfortable little supper. Boswell, drowsy with Lichfield ale, found the two-bedded chamber "tolerable," but evidently not quite to his taste, for the next day, when Peter Garrick invited them to take beds at his house, Boswell regretted Johnson's refusal. Johnson loved the freedom of an inn more than a soft bed.

The next morning, Saturday, Boswell was taken to Redcourt, which he describes as a stately house with a handsome garden, to meet Lucy Porter, "now an old maid with much simplicity of manner." Boswell was pleased to note that the relationship between Lucy and her stepfather was respectful and tender. Next came a visit to Peter Garrick's, David's brother, whom Boswell had already met at Dr. Johnson's in

London and at the Thrales'. Peter obligingly walked Boswell about the town and about the garden of his sister, Mrs. Docksey. Greene's Museum was visited and it was on this occasion that Greene claimed relationship with Johnson. Boswell found Greene a bustling, good-humored little man. Tea and coffee at Peter Garrick's concluded a busy day.

Sunday started off with breakfast at the Friary, "a sweet old sequestered place," with Mrs. Cobb and her niece Mary Adey. Boswell went to the Cathedral, and Johnson to St. Mary's. They dined at Peter Garrick's, finding their host in fine form for telling stories, and went together to the Cathedral. Boswell returned to the Garrick house for tea and coffee, and afterward joined Johnson at the Palace where he received a very good impression of Dr. Seward and met Anna. His verdict on her was that she was a rather pretty woman with bright eyes and a bad mouth. Did he mean a sharp tongue?

Monday was as full of engagements—breakfast at Lucy's, dinner at Mrs. Gastrell's, "a good, chatty, hospitable lady"; theatre in the evening; and, as guests to supper at the inn, Dr. Seward and Lucy's friend, Mr Pearson, "a modest, well-behaved young man much esteemed by Mrs. Porter."[4]

Two dinners this week were sufficiently important to receive special mention in Boswell's record. On Saturday the travelers entertained an old school friend of Johnson, Mr. Harry Jackson, who made a poor impression on Boswell. He wore a coarse grey coat, a black waistcoat, greasy leather breeches, and Boswell thought he looked like a heavy drinker. Boswell found him dull and stupid, and indeed the conversation must have been boring, for it was a long account of Jackson's business failures as a cutler in Birmingham, and a confused scheme for improving his fortunes by a new method of dressing leather. Boswell noted Johnson's kindness and humanity in listening with patient attention and giving advice.

Monday's dinner was at Mrs. Gastrell's house. Boswell, who

had not met the lady, was not invited and he was aggrieved that Johnson went blithely off without a word of apology, considering it very bad manners on Johnson's part not to have him included. Before long came a note informing him that Mrs. Gastrell in the lower house on Stowe Hill desired Mr. Boswell's company at dinner at two, and Boswell's enthusiasm for his friend revived.

All pleasure was dulled by the receipt of a letter telling of the death of the Thrales' only son. The following morning the two went on to Ashbourne in Dr. Taylor's roomy chaise drawn by four stout horses driven by two postillions, and after a couple of days spent with Dr. Taylor they returned to London.

Boswell, visiting Lichfield later on without Dr. Johnson, reported to him by letter. Boswell was traveling with a Col. Stuart who was rejoining his regiment in Chester but kindly stayed over in Lichfield a half day to afford Boswell time for a run-around among his acquaintances. Col. Stuart preferred to stay at the George Inn which was smarter than the Three Crowns kept by Dr. Johnson's favorite inn-keeper, Mr. Wilkins. George Farquhar, the playwright, had put up at The George when billeted in Lichfield on recruiting service years before, and the inn is the scene of his play, *The Beaux Stratagem.* The innkeeper of that day and his daughter are featured in the comedy and Boniface puffs his ale as the best in Staffordshire, smooth as oil, sweet as milk, clear as amber, and strong as brandy.

The day after Boswell's arrival, a Tuesday in late October, 1779, was so rainy that he ordered a post-chaise to take him on his round of visits. He set out between eight and nine, and in two hours called on Mr. Greene of the Museum (who was out attending a visiting Bishop with gout), Mrs. Cobb (who was flurried at being caught at breakfast), Peter Garrick (who invited him to stay a week), Dr. Seward (who was in bed with a cold, wearing a white flannel night-gown over a black one, but good-humored and polite), Mrs. Gastrell (whose conversation he was loathe to leave), Mrs. Aston (whose health was better), and finally Mrs. Lucy Porter (a visit of sincere satisfaction on both sides). Dr. Johnson was the subject of the conversation at each house and all competed in praising him. In the rhetoric of the period one may say that guest and hostesses rode the sea of friendship on a raft of compliments, blown before a gale of adulation. Boswell asserted that never had he passed two hours with more self-complacency than these, as the friend of Dr. Johnson.

Dr. Johnson's death occurred in 1784, less than two months after his last visit to his home town. (David Garrick had died first of all the Johnson group in 1779.) Mrs. Aston died, following a long illness, the next year, and Lucy Porter the year after. Mrs. Gastrell lived till 1791, and Mrs. Cobb till 1795. Their last years were full of illness and loneliness except perhaps in the case of Mrs. Cobb who had a lively spirit and a dutiful niece. Dr. Taylor lived four years longer that Dr. Johnson. Peter Garrick was vigorous and hearty until his mind failed pathetically a few years before his death at the age of eighty-five.[5]

Of the younger group most of whom must be classed as acquaintances rather than intimates of Johnson—Erasmus Darwin, Anna Seward, John Saville, Sir Brooke Boothby, and Henry White—all lived into the next century. These junior associates kept up their interest in music, attending musical festivals in the nearby cities, staging their own amateur concerts, and enjoying musical house parties in the homes of the neighboring gentry. They got in a fair amount of travel in their own

chaises drawn by hired post horses, and they contributed their
share of published prose and poetry. Yet they had plenty of
sadness and pain. Saville's death was a shattering blow to
Anna Seward.[6] She showed the essential nobility of her nature
by assuming the financial support of his family, including his
estranged wife.[7] Sir Brooke Boothby, marrying a small,
crippled, pleasant woman, secured a fortune to replace the
two he had spent, but they lost their only child, a darling
little girl named Penelope, the idol of their hearts.[8] Another
associate must be mentioned; one who was in the group but
not of it—Francis Barber, Dr. Johnson's Negro servant. After
his master's death, Barber came with his family to live in
Lichfield. So long as the money left him by the doctor lasted
he lived in Stowe Street and occupied himself with gardening,
reading, and fishing in Stowe Pond. Later he moved to a
neighboring hamlet where he kept a school. After his death
his wife returned to Lichfield and herself opened a school,
probably a dame school for young children.[9]

Dr. Johnson's Lichfield friends were bound together by belonging to the same race, the same nation, and to the same
class of society, as well as by common Lichfield memories and
interests. Their relation to each other was that of the fingers
of an outstretched hand, held together by a common attachment to a palm which they did not choose but accepted as
inevitable. These people had the same background of social
customs, domiciliary habits, urban government, educational
training, church affiliations, ethical standards, religious habits,
and current prejudices. Basically they were alike, but indivi-
dually they differed. The group reminds one of a huge family
portrait piece in which a household poses on the lawn, each
member ostentatiously preserving his own personality: the
father is accompanied by his pointer, the mother holds the
littlest baby in her arms, toddlers cling to her skirts, the heir
is gallantly mounted, the oldest daughter is beautiful, assorted

children treasure hoops and whips and apples, and a couple of servants busy themselves with a tea equipage. The family resemblance is striking, yet no one member could be mistaken for another.

Notes and References

CHAPTER I

1 LAITHWAITE, PERCY, M. Sc. *A History of St. Chad's Church.* Privately printed, Lichfield, 1938. St. Chad's Well which had been long neglected was restored in 1949, its grounds made into a garden, and a caretaker's cottage built.

2 HARWOOD, REV. THOMAS *History and Antiquities of the Church and of Lichfield.* London, 1806. pp. 2–4; 509.

3 Ibid, pp. 19–26. Also Warner, Rev. Richard. *A Tour Through the Northern Counties of England and Borders of Scotland.* London, 1802. Vol. I, p. 11.

CHAPTER II

1 DEFOE, DANIEL *A Tour Through the Whole Island of Great Britain,* By a Gentleman. 4 Vols. London, 1753. Vol. II, p. 389. 5th Edition.

2 MORITZ, CARL PHILIP *Travels in England,* ed. by P. E. Matheson. New York, 1924. p. 186.

3 LAITHWAITE, PERCY, M. Sc. *The History of the Lichfield Conduit Lands Trust, 1546—1946.* Privately printed, Lichfield, 1947. In honor of the 400th anniversary of the Trust, Percy Laithwaite, Esq., Honorary Secretary of the Johnson Society, wrote a brochure on its history, having dug out information from a four-hundred-year mass of nearly undecipherable records stored in an ancient chest, safeguarded by three locks, the keys of which were kept in the respective custody of a sideman, a constable and a warden.
   The Trust was devised to save from the greedy fingers of Edward VI the lands containing the headwaters at Aldershaw

and the fields through which water pipes ran to the town. Henry VIII had dissolved the religious orders, including Lichfield's Order of the Friars Minor and sold or given to favorites houses, lands, and riches. Lichfield knew what impended when Edward began looting guilds, which, as governing bodies of the smaller cities, held property in trust for the citizens. Hector Beane, the Lichfield Guildmaster, shrewdly circumvented the royal thief by transferring the ownership of essential lands to a committee of trustees. Although the duties of the Trust have been somewhat rearranged during the past four hundred years, the agency still functions and maintains high standards of efficiency and usefulness.

The property at first consisted of only five houses and their acres which the committee leased to tenant farmers, but so well administered were the rents that they not only covered the expense of maintaining the water system, but as the years went by enabled the trustees to buy more land, enlarge the system, and finally to contribute to the welfare of citizens by grants of money to individuals and by cooperation with other agencies.

4 READE, ALEYN LYELL *Johnsonian Gleanings.* 10 vols. Privately printed, London. Vol. X, pp. 4–12.

5 HARWOOD op. cit. p. 536–8.

6 READE op. cit. Vol. X, pp. 5, 6, 16, 18–20. Also, Hill, George Birkbeck, ed. *Boswell's Life of Johnson.* 6 Vols. Oxford, 1887. Vol. I, pp. 35ff, 80; IV, p. 372n2.

7 HARWOOD op. cit. pp. 299, 380. From 1386 the title was "Lichfield and Coventry"; in 1836 Coventry was annexed to Worcester and the title became "The Diocese of Lichfield."

8 READE, ALEYN LYELL *The Reades of Blackwood Hill . . . Dr. Johnson's Ancestry His Kinfolk and Family Connexions.* Privately printed, 1906, pp. 171ff.

CHAPTER III

1 READE op. cit. Vol. I, p. 110.

2 The property of Mr. Pennant of St. Asaph, Wales, whose ancestor received it from Lucy Porter.

3 READE, ALEYN LYELL *The London Times Literary Supplement,* June 17, 1947. Also: Ellic Howe, letter in same periodical, June 24, 1949.

4 Ibid.

5 The John Rylands Library, Manchester, England   Eng. Ms. No. 565. Letter 3. f. 1a. 1b. 2a. *Letter from Anna Seward to Mrs. Piozzi,* accompanying a packet of letters written by Dr. Johnson to Hill Boothby. Also: Seward, Anna. *Letters of Anna Seward.* 6 Vols. Edinburgh, 1811. Vol. II, pp. 103, 349. Also: Croker, John Wilson, ed. *Boswell's Life of Johnson.* 10 Vols. London, 1872. pp. 57ff.

6 SEWARD   op. cit. Vol. II, pp. 347–8. Also: Reade, op. cit., Vol. 10, p. 137. Also: Smith-Dampier, L. J. *Who's Who in Boswell.* Oxford, 1935. p. 27.

CHAPTER IV

1 DODSLEY, ROBERT, ED.   *A Collection of Poems by Several Hands.* 6 Vols. London, 1763. pp. 294–301. This volume contains two other poems by Dr. Seward.

2 The principal works of the Lichfield and closely associated writers are: Sir Brooke Boothy: *Sorrows Sacred to the Memory of Penelope* (1792), Brittanicus, *Fables and Satires* (1803) and political pamphlets. Dr. Erasmus Darwin: *The Botanic Garden* (1781 and 1789), *Zoomania, or the Laws of Organic Life* (1794–6) *Phytologia; or the Philosophy of Agriculture and Gardening* (1791). Anna Seward: *Monody on Major André* (1781), *Sonnets* (1772–1799) *Louisa* (1781), *Life of Dr. Darwin* (1804), *Letters* (posthumously published 1811–3). Thomas Day: *Sanford and Merton* (1783–9). Richard Lovell Edgeworth, educational books. Thomas Sedgewick Whalley: *Edwy and Edilda* (1779), *The Castle of Montval* (1781), *Kenneth and Fenella* (1809). William Hayley: *The Triumphs of Temper* (1781).

3 SCHIMMELPENNICK, MARY ANN   *Life of Mary Ann Schimmelpennick,* ed. by C. C. Hankin. London, 1858.

CHAPTER V

1 The Johnson Birthplace Collection of Letters. *Letter from Anna Seward to Unknown Correspondent.* n. d. The final paragraph

in slightly altered form is reproduced in *Works of Anna Seward,* ed. by Sir Walter Scott. 3 Vols. Edinburgh, 1810. Vol. I, p. lxxxv.

2 The R. B. Adam Collection of manuscripts, temporarily in the Rush Rees Library, University of Rochester, New York State, now owned by Mr. and Mrs. Donald Hyde, Somerville, N. J. *Letter from Dr. Seward to Sarah Seward.* July 14, no year.

3 Birthplace Collection, op. cit. *Letter from Sarah Seward to Mary Adey.*

CHAPTER VI

1 Johnson Birthplace Collection, op. cit. *Letter of Anna Seward to Mrs. Sykes.* 1773.

2 Ibid. *Letter of Anna Seward to her Publisher.* June 14, 1802.

CHAPTER VII

1 The Rev. Sir John Every, 7th baronet, Rector of Waddington, Co. Lincoln; b. 1709; married Dorothy Parkman; d. 1779.

2 Robinson, Rev. Richard George, Chancellor's Vicar, Lichfield Cathedral. Manuscript, in possession of the writer, dated 27th October, 1812.

3 WOODEFORDE, REV. JAMES *Passages from the Diary of a Country Parson,* ed. by John Beresford. Oxford, 1955. pp. 173ff, 421ff.

4 SHERWOOD, MARY MARTHA *The Life of Mrs. Sherwood,* ed. by Sophia Kelly. London, 1887. p. 11.

CHAPTER VIII

1 READE op. cit. Vol. II, p. 113. Also: Ashmun, Margaret. *The Singing Swan.* Yale University Press, 1931. pp. 5–6.
Entries in the Seward Family Bible, some dates being incorrect: Thomas Seward was married to Elizabeth Hunter at Newton-in-the-Thistle in Warwickshire on the 27th. Oct., 1742.
    And to them was born a daughter on the 1st Dec. 1744. She was baptised Anne on the 28th of the same month, her Sponsors were her Uncle Norton, her Aunt Martin, and Mrs. Jackson of Burton.

To them was born another Daughter 17th March, 1746. She was baptised Sarah on 25th May, her Sponsors were her Uncle Seward, her Aunt Norton, and Mrs. Simpson of Lichfield.

(Then follow entries of five births and early deaths.)

Sarah Seward departed this Life June 13th. 1764, aged Nineteen years, two Months and Sixteen Days. Buried in the Lady Choir of the Cathedral in Lichfield.

(The above is in Dr. Seward's handwriting. The two following entries are in Anna's hand.)

On the last day of July 1780 Elizth. Wife of Thomas Seward departed this Life, aged 66, and was buried in the Lady Choir, ...

On Thursday the 4th of March, 1790, the Revd. Thomas Seward departed this Life aged 81 and was buried in the Choir. . . . . .

(The final entry is in the handwriting of Nancy Hall, friend and servant in the Seward family.)

On the 25th March 1809 Anna Seward departed this Life aged 65. She was buried in the Choir . . .

Also: Scott, op. cit. Vol. I, p. lxxxviii. Anna wrote to a friend that she "took an eternal farewell of teens" on Dec. 12, 1763.

See also: *Modern Philology,* Nov. 1941: an article by Dr. James L. Clifford, *The Authenticity of Anna Seward's Published Correspondence.*

2 Information from LAITHWAITE op. cit.

3 Information from James R. Beard, Esq., great-great-great-grandson of John Saville.

4 *Aris's Birmingham Gazette,* Sept. 5, 1796.

5 SHENSTONE, WILLIAM *Verses Written toward the Close of the Year 1748.* (Anna Seward misquoted the verse.)

6 HARWOOD op. cit. pp. 271ff. The Vicars Choral were of two types; priest-vicars who deputized for the Canons, and lay-vicars who were the men of the Cathedral choir. The Vicars Choral was a specifically chartered corporation with a common hall, a mace, and a seal, from at least as early as 1240. These gentlemen were a lively bunch with ideas as to their rights and privileges. The Vicars Choral had a dust-up with the Dean and Chapter after the Restoration when they called attention to the fact that they

who had numbered sixteen for over four hundred years were now only six and that three of their sixteen dwellings had been demolished besides their common hall. They pointed out that they kept the Vicars' Close clean while the Great Close was filthy from swine being kept by the inhabitants.

7   From unpublished letters, by permission of Prof. Harold E. Butler.

8   WHALLEY, DR. THOMAS SEDGEWICK   *Journals and Correspondence,* ed. by Rev. Hill Wickham. 2 Vols. London, 1863. Vol. I, p. 344.

9   Johnson Birthplace Collection, op. cit. *Letter from Anna Seward to Mrs. Sykes.*

10   WHALLEY   op. cit. Vol. I, p. 344.

11   PIOZZI, HESTER THRALE   *Letters to and from the Late Samuel Johnson.* 2 Vols. London, 1788. Vol. II, p. 359.

12   NICHOLS, JOHN   *Literary Anecdotes of the Eighteenth Century* 8 Vols. London, 1812–15. Vol. VIII, p. 432.

13   SEWARD   *Letters,* op. cit. Vol. I, p. 181.

14   Johnson Birthplace Collection, op. cit.   *Letter from Anna Seward to Charles Simpson,* 1800.

15   Ibid.   *Letter from Anna Seward to Mrs. Sykes,* 1773.

16   Ibid.   *Letter from Dr. Seward to Anna,* Nov. 12, 1771.

17   ROYDE-SMITH, NAOMI   *The State of Mind of Mrs. Sherwood.* London, 1946. p. 43.

18   Birthplace Collection, op. cit.   *Letter from Anna Seward to Mrs. Sykes,* August 29, 1778.

19   Permission of George Birch, Esq.

CHAPTER IX

1   HILL, GEORGE BIRKBECK, ED. *Letters of Samuel Johnson, LL.D.* 2 Vols. Harper's, New York, 1892. Vol. I, pp. 101–8. Also:

Journal of the Derbyshire Archaeological and Natural History Society, No. LX. 1939. New Series Vol. XIII. Also: any edition of Boswell's *Life*.

2 HAYWARD, A., ED. *Autobiography, Letters, and Literary Remains of Mrs. Piozzi* (Thrale). 2 Vols. London, 1861. Vol. I, pp. 111, 118. Also: Gaussen, Alice, ed. *A Later Pepys*. 2 Vols. London, 1894. Vol. I, pp. 50, 61.

3 WRIGHT, J. D., ED. *Some Unpublished Letters to and from Dr. Johnson*. Manchester University Press, 1932. pp. 17–24. Also: Taylor, John. *Records of my Life*. New York, 1833. Also: Polewhele, Richard. *Traditions and Recollections*. 2 Vols. London, 1826. Vol. II, pp. 566–73. Also: Johnson Birthplace Collection, op. cit. *Correspondence between Anna Seward and Pratt*. Also: Whalley, op. cit. Vol. I, pp. 322, 386, 437, 493, Vol. II, 28.

4 DARTON, J. HARVEY *The Life and Times of Mrs. Sherwood*. London, 1910. p. 78. Also: Bagot, Mrs. Charles. *Links with the Past*. London, 1901. Salop is the old name for Shropshire.

5 WHALLEY op. cit. and Seward, *Letters*, op. cit., in all volumes. Also: Knapp, Oswald G. *The Intimate Letters of Hester Piozzi and Penelope Pennington*. Lane, London, 1913. pp. 171–2. Also: De Quincey, Thomas. *Writings*, ed. David Masson. 14 Vols. Edinburgh, 1889. Vol. II, pp. 447–50.

6 SEWARD *Letters*, op. cit. and Whalley, op. cit. Much information in all volumes. The Burt episode, Whalley, Vol. II, p. 48ff. The Hayley episode, especially Seward; Vol. II, pp. 317–8.

CHAPTER X

1 SARGENT, WINTHROPE *Major John André*. Boston, 1860. The quotations from André's letters are from this book.

2 Johnson Birthplace Collection, op. cit. *Letter from Anna Seward to Mrs. Sykes*, Dec. 10, 1775.

3 Ibid. *Letter from Eliza Cottman to Anna Seward*, May 2, 1784. No published work of Miss Cottman has been found. She was probably one of the many ladies who sent their poems around in letters.

NOTES AND REFERENCES

CHAPTER XI

1 Robinson manuscript, op. cit.

2 Johnson Birthplace Collection. All the quoted letters from Day to Anna Seward are in this collection.

CHAPTER XII

1 Unpublished *Letter from Anna Seward to Mary Powys*. n. d. Permission of Prof. Harold E. Butler.

2 Johnson Birthplace Collection, op. cit. *Letter from Anna Seward to Mrs. Sykes*, July 27, 1773.

3 Ibid. June 16, 1776.

4 Ibid. n. d.

CHAPTER XIII

1 KRAUSE, ERNST *Erasmus Darwin*, translated by W. S. Dallas. Appleton, New York, p. 29.

2 GARDINER, DOROTHY *English Girlhood at School*. Oxford Press, 1929. pp. 347–8.

CHAPTER XIV

1 DELANY, MRS. PATRICK *The Autobiography and Correspondence of Mrs. Delany*, ed. by Sarah Chauncey Woolsey. 2 Vols. bound together. Boston, 1898. Vol. II, p. 224.

2 SHAW, REV. STEBBING *History of Staffordshire*. 2 Vols. London, 1798. Vol. II, p. 346.

3 The Close water system, which was distinct from that of the City, collected water from these springs some half mile away at Maple Hayes.

4 It was sometimes difficult to determine the author of some poem which was passed from hand to hand in manuscript. The common

practice of tinkering with each other's verses confused the owner-ship. Edgeworth stated in his memoirs that Darwin wrote much of Anna Seward's *Elegy on Captain Cook*. Samuel Pratt had all his friends revising his *Sympathy,* published it anonymously with intimations that it was Whalley's, then that it was Hayley's, and after it had been well received, claimed it as his own.

The genteel practice of publishing anonymously, the weakness of the copyright law, pirating by publishers, and the fact that magazines seldom paid for the verses they accepted, all added to the confusion. One of Dr. Seward's poems appeared in print some twenty years after it was written and no one knew how it had wandered into the editorial office. Anything in print was used without credit. Day in one of his prefaces wrote: "As to the histories themselves, I have used the most unbounded license; altering, curtailing, adding . . . those who are acquainted with literature will easily discover where I have borrowed, where I have imitated, and where I have invented; and to the rest of the world it is of little consequence. . . ."

CHAPTER XV

1 PARSONS, MRS. CLEMENT *Garrick and his Circle.* London, 1905. p. 21.

2 LAITHWAITE op. cit. pp. 18–24. The convenience of taps in private houses was allowed provided the householder had already both a cistern and a well. Lucy Porter was one of the first to avail herself of this privilege. By the time the gravity system was inadequate for the growing town, the steam pump had been invented, improved and tested. About the same time coal deposits were discovered on lands owned by the Trust, the value of which offset the cost of installing pumps.

3 READE op. cit. Part II. Francis Barber was born in Jamaica in the Parish of St. Mary on the Orange River estate belonging to Col. Richard Bathurst, father of Johnson's friend, the physician, Richard Bathurst. The elder Bathurst brought the lad to England, had him baptised, sent him to school, passed him on to his son, the doctor, who in turn consigned him to the care of Dr. Johnson.

4 BOWDEN, WITT *Industrial Society in England toward the End of the Eighteenth Century.* Macmillan, New York, 1925. pp. 295–303.

5 Johnson Birthplace Collection, op. cit.

6 Ibid.

7 Harwood op. cit. p. 353. Also: Thiselton, T. E. *British Popular Customs*. London, 1891. p. 173.

8 KRUTCH, JOSEPH WOOD *Samuel Johnson*. Holt, 1944. pp. 139–44.

9 When Croker, in his edition of Boswell's Life, printed this story from Johnsoniana, he added an editorial note; "Dr. Harwood informs me that Mr. Wickins was a respectable draper in Lichfield. It is very true that Dr. Johnson was accustomed to call on him during his visits to his native town. The garden attached to his house was ornamented in the manner he describes, and no doubt was ever entertained of the exactness of his anecdotes."

CHAPTER XVI

1 Adam Collection, op. cit. *Letter of William Hayley to Anna Seward,* Nov. 14, 1784.

2 CLIFFORD, JAMES L. *London Times Literary Supplement,* Aug. 28, 1937.

CHAPTER XVII

1 From a syllabus of Greene's Museum compiled 1777.

2 Johnson Birthplace Collection, op. cit. *Letter of Rev. Joseph Greene,* Dec. 21, 1757.

3 LAITHWAITE *Conduit Lands,* etc. op. cit. pp. 46–7.

4 BOSWELL, JAMES *Private Papers of James Boswell from Malahide Castle,* ed. by Geoffrey Scott and Frederick Pottle. 18 Vols., privately printed for Col. Isham, 1928-34. Vol. XI, p. 188 ff. Also, p. 184.

5 Peter Garrick in 1791, being then of a sane mind, drew up a will leaving most of his fortune of nearly 30,000 pounds to his sister,

Merrial Garrick Docksey. This will is filed at Somerset House, London, in the 1791 volume, call number Lichfield May 248. After his mind failed he fell under the influence of Stephen Panting, a Lichfield apothecary. When Peter died, Dec. 19, 1795, Panting produced a deed of gift, a codicil, and a will, drawn in 1795, leaving the fortune to Panting. Mrs. Docksey brought suit and the case was tried at the Stafford Assizes, March, 1796. Mrs. Docksey won the case and the 1791 will was proved at London, May 20, 1796.

6 John Saville died August 2nd, 1803, aged sixty-seven, having served as Vicar Choral for 48 years. His will is at the Probate Court of Birmingham, drawn Feb. 9, 1792, eleven years before his death. The will was proved Feb. 1, 1804. He bequeathed "To my wife Mary Saville all my property whatsoever and wheresoever, after lawful debts are paid, and after such of my papers and books as Anna Seward of the Close of the said Cathedral Church, spinster, shall choose to take for her own use". The proved estate was less than six hundred pounds.

7 Anna Seward died March 25, 1809. Anna drew up her own will, a long one, leaving gifts and mementoes to a wide circle of friends. She left to Mrs. Saville, with reversion to her daughter, Elizabeth Saville Smith, the house which she had bought for Saville when because of his failing health he needed a house large enough to accommodate his daughter also. She had been able to acquire the building because although most of the houses belonged to the Dean and Chapter, some remained in private hands. This house is now numbered "8, The Close", and the head-verger of the Cathedral lives in it. She settled an annuity of a hundred pounds on Elizabeth which with a fifty-pound annuity which she already received safeguarded her for life. Anna left a trust fund for Saville's granddaughter.

8 Penelope Boothby is said to have been an especially beautiful child. Her monument in the Ashbourne Church, executed by Thomas Bank, is lovely. On the sides of the pedestal which supports a sculptured marble child are infinitely touching inscriptions, one of which concludes with the words; "The unfortunate parents ventured their all on this frail bark, and the wreck was total." This inscription was severely criticised as unchristian. Wordsworth held that it had three gross faults: it expressed rebellious grief; it expressed violent, transitory passion; the "vicious sentiment"

was expressed fancifully and therefore out of place on a sculptured record. De Quincey, Thomas. *Collected Writings*, ed. by Masson. 14 Vols. Edinburgh, 1890. Vol. XI, p. 180n.

9   SHOLES, PERCY A.   The Great Dr. Burney. 2 Vols. Oxford Press, 1948. Vol. II, p. 163.

Bibliography

BIOGRAPHIES

JOHNSON, DR. SAMUEL:

Letters of Dr. Samuel Johnson, LL.D.—Ed. by George Birkbeck Hill. 2 Vols. London, Oxford Press, 1892.

Letters to and from the Late Samuel Johnson, LL.D.—Ed. by Hester Thrale Piozzi. 2 Vols. London, 1788.

The Queeney Letters.—Ed. by The Marquis of Lansdowne. London, Cassell, 1934.

Boswell's Life of Johnson.—Ed. by George Birkbeck Hill. 6 Vols. Oxford, 1887.

Boswell's Life of Johnson.—Ed. by John Wilson Croker. 10 Vols. London, 1872.

Anecdotes of the Late Samuel Johnson, LL.D.—In the Croker edition of the *Life,* op. cit.

Autobiography, Letters and Literary Remains of Mrs. Piozzi (Thrale).—Ed. by A. Hayward. 2 Vols. London, 1861.

Johnsonian Gleanings.—By Aleyn Lyell Reade. 10 Vols. Privately Printed. London, 1909–1946. Also: Reade's *The Reades of Blackwood Hill and Dr. Johnson's Ancestry.* London, privately printed, 1906.

BIBLIOGRAPHY

DARWIN, ERASMUS:

Erasmus Darwin.—By Ernst Krause. New York, Appleton, 1880.

Charles Darwin.—By H. Wells. Yale University Press, 1938.

Scientific Correspondence of Joseph Priestly.—By H. C. Bolton. New York, 1892.

Memoirs of the Life of Dr. Darwin.—By Anna Seward. Philadelphia, 1804.

ANNA SEWARD:

The Singing Swan.—By Margaret Ashmun. Yale University Press, 1931.

Letters of Anna Seward.—6 Vols. Edinburgh, 1811.

Complete Works of Anna Seward.—Ed. by Sir Walter Scott. Edinburgh, 1810.

MARY MARTHA BUTT SHERWOOD:

Three lives based on her own manuscript autobiography:

The Life of Mrs. Sherwood.—Ed. by Sophia Kelly. London, 1887.

The Life and Times of Mrs. Sherwood.—Ed. by J. Harvey Darton. London, 1910.

The State of Mind of Mrs. Sherwood.—By Naomi Royde Smith. London, Macmillan, 1946.

GENERAL:

Major John André.—By Winthrope Sargent. Boston, Tichnor, 1860.

The Exemplary Mr. Day.—By Sir S. H. Scott. New York, Putnam, 1935.

A Life of Thomas Day.—By George Gignilliat. Columbia University Press, 1932.

Memoirs of Richard Lovell Edgeworth.—By Richard Lovell and Maria Edgeworth. 2 Vols. Boston, 1821.

Intimate Letters of Hester Piozzi and Penelope Pennington—Ed. by Oswald G. Knapp. London, John Lane, 1913.

Journals and Correspondence of Thomas Sedgewick Whalley.—Ed. by Rev. Hill Wickham. London, 1863.

Handel's Messiah.—By Robert Manson Myers. New York, Macmillan, 1948.

Anna Seward, an Eighteenth Century Handelian.—By the same author. Privately printed. 1947.

Traditions and Recollections.—By Rev. R. Polewhele. 2 Vols. London, 1826.

Who's Who in Boswell.—By J. L. Smith-Dampier. Oxford, 1935.

Passages from the Diary of a Country Parson, (Rev. James Woodeforde).—Ed. by John Beresford. Oxford, 1935.

Call Back Yesterday.—By Lady Charnwood. London, 1937.

The English Church and Its Bishops, 1700–1800.—By C. J. Abbey. London, 1887.

Reports of the Annual Dinners of the Johnson Society in Lichfield.

The English Landscape Garden.—By H. F. Clark. Pleiades Books, London, 1948.

HISTORIES AND TOPOGRAPHICAL BOOKS

The History and Topography of Ashbourn and Adjacent Villages—Anonymous. Ashbourn, 1839.

A Short Account of the Ancient and Modern State of the City and Close of Lichfield.—Anonymous. Lichfield, 1819.

BIBLIOGRAPHY

A Tour Through the Whole Island of Great Britain, by a Gentleman.— By Daniel Defoe. 4 Vols. 1753.

The History and Antiquities of Lichfield.—By Thomas Harwood, F. S. A., 1806.

Handbook of the City of Lichfield and Its Neighborhood.—By John Hewitt. 1884.

History of the City and County of Lichfield.—By John Jackson. 1795.

A Sentimental Journey. . . . City of Lichfield.—By Alfred A. Parker. Lichfield, Lomax, 1925.

A Topographical History of Staffordshire.—By William Pitt. Newcastle-under-Lyme. 1817.

Natural History of Staffordshire.—By Robert Plot. 1686.

History of Staffordshire.—By Rev. Stebbing Shaw. 2 Vols. London, 1798.

A Complete History of England.—By Tobias Smollet. London, 1757–65.

Tour Through the Northern Counties of England and Borders of Scotland.—By Rev. Richard Warner. London, 1802.

MANUSCRIPT COLLECTIONS

The R. B. Adam Library (manuscripts relating to Dr. Johnson), which was temporarily in the University of Rochester Library, and is now in the possession of Mr. and Mrs. Donald Hyde.
Johnsonian manuscripts in the John Rylands Library (English Manuscript Department), Manchester, England.
The Johnson Birthplace Collection of Letters, Lichfield, England.
An eight-page manuscript by Rev. Richard George Robinson, dated 1812, criticising Anna Seward's *Life of Darwin,* in the possession of Mary Alden Hopkins.

253

This book may be kept

SEVEN DAYS

A fine of TWO CENTS will be charged for each day
the book is kept over time.

Mar. 28			
Apr. 4			
Apr 25			
apr 20			
Apr 23			